teach yourself

beginner's french

catrine carpenter

advisory editor

paul coggle

Launched in 1938, the **teach yourself** series grew rapidly in response to the world's wartime needs. Loved and trusted by over 50 million readers, the series has continued to respond to society's changing interests and passions and now, 70 years on, includes over 500 titles, from Arabic and Beekeeping to Yoga and Zulu. What would you like to learn?

be where you want to be with **teach yourself**

For UK order enquiries: please contact Bookpoint Ltd, 130 Milton Park, Abingdon, Oxon, OX14 4SB. Telephone: +44 (0) 1235 827720. Fax: +44 (0) 1235 400454. Lines are open 09.00–17.00, Monday to Saturday, with a 24-hour message answering service. Details about our titles and how to order are available at www.teachyourself.co.uk

For USA order enquiries: please contact McGraw-Hill Customer Services, PO Box 545, Blacklick, OH 43004-0545, USA. Telephone: 1-800-722-4726. Fax: 1-614-755-5645.

For Canada order enquiries: please contact McGraw-Hill Ryerson Ltd, 300 Water St, Whitby, Ontario, L1N 9B6, Canada. Telephone: 905 430 5000. Fax: 905 430 5020.

Long renowned as the authoritative source for self-guided learning – with more than 50 million copies sold worldwide – the **teach yourself** series includes over 500 titles in the fields of languages, crafts, hobbies, business, computing and education.

British Library Cataloguing in Publication Data: a catalogue record for this title is available from the British Library.

Library of Congress Catalog Card Number: on file.

First published in UK 1992 by Hodder Education, part of Hachette Livre UK, 338 Euston Road, London, NW1 3BH.

First published in US 1992 by The McGraw-Hill Companies, Inc.

This edition published 2008.

The **teach yourself** name is a registered trade mark of Hodder Headline.

Typeset by Transet Limited, Coventry, England.
Printed in Great Britain for Hodder Education, an Hachette Livre UK Company, 338 Euston Road, London NW1 3BH, by CPI Cox and Wyman, Reading, Berkshire, RG1 8EX.

The publisher has used its best endeavours to ensure that the URLs for external websites referred to in this book are correct and active at the time of going to press. However, the publisher and the author have no responsibility for the websites and can make no guarantee that a site will remain live or that the content will remain relevant, decent or appropriate.

Hachette Livre UK's policy is to use papers that are natural, renewable and recyclable products and made from wood grown in sustainable forests. The logging and manufacturing processes are expected to conform to the environmental regulations of the country of origin.

Impression number   10 9 8 7 6 5 4 3 2 1
Year   2012 2011 2010 2009 2008

contents

about the course   vii

pronunciation guide   xi

01   **bonjour** *hello*   1

simple questions • refusing politely in French • calling the waiter's attention • how to be courteous • when to use **tu**; when to use **vous** • how to learn vocabulary

02   **c'est combien?** *how much is it?*   9

numbers up to ten • *a, an* • *the* – **le, la, l',** **les** – the definite article • *do you have ...?* • *some, any* • *one/a/an* • *how much is it?* • how to organize your learning

03   **je m'appelle ... et vous?** *my name is ... what's yours?*   17

numbers 11–20 • regular verbs ending in **-er** • two important verbs: *to have, to be* • the negative form • adjectives: their agreement • capital letters • *what, which ...?* • saying how old you are • be active in your learning

04   **vous habitez où?** *where do you live?*   27

numbers 20–70 • how to ask simple questions • *is it ...? is that ...?* • *is there ...? are there ...?* • some likely answers: *yes there is ... no there isn't* • more answers: *yes I have ... no I haven't ...* • other questions • *my, your, his* • create every opportunity to immerse yourself in the language

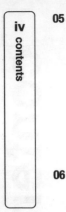

05 **quelle heure est-il?** *what time is it?* **35**
days of the week • months of the year •
numbers 70–90 • saying what you want/
want to do • asking what you can do;
asking for help • three different ways to
ask a question • questions starting with *what* •
verbs ending in **-ir** and **-re** • giving the date •
telling the time • *to do/to make* • *to take* •
experiment while learning

06 **pour aller à ...?** *the way to ...?* **46**
numbers 90 upwards • asking the way and
giving directions • *to go, to leave* • understanding
directions • when to use **à**; when to use **en** •
when **à** is followed by **le, la, l', les** •
locating the exact spot • *first, second, third* •
self-evaluation

07 **c'est comment?** *what is it like?* **58**
colours • *this, that, these, those* • saying
precisely what you want • how adjectives work •
making comparisons • learning to cope
with uncertainty

08 **vous aimez le sport?** *do you like sport?* **70**
asking and saying what you do as a hobby •
likes and dislikes • pronouns: *it, him, her, them* •
more negatives • when to use **savoir**; when
to use **connaître**: *to know* • *what's the weather
like?* • learn from errors

09 **qu'est-ce qu'il faut faire?** *what should I do?* **80**
asking for assistance • two very useful verbs:
to be able, to want • giving and understanding
instructions • learn to guess the meaning

10 **à l'avenir** *in the future* **89**
name of the seasons • saying what you usually
do using some reflexive verbs • saying what
you need • stating your intentions • the
pronoun **y**: *there* • *to go out, to come* •
using capital letters • when to use **visiter**

(*to visit*) • assess yourself and keep up
with grammar

11 les courses *shopping* 100
shops in France • food shopping • at the
market • shopping for other things • in a
clothes shop

12 se reposer, dormir *resting, sleeping* 111
choosing one's accommodation • looking for
a hotel • at the hotel • complaining • at the
caravan-campsite • the French alphabet •
booking online • sending an email

13 bien manger, bien boire *eating and
drinking well* 126
eating well • ordering a snack • at the
restaurant

14 les transports publics *public transport* 137
the Paris underground and tramway • taking
a taxi • travelling by bus • French railways •
at the information office • **le Vélib**

15 faire du tourisme *sightseeing* 149
getting information on things to see •
museums • going on an excursion

16 sortir *going out* 160
where to go • booking a ticket • booking a
tennis court

17 bonne route *safe journey* 170
French roads • asking for directions •
parking • traffic news • filling up the car
with petrol • breaking down

18 l'argent *money* 184
coins and banknotes in euros • getting small
change • changing money • an error in the bill

19 savoir faire face *troubleshooting* 193
chemist's in France • medical treatment •
using the post office, the phone and the
Internet • at the police station

taking it further	207
self-assessment tests	209
key to the exercises and tests	220
numbers	233
rôle-play scripts	234
French–English vocabulary	242
English–French vocabulary	251
index	257

about the course

Teach Yourself Beginner's French is the right course course for you if you are a complete beginner or wanting to make a fresh start. It is a self-study course which will help you to understand, read and speak most of the French you will need on holiday or a business trip.

Two key elements

The book has two parts. The first ten units introduce you to the basic structures and grammatical points you'll need in everyday situations. Units 1–10 should be taken in order, as each builds on the previous one.

Units 11–19 deal with everyday situations such as shopping, eating, booking a room, travelling and give you the opportunity to put into practice the language you've acquired in the first part. These units may be taken in any order.

The course is best used together with the accompanying recording, but is not dependent upon it. You are recommended to obtain and use the recording if possible. The recorded dialogues and audio exercises give you plenty of practice in understanding the basic language; they will help you develop an authentic accent and increase your confidence in saying simple phrases. Readers without the recording will find that some units include one activity that cannot be done with the book alone, but in such cases the material is always adequately covered by the other activities in the unit.

About Units 1–10

The first page of each unit tells you what you are going to learn and there is an easy exercise, *Essayez!* **Have a go!** which gets you speaking straight away.

Key words and phrases contain the most important words and phrases from the unit. Try to learn them by heart. They will be practised in the rest of the unit and the later units.

Dialogue Listen to the dialogue once or twice without stopping or read through it without looking anything up; try to get the gist of it. The notes underneath each dialogue will help you to understand it. Then, using the pause button, break the dialogue into manageable chunks and try repeating each phrase aloud. This will help you acquire a more authentic accent. Words and phrases listed in bold appear in the subsequent vocabulary box.

The sections marked with the **ⓘ** symbol provide cultural information or help you to develop your own 'techniques' to become a better learner, giving you tips on how to master the grammar, learn the vocabulary, improve your listening and reading skills and develop confidence in speaking.

Grammar In this section, you may want to start by reading the example(s) then work out the grammatical point, or you may prefer to read the **Grammar** section first and see how the rule applies. Once you feel confident about a particular grammar point, try to create your own examples.

Activities Each activity in this section allows you to practise one of the points introduced in the **Grammar** section. In some activities you will need to listen to the recording. It is not essential to have the recording in order to complete this course, as most of the activities are not dependent on it. However, listening to the recording will make your learning much easier.

Mini-test At the end of each unit you can test yourself on the last two or three units.

Score At the end of Units 3, 7 and 10 you can keep your own score in the space provided and see how well you did in the short self-assessment tasks.

About Units 11–19

The first page of each unit tells you what you are going to learn. There is also a checklist of structures which you have already learnt and will be practising in the unit. You'll also find in most units a short text in French about the topic.

Key words and phrases contains the basic vocabulary you'll need when coping, in real life, with practical situations such as checking into a hotel, ordering a snack, asking for a train timetable, going on an excursion.

Dialogues There are several short dialogues, each dealing with a different aspect of the topic. Remember to listen to the dialogues first and use the pause button to practise the new words and phrases out loud.

Activities The activities are mostly based on authentic French material. Here you can develop a feel for how things work in France, as well as practising your reading skills. You will then have more confidence to cope with the real situations.

Mini-test As in Units 1–10.

Score As in Units 1–10.

Key to the exercises and tests

The answers to the questions on the **Dialogues** in Units 1–10, Activities, *Essayez!* **Have a go!**, *Pratiquez!* **Practise!**, **Mini-tests**, **Self-assessment tests** can be found at the back of the book.

Be successful at learning languages

1 **Do a little bit every day,** between 20 and 30 minutes if possible, rather than two or three hours in one session.

2 **Try to work towards short-term goals,** e.g. work out how long you'll spend on a particular unit and work within this time limit.

3 **Revise and test yourself regularly** using the **Mini-test** at the end of each unit and the two **Self-assessment tests** at the back of the book.

4 **Make use of the tips** given in the book and try to say the words and phrases out loud whenever possible.

5 **Use every opportunity to speak the language.** Attend some classes to practise your French with other people, get some help from a French speaker or find out about French clubs, societies, etc.

6 **Don't worry too much about making mistakes.** The important thing is to get your meaning across and remember that making mistakes in French will not stop a French person understanding you. Learning can be fun particularly when you find you can use what you have learnt in real situations.

At the back of the book

At the back of the book is a section which contains:

- A **Taking it further** section to direct you to further sources of French.

- Two **Self-assessment tests** based on Units 1–10 and 11–19 giving you an opportunity to assess your progress as you go along.

- **Key to the exercises and tests.**

- **Numbers.**

- Rôle-play scripts for Units 4–10 and self-assessment tests.

- A **French–English vocabulary** list containing all the words in the course.

- An **English–French vocabulary** list with the most useful words you'll need when expressing yourself in French.

- An **Index** to enable you to look things up in the book.

About symbols and abbreviations

 This indicates that the recording is needed for the following.

This indicates cultural information or draws your attention to study tips and points to be noted.

(m)   masculine
(f)   feminine
(sing) singular
(pl)   plural
(lit.) literally

pronunciation guide

The **Pronunciation guide** is on the recording at the end of Unit 1.

▶ 1 How to sound French

Here are a few rules that will help you to sound French right from the beginning:

1 In French, unlike in most English words, it is the last part of the word that bears a heavy stress:
   res-tau-**rant**, o-**range**, ca-**fé**, té-lé-**phone**

2 French words that are spelt like English words are almost always pronounced differently:
   pardon, important, parking, sandwich, ticket

3 In general, consonants at the end of a word such as **d g p s t x z**, and the letter **h**, are silent.
   vous   anglais   nuit   dames   messieurs   hôtel

▶ 2 French sounds

Here is the list of the **French vowels** with a rough English equivalent sound. You'll see that an accent on an e or an n changes the way the letter is pronounced.

letter	rough English sound	French example
a à	cat	madame
e	1 above	le ne
	2 best (before two consonants or x)	merci
	3 may (before z, r)	parlez
é	may	café

letter	rough English sound	French example
è ê	pair	père fête
i î y	police	merci dîner typique
o	dot	olive
u	a sound not found in English – first say **oo**, but then keeping the lips in that position try saying **ee**	une du
ai	as è ê above	lait s'il vous plaît
ô au eau	pronounced as **o** but with rounded lips	hôtel autobus beaucoup
eu oeu	sir	leur soeur
oi	the **wa** sound at the beginning of **one**	bonsoir
ou	moo	vous

Many **consonants** are similar to English, with a number of exceptions and variations:

letter	rough English sound	French example
ç	sit	ça français
ch	shop	chic
g	leisure (before **i**, **e**)	Brigitte
gn	onion	cognac
h	not pronounced	hôtel hôpital
j	leisure	je bonjour
l ll	yes (often when **i** precedes **l**, **ll**)	fille travail
qu	care	question
r	pronounced at the back of the throat with the tongue touching the bottom teeth	rat Paris
s	desert (between vowels)	mademoiselle
t	(before **ion**) pass	attention
th	tea	thé
w	1 what 2 van	whisky wagon-restaurant

Here are the **nasal sounds** formed usually with vowels followed by **m** or **n**. Speak through your nose when you pronounce them and listen carefully to the recording.

ein im in ain	{ bang (stop before the g) }	frein important vin train impossible

en an	long (stop before the g)	encore Jean restaurant
on	as above but with lips pushed forward	pardon on non
un um	similar to ein im in ain	parfum un

▶ 3 How to link the sounds together

To make the words run more smoothly the final consonants of words which are usually silent are sounded when the next word starts with a vowel or h, e.g. très_important (trayzimportan). This is called a liaison. In some cases, as above, liaisons are essential; in other cases they are optional. To help you recognize when the liaisons are essential they'll be indicated with a linking mark (_) in Units 1–10.

When making liaisons all French people:

1 pronounce s and x like z: les_oranges   deux_heures
2 pronounce d and t like t, but the t of et (*and*) is never sounded: le grand_homme   c'est_ici   un café et une bière
3 link n in the nasal un when the next words starts with a vowel or a silent h: un_enfant   un_hôtel

4 A few tips to help you acquire an authentic accent

It is not absolutely vital to acquire a perfect accent. The aim is to be understood. Here are a number of techniques for working on your pronunciation:

1 Listen carefully to the recording or a native speaker or a teacher. Whenever possible repeat aloud, imagining you are a native speaker of French.
2 Record yourself and compare your pronunciation with that of a native speaker.
3 Ask native speakers to listen to your pronunciation and tell you how to improve it.
4 Ask native speakers how a specific sound is formed. Watch them and practise at home in front of a mirror.
5 Make a list of words that give you pronunciation trouble and practise them.

6 Study the sounds on their own then use them progressively in words, sentences and tongue-twisters.

Try this one! **Panier-piano, panier-piano, panier-piano** (**panier** is a basket in French).

▶ 5 And now practise ...

Starting with **Paris** go round anti-clockwise saying each of the 14 towns out loud. Pause after each town and check your pronunciation with the recording.

01

hello

bonjour

In this unit you will learn how to
- say 'hello' and 'goodbye'
- exchange greetings
- observe basic courtesies
- ask people to speak more slowly

Before you start

Read the **Introduction** to the course. This gives some useful advice on studying alone and how to make the most of the course.

Different people have different ways of learning: some need to know rules for everything, others like to feel their way intuitively. In this unit you'll be given the opportunity to find out what works best for you, so look out for the symbol **i**.

Make sure you've got your recording ▶ next to you as you'll need it to listen to the **Pronunciation guide** and **Dialogues** sections. If you don't have the recording, use the **Pronunciation guide** in the book.

i Study tips

Remember that studying for 20 minutes regularly is better than occasionally spending two hours in one go.

1 Listen to the **Dialogues** once or twice without the book (read them if you haven't got the recording).

2 Go over each one, bit by bit, in conjunction with the **Key words and phrases** and notes underneath the dialogues.

3 Read the **Grammar** section very carefully and study it.

4 Read the tips on **How to learn vocabulary** and **How to pronounce**.

5 Go back to the **Dialogues** and **Key words and phrases** for more listening and studying, this time using the pause button and repeating aloud after the recording.

6 Do the **Activities**, check your answers in the **Key to the exercises** and test yourself with the **Mini-test**.

Essayez! **Have a go!** Can you think of any French words you know such as the words for 'hello' and 'thank you'? Say them out loud, and then look at the sections **Key words and phrases** to check the answers.

Key words and phrases

bonjour	*good morning/afternoon, hello*
bonsoir	*good evening* (after 5.00 p.m.)
bonne nuit	*good night* (when going to bed)
au revoir	*goodbye*
bonjour, Madame	*good morning (Madam)*
bonjour, Mademoiselle	*good morning (Miss)*
bonsoir, Monsieur	*good evening (Sir)*
au revoir, Messieurs-dames	*goodbye ladies and gentlemen*
oui	*yes*
non, merci	*no, thank you*
merci	*thank you*
merci beaucoup	*thank you very much*
s'il vous plaît	*please*
d'accord	*OK*
pardon	*sorry* (to apologize), *excuse me*
comment ça va? ça va (informal)	*how are things? fine*
(très) bien merci	*(very) well thank you*
comment vas-tu?	*how are you?*
comment_allez-vous? (formal)	*how are you?*
je vais bien et toi?	*I am well – how about you?*
et vous? (formal)	*and you?*
vous parlez_anglais?	*do you speak English?*
parlez plus lentement	*speak more slowly*

i When you see a linking mark '_' between two words, sound the last letter of the first word as though it were attached to the next word: vous **parlez_anglais?**

▶ Dialogues

Listen to the recording and hear people practising saying 'hello' and greeting each other in French. Press the pause button after each sentence and repeat aloud.

Dialogue 1 Saying 'hello'

Jane   Bonjour, Messieurs-dames.

Michel   Bonjour, Mademoiselle.
Jane   Bonjour, Monsieur.

| Roger | Bonsoir, Madame. |
| Nathalie | Bonsoir, Monsieur. |

Roger	Comment ça va, Jane?
Jane	Très bien, et toi?
Roger	**Moi aussi**, ça va bien.

| Rosine | Comment vas-tu? |
| Jane | Je vais très bien Rosine, et toi? |

Mme Dubois	Comment_allez-vous, Monsieur Dubosse?
M. Dubosse	Très bien merci, et vous?
Mme Dubois	Très bien.

Dialogue 2 Saying 'goodbye'

| Michel | Au revoir, Madame et ... merci beaucoup. |
| Nathalie | Au revoir, Monsieur. |

▶ Dialogue 3 When things get difficult ...

| Jane | Pardon, Monsieur, vous parlez_anglais? |
| Garçon | Ah, non, **je regrette** ... |

Garçon	Bonjour, Madame. **Qu'est-ce que vous désirez?**
Nathalie	Parlez plus lentement, s'il vous plaît.
Garçon	D'accord ... Qu'est-ce que vous désirez?

moi	*me, I*
aussi	*also, too*
garçon	*waiter*
je regrette	*I'm sorry*
Qu'est-ce que vous désirez?	(lit.) *What do you wish?*
	but used in shops it means
	Can I help you?

ℹ How to pronounce ...

- As a general rule don't pronounce **d g p s t x z** at the end of a word, e.g.: beaucou**p** vou**s** nui**t** plaî**t**.

- The letter **e** often gets swallowed as in **mad'moiselle**.

- The stress, in French, is on the last part of the word: par-d**on** mer-**ci** mad'-moi-**selle** mon-**sieur**.

- **ç** placed before **o, u, a** is pronounced **s** as in *sit*: gar**ç**on, **ç**a va?

- The **s** in monsieur is pronounced as **ss** in *pass*.

Grammar

1 Simple questions

The simplest way of asking something in French is to raise your voice on the last syllable (part of a word):

Vouz parlez_anglais?⟋   Pardon?⟋   Ça va?⟋

Now practise saying pardon?⟋ (to have something repeated) and

pardon⟍ (to apologize or attract someone's attention).

2 Refusing politely in French

If you want to refuse something in France, you can say non merci or merci on its own.

3 Calling the waiter's attention

Although garçon is the word for waiter, today you would usually say Monsieur to attract his attention. For a waitress, you say Madame or Mademoiselle as you think fit or just look expectant and say s'il vous plaît.

4 How to be courteous

In France when you're talking to someone you don't know very well, it's polite to add Monsieur, Madame, Mademoiselle particularly after short phrases like oui, non, bonjour or merci.

The French shake hands with good friends and acquaintances every time they meet or say goodbye. Kissing (on both cheeks) is reserved for family and close friends.

5 When to use tu (you) and when to use vous (you)

The equivalent of *you* in French can be either tu or vous. French people use tu when speaking to children, teenagers, relations and close friends. They use vous in work and business situations or when speaking to senior or old people: vous is also used to address a group of people to whom one might say tu individually. The best advice is to say vous until you are addressed as tu or asked to use the tu form: on se tutoie? *shall we call each other* tu?

ℹ️ How to learn vocabulary

There are several ways of learning vocabulary. Find the way that works best for you; here are a few suggestions:

- Say the words out loud as you read them.
- Write the words over and over again.
- Listen to the recording several times.
- Study the list from beginning to end then backwards.
- Associate the French words with similar sounding words in English, e.g. **parlez** with *parlour*, a room where people chat.
- Associate the words with pictures or situations, e.g. **bonjour**, **bonsoir** with shaking hands.
- Use coloured pencils to underline/group the words in a way that will help you to remember them.
- Copy the words on to small cards or slips of paper, English on one side, French on the other. Study them in varying order giving the French word if the card comes out with the English on top, or vice versa.

Activities

1 How would you say *hello* in the situations below? Remember to add **Monsieur, Madame, Mademoiselle**. Write your answer underneath each picture.

a Bonjour Madam
b Bonjour Monsieur
c Bonsoir Mademoiselle
d Bonjour Messieurs-dames
e Bonsoir Monsieur
f Bonsoir Messieurs-dames

2 You're arriving late at a hotel one evening; greet the person behind the reception desk by choosing the right box below.

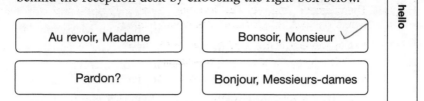

Au revoir, Madame	Bonsoir, Monsieur ✓
Pardon?	Bonjour, Messieurs-dames

3 A person at the bus stop asks you a question that you do not hear properly. What do you say? Choose **a, b** or **c**.

a **s'il vous plaît**
b **non merci**
(c **pardon?**)

4 You are staying the night with some friends. It's late and you decide to go to bed. You say:

Au revoir	Comment ça va?	(Bonne nuit)

5 You meet up with a French-speaking colleague. How do you ask: *How are you?*

Comment ça va?

The answer is *Very well, thank you.* What is it in French?

Très bien merci

6 Use the clues to complete the grid. When you've finished, the vertical word will be what you say if you step on someone's foot!

a The French translation for *please*
b Your answer to a friend who asks how you are
c *Goodbye*
d Calling the waitress' attention
e Greeting someone after 5p.m.
f Refusing politely

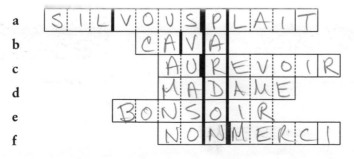

a S I L V O U S P L A I T
b C A V A
c A U R E V O I R
d M A D A M E
e B O N S O I R
f N O N M E R C I

7 Choose the appropriate word or group of words.

a How would you greet
several people?

    i Bonjour Madame
    ii Au revoir
    iii Bonjour Messieurs-dames

b How would you refuse
politely?

    i D'accord
    ii Non merci
    iii Pardon

c To ask someone if s/he
speaks English you say:

    i Parlez plus lentement
    ii Au revoir Messieurs-dames
    iii Vous parlez_anglais?

d To wish someone
good night you say:

    i Bonjour
    ii Bonsoir
    iii Bonne nuit

Remember to check your answers at the end of the book. If you have a number of wrong answers look back at the tips for learning vocabulary.

Mini-test

You've arrived at the end of Unit 1. Now you know how to say 'thank you' and exchange greetings and you've also learnt a little about French sounds. How would you:

1 Say 'hello' to your friend and ask how things are?
2 Ask someone to slow down when speaking French? (Don't forget to add *please* at the end.)
3 Apologize as you step on someone's foot?
4 Say you agree?

You'll find the answers to the **Mini-test** in the **Key to the exercises and tests** at the end of the book. If they are correct you are ready to move to Unit 2. If you found the test difficult, spend more time revising Unit 1.

02

c'est combien?

how much is it?

In this unit you will learn how to
- count up to ten
- ask for something
- say how much you want
- ask the price

Before you start

In this unit we will show you that it is nearly always possible to ask for what you want with just two words, **je voudrais** (*I would like*) and **s'il vous plaît** at the end.

The dialogue is short but there are a lot of new words including useful things you may need in France. Try to learn the words by heart using one of the techniques described in Unit 1 in the section **How to learn vocabulary**.

Essayez! **Have a go!** You are in a **pâtisserie** (*cake shop*) in France to buy a **baguette** (*French stick*). How would you greet the woman behind the counter? How would you ask for a French stick?

Key words and phrases

For you to say

un café	*a coffee/a café*
un thé	*a tea*
un coca-cola	*a coca-cola*
un_euro	*a Euro*
un journal	*a newspaper*
un plan	*a map, plan*
une baguette	*a French stick*
une bière	*a beer*
une chambre	*a room*
une pharmacie	*a chemist's*
une station-service	*a petrol station*
le timbre	*the stamp*
la carte postale	*the postcard*
la gare	*the station*
l'hôtel (m)	*the hotel*
l'hôpital (m)	*the hospital*
l'eau minérale (f)	*the mineral/bottled natural water*
gazeuse/plate	*sparkling/still*
l'addition (f)	*the bill*
les toilettes	*the toilets*
je voudrais	*I would like*
vous_avez ...?	*do you have ...?*
ça	*this/that*
du pain	*some bread*

du vin	*some wine*
de la limonade	*some lemonade*
de l'aspirine (f)	*some aspirins*
des sandwiches	*some sandwiches*
c'est combien?	*how much is it?* (lit. *it is how much?*)
un kilo	*one kilo*
un demi-kilo	*half a kilo*
un paquet	*one pack*
une bouteille	*one bottle*
une boîte	*one tin, box*

For you to understand

fermé	*shut*
je n'en_ai pas	*I haven't got any*
avec ça?	*will that be all?* (lit. *with that?*)
c'est tout?	*is that all?*

▶ Numbers 1–10

1 **un**	4 **quatre**	7 **sept** (the **p** is not pronounced)
2 **deux**	5 **cinq**	8 **huit**
3 **trois**	6 **six**	9 **neuf**
		10 **dix**

▶ Dialogue

Jane is in **une alimentation** (*grocer's shop*). *What does she want to buy? Does she get what she wants? Listen to the recording first, answer the questions, then check your answers.*

Jane	Vous_avez de la bière?
Vendeuse	Ah non, je regrette, je n'en_ai pas.
Jane	Et du vin?
Vendeuse	Euh oui. **Quel vin** désirez-vous?
Jane	Je voudrais une bouteille de Muscadet.
Vendeuse	Oui, **voilà** … et avec ça?
Jane	Deux bouteilles d'eau minérale.
Vendeuse	De la gazeuse ou de la plate?
Jane	De la plate.
Vendeuse	Bon, très bien. C'est tout?
Jane	Oui, merci. C'est combien?
Vendeuse	Pour le Muscadet, c'est 6€50 et pour l'eau minérale, 1€30 la bouteille.

la vendeuse	*the shop assistant (female)*
quel vin?	*which wine?*
voilà	*there you are*

ℹ️ How to pronounce ... *six et dix*

- when **six** and **dix** are on their own as numbers the **x** is pronounced as **s** and they rhyme with 'peace': **vous_avez des timbres? Oui, six.**

- when followed by a word starting with a consonant the **x** is not pronounced and they sound like 'dee' and 'see': **dix kilos, six bières.**

- when followed by a word starting with a vowel or **h** pronounce the **x** and **s** as **z**: **six_euros, dix_hôtels.**

Grammar

1 Words for 'a, an': *un, une*

The word *a* or *an* is **un** in front of a masculine noun and **une** in front of a feminine noun. All French nouns belong to one of the two groups: masculine or feminine. Sometimes it is obvious as in **un Français** *a Frenchman*, **une Française** *a Frenchwoman* while other times it is not obvious as in **un café** but **une bière**.

There is no rule to tell you to which group a noun belongs, although the ending of a noun often acts as a guide. For example:

- words ending in **-age**, **-ment** are often masculine, as in **le village, le moment.**

- words ending in **-lle**, **-tte**, **-ion**, **-ée** are often feminine as in **une bouteille, une cigarette, une alimentation, une année.**

2 Words for 'the': *le, la, l', les*

There are four different ways of saying *the*:

le with masculine nouns	**le** timbre
la with feminine nouns	**la** gare
l' with nouns starting with a vowel or an **h**	**l'**hôtel (m)
	l'eau (f)
les with plural nouns	**les** toilettes

i Plural nouns usually take an **s** at the end. Make a habit of learning words together with **le** or **la** before them. If they start with a vowel or **h**, they are followed by (m) or (f) in **Key words and phrases** to indicate if they are masculine or feminine.

3 *Vous avez ...?* Do you have ...?

To check if they have what you want, start your request with **vous avez** (*do you have*). To indicate that it is a question raise the voice on the last syllable of the sentence:

Vous_avez un plan?   *Do you have a room?*

4 Words for 'some, any': *du, de la, de l', des*

When **de** (*of*) is used in combination with **le, la, l', les** it changes its form and can mean *some* or *any* according to the context:

de + **le** becomes **du**   **de l'** remains unchanged
de la remains unchanged   **de** + **les** becomes **des**

Compare the examples below:

Je voudrais **du** vin.   *I would like **some** wine.*
Je voudrais **le** vin.   *I would like **the** wine.*
Vous_avez **de la** bière?   *Do you have **any** beer?*
Vous_avez **la** bière?   *Do you have **the** beer?*
Vous_avez **de l'**eau minérale?   *Have you **any** mineral water?*
Vous_avez **l'**eau minérale?   *Do you have **the** mineral water?*
Je voudrais **des** timbres.   *I would like **some** stamps.*
Je voudrais **les** timbres.   *I would like **the** stamps.*

i In English we often omit the word *some*. In French, **de** + the definite article (**le, la, l'** or **les**) is almost always used.

5 *Un kilo de* A kilo/one kilo of

To ask for one of something use un with masculine nouns and **une** with feminine nouns:

un kilo de sucre   *one kilo of sugar* or
                              a kilo of sugar

une boîte de sardines   *one tin of sardines* or
                                   a tin of sardines

6 *C'est combien?* How much is it?

You need only two words to ask for the price: **C'est combien?** *How much is it?* (lit. it is how much) followed by whatever you want to know the price of:

C'est combien la carte postale?   *How much is the postcard?*

C'est combien la baguette?   *How much is the French stick?*

ℹ How to organize your learning

It may help you to remember the new vocabulary, pronunciation and grammar rules that you learn in the book if you create your own system to organize this information, perhaps using one or more of the following ideas.

- You could group new words under:

  a generic categories, e.g. *food*, *furniture*.

  b situations in which they occur, e.g. under *restaurant* you can put *waiter*, *table*, *menu*, *bill*.

  c functions: greetings, parting, thanks, apologizing, etc.

- When organizing the study of pronunciation you could keep a section of your notebook for pronunciation rules and practise those that trouble you.

- To organize your study of grammar you may like to write your own grammar glossary and add new information as you go along.

Activities

1 Look at the objects below, and write their names in French preceded by **un**, **une** or **des**.

a

un café

b

une bière

c

un journal

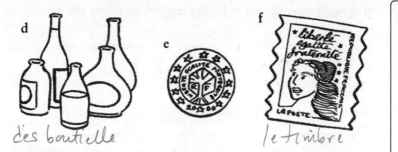

d

des bouteille

e

f

le timbre

2 You've arrived at a French hotel; you would like three things. What are they? You will find them hidden in the string of letters below:

motunechambrepozowiuncafémoghttunjournaldfc

3 Before you leave the hotel you want to buy a few things: how would you ask for them in French?

a I would like four cards, please.

Je voudrais quatre la carte postale

b Do you have four stamps for England?

Vous avec quatre les timbre pour l'Angleterre?

c And some aspirin, please.

et des l'aspirin

d How much is it?

C'est combien

4 All the numbers 'one' to 'ten' are listed in this wordsearch except for one. Which is missing? Read horizontally or vertically, either forwards or backwards.

E	Y	S	N	I	S
R	S	E	P	T	R
T	M	I	D	I	X
A	O	N	E	U	F
U	L	U	U	H	I
Q	S	H	X	I	S

Missing trois

5 Match the words in the left-hand column with the ones in the right.

a deux bouteilles ii   i   chewing gum
b un kilo IV   de   ii vin
c une boîte III   iii sardines
d un paquet i   iv sucre

▶ 6 Michel, sitting at a café, is ordering some drinks with his friends. He then asks for the bill. Using the words in the box, complete the script then check your version with the recording and/or the **Key to the exercises and tests.**

a Garçon   Bonjour... _Messieurs/dames_
b Michel   Je voudrais un ... _café_ ...
           et vous, Marie?
c Marie   Moi, une ... _bière_ ...
d Sylvie   Je ... _voudrais_ ... une limo-
           nade.
e Michel   Et je voudrais aussi l' _addition_
           s'il vous plaît.

> café
> voudrais
> addition
> Messieurs-dames
> bière

▶ 7 As numbers are very important, here's another chance to practise them. Write your answers to the sums below (in words, not figures).

a deux + trois = _cinq_   e dix   – huit = _deux_
b cinq + quatre = _dix_   f sept – trois = _trois_
c neuf + un = _dix_   g trois × trois = _neuf_
d six + trois = _neuf_   h quatre × deux = _huit_

Check your answers by listening to the recording, **Activity 7.** If you do not have the recording, check them in the the **Key to the exercises and tests,** then test yourself on Units 1 and 2 with **Mini-test.**

Mini-test

1 If a waiter said to you **Je n'en_ai pas** what would he mean?
2 How would you ask for the bill? _Je voudrais l'addition s'vous_
3 You have a headache. Stop at the chemist's and ask politely for what you need, then thank the chemist and say goodbye.
4 How would you ask for a bottle of mineral water?

03

je m'appelle ... et vous?

my name is ... what's yours?

In this unit you will learn how to
- count up to 20
- talk about yourself and your family
- say that things are not so
- say how old you are

Before you start

Speaking about yourself and your family in French is fairly easy once you know the vocabulary to describe your home and family and you know how to say what you do or don't have (**j'ai, je n'ai pas**) and what you are or aren't (**je suis, je ne suis pas**).

As we said in the introduction, to be successful at learning languages try to work towards short-term goals. In this unit concentrate on mastering **avoir** and **être**, the two most useful verbs in French. Keep practising them out loud: in the car, the bus, the bath. Aim at saying them without thinking.

Essayez! **Have a go!** You've just arrived in France. You stop at **une alimentation** to buy something to drink. How would you ask for two bottles of beer and one kilo of oranges? **Je ...**

Key words and phrases

quel est votre nom?	*what is your name?*
je m'appelle ... et toi/vous (formal)?	*my name is ... what's yours?*
tu es français?	*are you French?* (to a man)
vous_êtes française?	*(to a woman, formal)*
je suis_anglais/anglaise	*I'm English* (a man/a woman)
tu es marié?	*are you married?* (to a man)
vous_êtes mariée?	*(to a woman, formal)*
non, je ne suis pas marié	*no, I am not married*
je suis divorcé/e	*I am divorced* (man/woman)
Jane a un copain/petit_ami	*Jane has a boyfriend*
il a une copine/petite_amie	*he has a girlfriend*
vous avez des_enfants?	*do you have any children?*
oui, deux filles et un garçon	*yes, two girls* (or daughters) *and a boy*
ils_ont dix et six ans	*they are ten and six years old*
non, je n'ai pas d'enfants	*no, I have no children*
la fille/le fils	*daughter/son*
la soeur/le frère	*sister/brother*
le père/la mère	*father/mother*
les parents/les grands-parents	*parents/gandparents*
le grand-père/la grand-mère	*grandfather/grandmother*
j'habite en_Angleterre	*I live/I'm living in England*

avec ma famille	*with my family*
je travaille à New York	*I work in New York*
je viens/suis de Vancouver	*I am/come from Vancouver*
elle est secrétaire/comptable	*she is a secretary/an accountant*
elle travaille dans une banque	*she works in a bank*
il travaille pour IBM	*he works for IBM*
à mi-temps/à temps plein	*part-time/fulltime*

i In English *a* is used before a profession. In French it is always omitted:

Elle est professeure.   *She is a teacher.*

▶ Numbers 11–20

11	onze	16	seize
12	douze	17	dix-sept
13	treize	18	dix-huit
14	quatorze	19	dix-neuf
15	quinze	20	vingt (*pronounced as French 'vin'*)

▶ Dialogue

Jane is sitting on the terrace of a café reading an English magazine. A Frenchwoman has struck up a conversation with her. Listen to the recording or read the dialogue below. Does the Frenchwoman work? Has she got any children? Is Jane married?

Frenchwoman   Vous_êtes_anglaise?

Jane   Je suis_anglaise et **irlandaise**. J'ai un père anglais et une mère irlandaise.

Frenchwoman   Ah c'est bien. Et vous habitez Londres?

Jane   Non. Je suis de Londres mais j'habite Brighton.

Frenchwoman   C'est où ça, Brighton?

Jane   Dans le sud de l'Angleterre. Et vous, vous_êtes française?

Frenchwoman   Oui, je suis de Lille dans le nord de la France, mais j'habite Paris avec ma famille.

Jane   Vous_êtes mariée?

Frenchwoman   Divorcée, mais **je vis** avec un copain **depuis cinq ans**.

Jane	Et vous_avez des_enfants?
Frenchwoman	Oui, j'ai trois_enfants, une fille et deux garçons.
Jane	Ils_ont quel âge?
Frenchwoman	La fille a dix_ans et les garçons ont huit_ans et six_ans.
Jane	Ah, très bien.
Frenchwoman	Et vous, vous_êtes mariée?
Jane	Non, je ne suis pas mariée, mais moi **aussi** j'ai un petit_ami.
Frenchwoman	Il est_anglais?
Jane	Non, il est_américain. Il travaille pour IBM en Angleterre.
Frenchwoman	Ah c'est bien. Et vous, vous travaillez?
Jane	Oui, je suis dentiste.
Frenchwoman	Moi aussi, je travaille à mi-temps dans **une agence de voyages**.
Jane	C'est bien votre travail?
Frenchwoman	Oui, très. Je parle beaucoup anglais avec les touristes. Mais vous, vous parlez très bien français.
Jane	Non, **seulement un petit peu** ...

irlandais/e	*Irish*
je vis ... depuis cinq ans	*I have been living ... for five years*
aussi	*also*
une agence de voyages	*a travel agency*
seulement un petit peu	*only a little*

ℹ️ How to pronounce ...

- **nom** (*name*) is pronounced like **non** (*no*).

- **fille** is pronounced 'fee-ye' and **fils** is pronounced 'fee-sse'.

- Look at the **Key words and phrases** section and try to practise linking the words with a linking mark, e.g. **vous_êtes** (pronounce 'vou zêtes').

- To pronounce **secrétaire** French people will tend to pinch their lips for **se**, open the mouth up for **cré** and relax the mouth for **taire**. If you haven't got the recording check with the **Pronunciation guide**.

Grammar

1 Regular verbs ending in -er, e.g. parler, to speak

In English *to speak* is the infinitive of the verb (this is the form of the verbs you find in the dictionary). In French the equivalent infinitive is **parler**. It follows the same pattern as many other verbs with infinitives ending in -er. Here is the present tense of **parler**:

parler *to speak*		
je	parl**e**	*I speak, I'm speaking*
tu	parl**es**	*you speak, you're speaking*
il/elle/on	parl**e**	*he/she/one speaks, is speaking*
nous	parl**ons**	*we speak, we're speaking*
vous	parl**ez**	*you speak, you're speaking*
ils/elles	parl**ent**	*they speak, they're speaking*

i
- The present tense in French makes no distinction between *I speak* and *I'm speaking*.
- Before a vowel or **h**, **je** becomes **j'**: **j'habite** *I live*.
- **On** is commonly used in French when people talk about themselves. In a general sense it is the equivalent of *one, you, we*.
- **Ils** is used when the group of people is mixed or all males.
- **Elles** is for an all-female group.
- Pronunciation: the **je tu il elle on ils elles** forms of the present tense of any regular **-er** verb sound the same. Do not pronounce the 3rd person plural ending **-ent**. If you do, people may not understand you.

Pratiquez! Practise! Can you work out the present tense of **travailler**? Write it down and read it aloud. Remember the pronunciation tips above.

2 Two important verbs: *avoir* to have; *être* to be

Avoir and être are irregular, i.e. they do not follow the normal pattern. They are the two most common verbs in French and need to be learnt individually:

avoir *to have*		être *to be*	
j'ai	*I have*	je suis	*I am*
tu as	*you have*	tu es	*you are*
il/elle/on_a	*he / she /one has*	il/elle/on_est	*he / she / one is*
nous_avons	*we have*	nous sommes	*we are*
vous_avez	*you have*	vous_êtes	*you are*
ils/elles_ont	*they have*	ils/elles sont	*they are*

Pratiquez! **Practise!** Practise the verbs **avoir** and **être** in sentences using some of the key words you already know. Remember that for a question, you need to raise the voice on the last syllable. For example:

J'**ai** un_enfant.

Tu **as** des_enfants?
Il **a** trois frères.
Nous_**avons** …

Je **suis** marié.

Tu **es**_anglaise?
Elle **est** professeure.

3 The negative form: *ne … pas*

To say something is not so in French, you put **ne … pas** round the verb: je **ne** comprends **pas** *I don't understand*.

- **Ne** becomes **n'** if the following verb starts with a vowel or **h**: j'habite Paris *but* je **n'habite** pas Paris.

- After a negative form **du, de la …** becomes **de**: J'ai **du** vin *but* je n'ai pas **de** vin.

- **Ne** is often omitted in French conversations: **Je parle pas anglais.**

4 Adjectives: how they agree

To describe things in detail or talk about yourself you need to add descriptive words (called adjectives) to nouns; an adjective describing a masculine noun has a masculine form, and one describing a feminine noun has a feminine form. As a general rule, feminine adjectives end in -e and the plural adjectives take an -s:

J'ai un_ami américain.	*I have an American friend.*
J'ai une amie américaine.	*I have an American friend.*
Mes_amis sont_ américains.	*My friends are American.*

5 Capital letters

In French, adjectives of nationality and names of languages are not written with a capital letter (unless they start a sentence):

Vous parlez français?	*Do you speak French?*
Je suis canadien.	*I am Canadian.*
but: un(e) Anglais(e)	*an Englishman/woman*
un(e) Américain(e)	*an American*
un(e) Français(e)	*a Frenchman/woman*

6 *Quel est votre nom?* What's your name?

Quel, meaning *what* or *which*, is a useful word to remember; it is always pronounced '*kel*' but it is spelt differently to agree with the noun to which it refers:

Quel est votre nom?	*What's your name?*
Nom is a masculine noun.	
Quelle est votre **adresse?**	*What's your address?*
Adresse is a feminine noun.	
Quels vins?	*Which wines?*
Vins is a masculine plural noun.	
Quelles bouteilles?	*Which bottles?*
Bouteilles is a feminine plural noun.	

7 Saying how old you are

Start with **j'ai** (not **je suis**), add your age followed by **ans** (*years*):

Vous_avez quel âge?	*How old are you?*
J'ai dix-sept ans.	*I am 17.*

ⓘ Be active in your learning

As all language teachers will assure you, the successful learners are those students who overcome their inhibitions and get into situations where they must speak, write and listen to the foreign language. Here are some useful tips to help you practise French:

Rehearse in the foreign language.

- Hold a conversation with yourself, using the dialogues of the units as models and the structures you have learnt previously.
- After you have conducted a transaction with a salesperson, clerk or waiter in your own language, pretend that you have to do it in French, e.g. buying petrol, groceries, ordering food, drinks and so on.
- Look at objects around you and try to name them in French.
- Look at people around you and try to describe them in detail.

Activities

▶ **1** On the recording, you will hear some numbers between 1 and 20. Repeat and write them down in figures.

a ....   f ....

b ....   g ....

c ....   h ....

d ....   i ....

e ....   j ....

2 This time practise these sums aloud and write the answers in words. (+ is **plus** in French and – is **moins**)

a 10 + 3 = *treize*   f 19 – 8 = *onze*

b   7 + 8 = *quinze*   g 11 – 6 = *cinq*

c 15 + 5 = *vingt*   h 16 – 10 = *six*

d   4 + 9 = *treize*   i 12 – 8 = *quatre*

e 13 + 6 = *dix-neuf*   j 15 – 3 = *deuze*

3 Look at the family tree below and fill in the sentences:

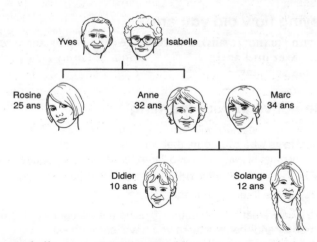

Yves   Isabelle

Rosine
25 ans

Anne
32 ans

Marc
34 ans

Didier
10 ans

Solange
12 ans

a Isabelle .... mariée avec Yves.
b Ils .... deux filles.
c .... s'appellent Rosine et Anne.
d Anne et Marc ont deux .... , une fille et .... fils.

e Rosine .... d'enfants.
f Elle .... mariée.
g Didier a .... ans.
h Solange .... douze ....

4 You are being very negative and answer **non** … to all the following questions using **ne** … **pas**:

a Vous_avez des timbres?   Non, je ....
b Elle a du café?   Non, elle ....
c Il est marié?   Non, il ....
d Elle est secrétaire?   Non, elle ....
e Vous_avez une chambre?   Non, je ....
f Ils_ont quatre enfants?   Non, ils ....
g Brighton est dans le nord de l'Angleterre?
  Non, Brighton.................................
h Vous parlez français?   Non, je ....
i Il a 18 ans?   Non, il ....

▶ 5 As you listen to (or read if you haven't got the recording) the passage on **la famille Guise**, look back at the family tree in **Activity 3** to help you understand it better.

La Famille Guise

Monsieur et Madame Guise sont français. Ils_habitent Chaville, 15 rue de la Gare et ils travaillent à Paris. Yves est comptable et Isabelle travaille dans la publicité. Monsieur et Madame Guise ne parlent pas anglais. Ils_ont deux filles: Rosine qui a vingt-cinq ans et Anne qui a trente-deux ans. Rosine travaille dans une banque, elle est divorcée. Anne est secrétaire et travaille à mi-temps. Elle est mariée avec Marc qui est professeur de Math dans_une école. Ils_ont deux_enfants: une fille, Solange et un fils, Didier. Solange a douze ans, Didier a dix ans. Anne et Marc parlent anglais tous les deux.

Rôle-play

Now imagine you're Anne and that you've been asked to take part in a survey. What would you reply to the interviewer?

a Comment vous_appelez-vous?
b Vous_êtes célibataire?
c Vous_avez des_enfants?
d Des filles ou des garçons?
e Ils_ont quel âge?
f Où habitez-vous?
g Vous travaillez?
Merci beaucoup, Madame.

6 This time you are the interviewer, questioning a man. Here are his replies. What were your questions?

a .... Non, je suis divorcé.

b .... Non, je n'ai pas d'enfants.

c .... Oui, je suis professeur.

d .... Oui, j'habite Paris.

e .... Oui, j'ai deux frères et une sœur.

f .... Ils_ont 20 ans, 17 ans et 12 ans.

g .... Non, je suis canadien.

h .... Oui, je parle anglais.

Mini-test

1 How would you ask someone to speak more slowly?
2 **D'accord** means   **a** very much
                      b OK
                      c sorry
3 What does **je ne comprends pas** mean?
4 How would you ask for a bottle of wine? Je ....
5 You want to know what something costs. What would you say?..
6 And now say in French: **a** my name is …
                                 b I am not married.
                                 c I live in Brighton.
                                 d I work in London.

You'll find the answers in **Key to the exercises and tests**. If most of the answers are correct, you should congratulate yourself for doing so well. Before going on to Unit 4 take the **Self-assessment test 1** (Units 1–3) p. 210. Check your answers in **Key to the exercises and tests** and write your score in the box below. If you score between 40 and 50 points, you can go straight on to Unit 4. If your score is between 20 and 40 points, you need to spend more time revising the areas which require more work. Below 20 points, go back over Units 1, 2 and 3 and take the test again to see how much you have improved.

Self-assessment score (Units 1–3)

Points: _____/50

04

vous habitez où?

where do you live?

In this unit you will learn
- numbers from 20 to 70
- simple and useful questions and their likely answers
- how to say that things are yours or someone else's
- how to understand prices

Before you start

In this unit you will meet some simple questions which you will find useful when coping with everyday situations in France. Some are formed simply by raising the voice at the end of a statement, others by including a question word in the statement: **c'est loin, la gare?** *how far is the station?*, **c'est combien, le billet?** *how much is the ticket?*

Essayez! **Have a go!** At a party you meet a friend of a friend who only speaks French. You want to be friendly and try out your French. You know he/she is married and has a family. Can you think of at least four questions you could ask in French?

Key words and phrases

vous vous_appelez comment?	*what's your name?*
je m'appelle...	*my name is ...*
vous_habitez où?	*where do you live?*
le magasin est_ouvert?	*is the shop open?*
non, il est fermé	*no, it's closed*
c'est loin?	*is it far?*
c'est_au bout de la rue	*it is at the end of the street*
c'est près d'ici	*it is nearby*
c'est_à 50 mètres d'ici	*it is 50 metres away* (lit. 50 m from here)
c'est_à cinq minutes à pied	*it is five minutes away on foot*
c'est_une grande ville	*it is a big town*
c'est_une petite piscine	*it is a small swimming pool*
c'est gratuit, la brochure?	*is the brochure free?*
non, il faut payer	*no, you must pay* (lit. it's necessary to pay)
c'est combien, le billet?	*how much is the ticket?*
c'est où, l'arrêt d'autobus?	*where is the bus stop?*
c'est où, la station de métro?	*where is the tube (subway) station?*
c'est quand, le départ?	*when is the departure?*
c'est_à quel étage?	*what floor is it on?*
c'est_au premier étage	*it's on the first floor*
c'est cher/bon marché?	*it's expensive/cheap?*
il y a un car pour Caen?	*is there a coach for Caen?*
oui, il y en_a un	*yes, there is one*

il y a un train direct pour Paris?	is there a direct train to Paris?
non, il n'y en_a pas	no, there isn't any
un restaurant dans l'hôtel	a restaurant in the hotel
beaucoup de ...	a lot of ...

▶ Numbers 20–70

vingt	20	trente-deux	32
vingt_et un	21	quarante	40
vingt-deux	22	quarante et un	41
vingt-trois	23	quarante-deux	42
vingt-quatre	24	cinquante	50
vingt-cinq	25	cinquante et un	51
vingt-six	26	cinquante-deux	52
vingt-sept	27	soixante	60
vingt-huit	28	soixante et un	61
vingt-neuf	29	soixante-deux	62
trente	30	soixante-dix	70
trente et un	31		

▶ Dialogue

Jane has been invited to an office party. She strikes up a conversation with one of her friend's colleagues. Does he work? Does he live near Paris? Is he married? Has he got any children?

Jane	Vous vous_appelez comment?
Jean Durand	Je m'appelle Jean Durand et vous?
Jane	Moi, Jane Wilson. Vous_habitez où?
Jean Durand	**Dans la banlieue** de Paris, à Chatou.
Jane	Et ... c'est loin Chatou?
Jean Durand	C'est_à 45 minutes en train. Il y a un train direct Paris–Chatou.
Jane	Et ... vous travaillez?
Jean Durand	Oui, je suis_homme d'affaires et vous?
Jane	Moi, je travaille en_Angleterre, à Brighton ... je suis dentiste.
Jean Durand	Et vous_êtes_**en vacances**?
Jane	Oui, je suis_ici **depuis deux semaines. J'aime** beaucoup Paris. Vous_êtes marié?
Jean Durand	Oui.
Jane	Vous_avez des_enfants?
Jean Durand	J'ai trois_enfants: deux filles et un garçon.

Jane	Il y a **une école** à Chatou?
Jean Durand	Oui. Il y en_a une à dix minutes à pied.
Jane	**Votre femme** travaille?
Jean Durand	Oui, elle est professeure à l'école de Chatou.
Jane	C'est_une grande ville, Chatou?
Jean Durand	Oui, c'est grand. Il y a beaucoup de magasins, deux banques, une pharmacie, **un parc** et une piscine.
Jane	Il y a un cinéma?
Jean Durand	Non, il n'y en_a pas.

dans la banlieue	*in the suburbs*
un_homme d'affaires	*a businessman*
en vacances	*on holiday*
depuis deux semaines	*for two weeks*
j'aime	*I like/love*
une école	*a school*
votre femme	*your wife*
un parc	*a park*

Grammar

1 How to ask simple questions

As you already know, the easiest way to ask a question is to make a statement and raise the voice on the last syllable:

Vous_êtes marié?   *Are you married?*

2 *C'est ...?* Is it ...? Is that ...?

You can start the question with **c'est** (lit. *it is ...*) and raise the voice at the end of the sentence. To say that *it isn't* use **ce n'est pas**:

C'est loin?   *Is is far?*
Non, ce n'est pas loin.   *No, it isn't far.*

3 *Il y a ...?* Is there ...? Are there ...?

You can also start the question with **il y a** (*there is, there are*) and raise the voice at the end of the sentence. To say *there is no ...* or *there are no ...*, use **il n'y a pas de ...**

Il y a un restaurant dans
l'hôtel?
Non, il n'y a pas de
restaurant ici.

Is there a restaurant in
the hotel?
No, there is no restaurant
here.

4 Some likely answers: yes, there is; no, there isn't

To the question **il y a une banque près d'ici?** *is there a bank
nearby?* most people in France would answer **oui, il y en_a une**
yes there is one or **non, il n'y en_a pas** *no there isn't (one)*; **en**
which means *one, some, of it, of them,* can be omitted in English
but not French:

Il y a une banque à Chatou?
Oui, il y en_a une.
Il y a une cabine
téléphonique près d'ici?
Non, il n'y en_a pas.

Is there a bank at Chatou?
Yes, there is one.
*Is there a telephone box
near here?*
No, there isn't one.

5 More answers: yes, I have; no, I haven't

Similarly, to the question **vous_avez un/une …** you will hear the
answer **oui, j'en_ai un/une** or **non, je n'en_ai pas**:

Vous_avez un timbre?
Oui, j'en_ai un.
Vous_avez une voiture?
Oui, j'en_ai une.
Non, je n'en_ai pas.

Do you have a stamp?
Yes, I have.
Do you have a car?
Yes, I have.
No, I haven't.

6 Other questions

You can form other questions starting with **c'est** or giving a
statement and adding the question word afterwards:

C'est comment, le musée?
C'est combien, le billet?
C'est où, l'arrêt d'autobus?
C'est quand, les vacances?
Les magasins ferment
quand?
Les magasins ouvrent
quand?

What is the museum like?
How much is the ticket?
Where is the bus stop?
When are the holidays?
When do the shops shut?

When do the shops open?

7 *Mon, ton, son* My, your, his

Thing possessed	*my*	*your*	*his/her/its/ one's*	*our*	*your*	*their*
masc. sing.	**mon**	**ton**	**son**	**notre**	**votre**	**leur**
fem. sing.	**ma**	**ta**	**sa**	**notre**	**votre**	**leur**
masc. & fem. pl.	**mes**	**tes**	**ses**	**nos**	**vos**	**leurs**

Like all adjectives in French, these agree with the noun they refer to:

mon mari	*my husband*
ma femme	*my wife*
mes enfants	*my children*

Take care when using **son** and **sa** to make them agree with the thing being owned, and not the owner:

le fils de M. Durand becomes **son fils** (*his son*)
le fils de Mme Durand becomes **son fils** (*her son*)
la fille de M. Durand becomes **sa fille** (*his daughter*)
la fille de Mme Durand becomes **sa fille** (*her daughter*)

ℹ Create every opportunity to immerse yourself in the language

- **Try to practise your French with other learners or French speakers.**
  Find out about French societies, clubs or circles in your area (the library is a good place to find out information). They provide an opportunity to meet other people with whom you can practise your newly acquired language.

- **Listen to some French regularly.**
  Not only will it sharpen your comprehension skills but it will help you improve your pronunciation.

- **Read something in French.**
  Buy a French magazine and read the French press online and see how many words you can recognize. Try to get the gist of short articles by concentrating on the words you know, getting clues from photographs if there are any and using some guesswork.

- For more details refer to the **Taking it further** section on page 207.

Activities

1 Match the questions in the left-hand column with the answers on the right.

a C'est gratuit?

b C'est M. Martel?

c C'est_ouvert?

d Il y a des timbres?

e C'est loin?

f C'est cher?

g C'est combien?

h C'est près?

i Non, c'est Monsieur Durand.

ii Non, c'est bon marché.

iii Non, c'est_à dix minutes à pied.

iv Oui, c'est tout près.

v Non, il faut payer.

vi C'est 50€4.

vii Non, c'est fermé.

viii Non, il n'y en_a pas.

2 You've just arrived at an hotel. At the reception you find out about the hotel and the amenities in the area. Can you reconstruct the conversation?

a ....

Non, Monsieur, il n'y a pas de restaurant dans l'hôtel.

b ....

Oui, il y a une pharmacie au bout de la rue.

c ....

Oui, il y a beaucoup de magasins près d'ici.

d ....

Non, Monsieur, la banque est fermée maintenant.

e ....

Oui, il y a un train direct pour Paris.

f ....

Non, la gare n'est pas loin. Elle est_à cinq minutes à pied.

g ....

Les toilettes sont_au premier étage.

3 That night you have a nightmare; you are in town doing some shopping but it is a very strange town. Using the example as a model, describe what you see to your friend?

Example: Il y a des cartes postales mais il n'y a pas de timbres.

a .... une pharmacie .... aspirine.

b .... pâtisserie .... croissants.

c .... une gare .... trains.

d .... un arrêt d'autobus .... bus.

e .... un bar .... bière.

f .... une cabine téléphonique .... téléphone.

4 You overhear one side of a woman's conversation in a café. These are the answers, but what were the questions?

  a Oui, je suis_en vacances.
  b Oui, je suis mariée?
  c Non, je n'ai pas d'enfants.
  d Non, je n'habite pas Londres, j'habite Manchester.
  e Je travaille comme secrétaire.

5 Fill in the gaps using one of the following question words: **où, quand, comment, combien**.

  a C'est .... le journal?   C'est 2€11.
  b C'est .... l'arrêt d'autobus? C'est_au bout de la rue.
  c C'est .... les vacances?   C'est_en juin.
  d C'est .... le Sacré-Cœur? C'est_au nord de Paris.
  e C'est .... la Pyramide?   C'est près du Louvre.
  f C'est .... le film?   C'est super.

▶ 6 Listen to how much each item costs and fill in the price tags in Euros.

a	b	c	d	e

▶ 7 Rôle-play

You are stopped by a French tourist in your home town. She needs some information on the amenities of the town. Answer her.

Mini-test

1 Ask someone for his/her name.
2 Find out if he/she works.
3 Find out where he/she lives and say that you live in the suburbs of London.
4 Say how old you are.
5 Say that there is a bank nearby, at the end of the street.

05

quelle heure est-il?

what time is it?

In this unit you will learn

- the days of the week
- the months of the year
- some useful expressions of time
- numbers from 70 to 90
- how to say what you want to do
- how to ask what you can or cannot do
- how to ask for help
- the dates
- how to tell the time

Before you begin

For a successful holiday or business trip in France you need to know when things are happening or when shops open. You also need to be able to say what you want to do, find out if it can be done and ask for help. You will be able to achieve all this with the few structures introduced in this unit. You'll also be introduced to quite a lot of vocabulary: days, dates and times.

Essayez! Have a go!

1 You are in l'office du tourisme (*tourist office*) in Paris. How would you ask for a street map? Ask if there are a bank and telephone box nearby? Can you think of other questions to ask?

2 Revise the following numbers: say them aloud.

41 – 22 – 68 – 15 – 5 – 55 – 14 – 29 – 31 – 47 – 60 – 11

▶ Check your answers and your pronunciation with the recording. If you do not have the recording, check with **Numbers** at the back of the book.

Key words and phrases

à quelle heure ...	*at what time ...*
***quand est-ce que l'avion part?**	*when does the aircraft leave?*
***quand est-ce que le bus arrive?**	*when does the bus arrive?*
***quand est-ce qu'on rentre?**	*when do we come back?*
***quand est-ce qu'on peut prendre le petit-déjeuner?**	*when can we have breakfast?*
***quand est-ce qu'il y a un métro?**	*when is there a (tube, subway) train?*
***quand finit le concert?**	*when does the concert finish?*
quelle heure est-il?	*what time is it?*
il est ...	*it's ...*
qu'est-ce que vous faites dans la vie?	*what's your job* (lit. what do you do in life?)
dans dix minutes	*in ten minutes' time*
à dix heures du soir	*at ten o'clock in the evening*
je travaille ...	*I work ...*
tous les jours de la semaine	*every day of the week*
sauf le samedi et le dimanche	*except Saturdays and Sundays*
le lundi, le mardi	*on Mondays, Tuesdays*
et le mercredi	*and Wednesdays*

le jeudi et le vendredi	on Thursdays and Fridays
jusqu'à midi/minuit	until lunch/midnight
depuis dix heures du matin	since ten in the morning
pendant l'après-midi	during the afternoon
je regarde la télévision ...	I watch TV ...
quelquefois	sometimes
souvent	often
toujours	always
aujourd'hui	today
demain	tomorrow
maintenant	now

i You can make the same questions easier by placing the question word afterwards:

L'avion part quand?	*When does the plane leave?*
Le bus arrive quand?	*When does the bus arrive?*

Pratiquez! *Practise!* Can you work out a simpler way of asking the other questions marked with an asterisk?

▶ Les mois de l'année *The months of the year*

janvier	*January*	juillet	*July*
février	*February*	août	*August*
mars	*March*	septembre	*September*
avril	*April*	octobre	*October*
mai	*May*	novembre	*November*
juin	*June*	décembre	*December*

▶ Numbers 70–90

soixante-dix	70	quatre-vingts	80
soixante et onze	71	quatre-vingt-un	81
soixante-douze	72	quatre-vingt-deux	82
soixante-treize	73	quatre-vingt-trois	83
soixante-quatorze	74	quatre-vingt-quatre	84
soixante-quinze	75	quatre-vingt-cinq	85
soixante-seize	76	quatre-vingt-six	86
soixante-dix-sept	77	quatre-vingt-sept	87
soixante-dix-huit	78	quatre-vingt-huit	88
soixante-dix-neuf	79	quatre-vingt-neuf	89
		quatre-vingt-dix	90

▶ Dialogue

Jane is asking Mme Durand about her working week. Listen to the recording several times. At what time does Mme Durand start in the mornings and finish in the evenings? Where does she go for lunch?

Jane	Mme Durand, qu'est-ce-que vous faites dans la vie?
Mme Durand	Je suis professeure de biologie.
Jane	Vous travaillez tous les jours?
Mme Durand	Oui, je travaille à temps plein, donc tous les jours sauf le dimanche.
Jane	A quelle heure est-ce que vous commencez le matin?
Mme Durand	**Ça dépend**, le lundi, le mercredi et le vendredi, je commence à huit heures et demie, mais le mardi et le jeudi je ne travaille pas le matin.
Jane	A quelle heure finissez-vous l'après-midi?
Mme Durand	Je finis à cinq heures et demie le lundi, le mardi, le jeudi et le vendredi. Le mercredi après-midi je ne travaille pas **mais je reste** dans mon **bureau**. Le samedi, l'école finit à midi et c'est le week-end jusqu'au lundi matin.
Jane	Où est-ce que vous déjeunez à midi?
Mme Durand	Mes_enfants et moi, nous déjeunons_à l'école. Il y a une cafétéria **qui est_ouverte** toute la journée de neuf heures à cinq heures.
Jane	Et le week-end, qu'est-ce que vous faites?
Mme Durand	Ah, le week-end c'est **formidable** mais_**il passe trop vite**. Samedi après-midi je regarde souvent le football à la télévision avec mon **mari** et mes_enfants. Dimanche **on va** toujours à la piscine de Chatou.

ça dépend	*it depends*
mais je reste	*but I stay*
le bureau	*the office*
qui est_ouverte	*which is open*
formidable	*great*
il passe trop vite	*it goes too quickly*
mari	*husband*
on va	*we go*

Grammar

1 Saying what you want / want to do

Instead of saying **je veux** (*I want*), it's more polite to start with **je voudrais** (*I would like*). To say what you want to do, put the infinitive next. (**Je veux** and **je voudrais** are part of the verb **vouloir**.)

Je voudrais une chambre pour ce soir.	*I would like a room for tonight.*
Je voudrais acheter un timbre pour l'Angleterre.	*I would like to buy a stamp for England.*

2 Asking what you can do; asking for help

To ask if you can do something use **je peux** or **on peut** followed by the infinitive describing what you want to do. To ask for someone's help use **vous pouvez**. (**Je peux, on peut, vous pouvez,** are part of the verb **pouvoir**.)

Je peux changer de l'argent?	*Can I change some money?*
On peut prendre le petit déjeuner à quelle heure?	*At what time can I / we have breakfast?*
Vous pouvez répéter?	*Can you repeat that?*

3 Three different ways to ask a question

a By giving a questioning tone to what is really a statement:

Tu es française?	*Are you French?*

b By leaving the verb as it is and using **est-ce que** (pronounced *esker*) which is the equivalent of the English *do, does,* in sentences such as *do you speak English?*

Est-ce que tu travailles?	*Do you work?*
Où est-ce que tu habites?	*Where do you live?*

c By turning the verb round and joining the two parts with a hyphen:

Travailles-tu?	*Do you work?*

i Out of the three different ways of asking a question, the safest one is **b** as there are no situations in which **est-ce que** cannot be used; **a** is common in conversation but less so in written French; **c** is not usually used with **je**.

4 Questions starting with *Qu'est-ce que ...?* What ...?

Many questions start with qu'est-ce que ...? *what ...?*

Qu'est-ce que c'est?	*What's that?*
Qu'est-ce que vous désirez?	*What would you like?* (in a shop)
Qu'est-ce que vous faites dans la vie?	*What's your job?* (lit. what do you do in life?)

Qu'est-ce que can also be replaced by quoi and placed at the end like other question words (quand, où, comment):

C'est quoi?	*What's that?*
Vous désirez quoi?	*What would you like?*
Vous faites quoi dans la vie?	*What's your job?*

5 Verbs ending in *-ir* and *-re*

There are three main groups of regular verbs in French:

verbs ending in -er	e.g. travailler
verbs ending in -ir	e.g. finir
verbs ending in -re	e.g. attendre

To work out the present tense of -ir and -re verbs, knock the -ir and -re off the infinitives and then add the following endings:

finir *to finish*		attendre *to wait*	
je	finis	j'	attends
tu	finis	tu	attends
il/elle/on	finit	il/elle/on	attend
nous	finissons	nous	attendons
vous	finissez	vous	attendez
ils/elles	finissent	ils/elles	attendent

A quelle heure finissez-vous?	*At what time do you finish?*
Je finis à 5h.30.	*I finish at 5.30.*
L'école finit à midi.	*School finishes at lunchtime.*
J'attends le train de 7h.30.	*I'm waiting for the 7.30 train.*
Elle attend son petit_ami.	*She's waiting for her boyfriend.*

i Remember not to pronounce the last letters in: finis/finit/finissons/finissent; attends/attend/attendons/attendent.

6 Giving the date

The English talk about the 1st, 2nd, 3rd, 4th, etc. ... of the month. The French say 'the 1st' (**le premier** or **1er**) but 'the two', 'the three', 'the four', etc. ... of the month:

Quelle est la date?	*What's the date?*
Nous sommes **le 1er_octobre.**	*It's the 1st October.*
Aujourd'hui c'est **le deux_avril.**	*Today is the 2nd of April.*

7 Telling the time

a The 24-hour clock is used widely in France to distinguish between a.m. and p.m.

il est **treize heures**	*it's 1 p.m.*
il est **quatorze heures quinze**	*it's 2.15 p.m.*
il est **quinze heures trente**	*it's 3.30 p.m.*
il est **seize heures quarante-cinq**	*it's 4.45 p.m.*
il est **dix-sept heures cinquante**	*it's 5.50 p.m.*
il est **dix-huit heures cinquante-deux**	*it's 6.52 p.m.*
il est **dix-neuf heures cinquante-cinq**	*it's 7.55 p.m.*

b The 12-hour clock. To reply to the question **Quelle heure est-il?** *What time is it?*, one is more likely to use the 12-hour clock:

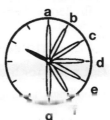

a il est **dix heures**
b il est **dix heures cinq**
c il est **dix heures dix**
d il est **dix heures et quart**
   (*lit. ten hours and a quarter*)
e il est **dix heures vingt**
f il est dix heures vingt-cinq
g il est **dix heures et demie**
   (*lit. ten hours and half*)

h il est **onze heures moins vingt-cinq**
   (*lit. eleven hours minus twenty-five*)
i il est **onze heures moins vingt**
j il est **onze heures moins le quart**
   (*lit. eleven hours minus the quarter*)
k il est **onze heures moins dix**
l il est **onze heures moins cinq**

To distinguish between 9 a.m. and 9 p.m. people say:

il est neuf heures **du matin**   *it's 9 a.m.*
il est neuf heures **du soir**   *it's 9 p.m.*

i Pronounce the **f** of **neuf** as a **v** when it is followed by a vowel or an **h**.

Noon and midnight are however distinguished from each other:

il est **midi**   *it's (12 p.m.) midday*
il est **minuit**   *it's (12 a.m.) midnight*

8 *Faire* to do/to make

Faire is an irregular verb as it does not follow the pattern of **attendre**. It is used in a number of expressions in French (can you think of a recent one you've seen?). Here is a new one: **faire la cuisine** *to do the cooking*:

je fais   nous faisons
tu fais   vous faites
il/elle/on fait   ils/elles font

9 *Prendre* to take

Prendre is also an irregular verb and needs to be learnt on its own. **Apprendre** *to learn* and **comprendre** *to understand* follow the same pattern as **prendre**:

je prends   nous prenons
tu prends   vous prenez
il/elle/on prend   ils/elles prennent

i Experiment while learning

Get a feel for the language

Learning a language is like learning any other skill. Take swimming for example: it is only when you go into the water and put into practice what you've read or been told, that real learning starts.

- Experiment with grammar rules: sit back and reflect on some of the rules you've been learning. See how they compare with your own language or other languages you may already speak. Try to find out some rules on your own and be ready to spot the exceptions. By doing this you'll remember the rules better and get a feel for the language.

- Experiment with words: use the words that you've learnt in new contexts and find out if they are correct. For example, you've learnt that **passe** can mean *go* in the context of time, e.g. **le dimanche passe trop vite**. Experiment with **passe** in new contexts. **Les vacances passent trop vite; la semaine passe ...** etc. Check the new phrases either in this book, a dictionary or with French speakers.

Activities

1 See how many sentences you can make using the verbs in the boxes below and adding a few words.

| je voudrais

je peux
on peut
vous pouvez | **+** | déjeuner ....
habiter ....
prendre ....
acheter ....
finir...............................
commencer ....
apprendre .... |

2 Put the correct endings to the verbs in brackets.

a Le matin je (prendre) le train à 7.30.
b Mes_enfants (commencer) l'école à 8.30.
c Le train (arriver) à huit heures du matin.
d Il (apprendre) le français depuis deux mois.
e A midi on (déjeuner) à la cafétéria.
f Qu'est-ce que vous (prendre) pour le petit-déjeuner?
g De huit heures à neuf_heures je (faire) la cuisine.
h Quelle heure (être)-il?
i Le mercredi, la journée (finir) à midi.
j Qu'est-ce que vous (faire) dans la vie?
k Nous (attendre) à l'arrêt d'autobus.
l Ils (comprendre) l'anglais.

3 Complete the questions by selecting the appropriate endings.

a Comment
b Quel âge
c C'est où
d Qu'est-ce que
e Il y a
f A quelle heure
g Vous_avez

i vous faites dans la vie?
ii une banque près d'ici?
iii vous_appelez-vous?
iv commencez-vous le matin?
v la cabine téléphonique?
vi combien d'enfants?
vii ont-ils?

4 Below is M. Durand's timetable for a typical day. However, the lines got muddled up. Can you put them in the right order, starting with the sentence in bold type?

a Il arrive au travail à 9 heures.
b Le soir, il regarde la télévision jusqu'à 22 heures.
c Il travaille de 9.15 jusqu'à 13 heures.
d Il finit la journée à 17.30.
e Il prend le train à 7 heures du matin.
f **Il prend le petit-déjeuner à 6.30 du matin.**
g A midi il déjeune au restaurant avec ses collègues.
h Il rentre à la maison vers 19.15.

5 Using the pictures to help you, fill in the missing words.

a Je .... le petit-déjeuner.

b Ils .... le train.

c Elle .... le travail à 9h.

d Il .... jusqu'à midi.

e A midi il .... à la cafétéria.

f Le soir il .... le travail à 17.30.

g Elle .... la cuisine.

h Ils .... la télévision.

6 Give the following dates in French:

| 1st May | 10th June | 3rd February | 13th October |
| 21st March | 30th September | 15th July | 6th August |

▶ **7** Listen to the recording. Michel is talking about what he's going to do this week. Fill in the gaps with the correct day of the week in French (**aller** = *to go*).

a .... je déjeune au restaurant avec Sophie
b .... je prends le train pour Manchester
c .... je regarde la télévision avec ma famille
d .... je réserve une chambre à l'Hôtel Nelson
e .... j'achète des fleurs pour ma femme
f .... je voudrais_aller au cinéma avec mes_enfants
g .... je travaille au bureau toute la journée

8 What time is it? Write out your answers in full, using the 12-hour clock. To differentiate between a.m. and p.m. you can use **du matin/de l'après midi/du soir**. Use also **midi** and **minuit** to distinguish between the middle of the day and the middle of the night.

▶ **9** Rôle-play
A journalist interviews you on your typical week. Take part in the interview.

Mini-test

1 Say the days of the week in reverse order starting with Sunday.
2 How would you ask (the easy and more difficult ways) 'When does the bank shut?'
3 Ask the ticket collector in Calais 'Is there a train for Lille?'
4 How would you ask if you can have breakfast in the hotel?
5 Give the date and the time.

06

pour aller à ...?
the way to ...?

In this unit you will learn
- how to count from 90 upwards
- how to ask for and understand directions
- useful verbs to describe what you do every day

Before you start

In **Key words and phrases**, Unit 4, you learnt to say how far somewhere is and how long it takes to go somewhere on foot and by car. Revise these structures as you will need them to understand the dialogue in this unit.

You now know how to ask where things are: **Où est ...?** or **C'est où ...?** Asking the way is also very simple; you start your question with the phrase **pour aller à** and raise the voice at the end of the statement.

Understanding the answer can be more tricky and you'll need to pick out the few essential words such as **tout droit, à gauche, à droite** out of the flow of other words.

As people give you directions, repeat after them, to make sure you have understood. If you do not understand, ask them to repeat or slow down.

Essayez! **Have a go!**

1 Ask someone:
   a to speak more slowly
   b to repeat

2 Talk about your typical day. Use the verbs in the box below to make it exciting and busy.

---

je reste ....   je travaille ....

               je regarde ....

                              je finis ....

je commence ....   je rentre ....

               je prends le déjeuner ....

Key words and phrases

To go straight on

pour_aller à ...	*the way to ...*
(vous) allez tout droit	*(you) go straight on*
continuez	*carry on*
descendez la rue	*go down the street*
montez l'avenue	*go up the avenue*

passez le magasin	go beyond the shop
traversez la place	cross the square
prenez la route de ...	take the road to ...

To turn

(vous) tournez à gauche	(you) turn left
tournez à droite	turn right
vous_allez prendre ...	you're going to take ...
la première rue à droite	the first street on the right
la deuxième sur votre gauche	the second on your left

Where it is

la place du marché est située ...	the market place is ...
au coin de la rue	at the corner of the street
à côté du supermarché	next to the supermarket
en face de la boulangerie	opposite the baker's
au centre ville	in the town centre
sur votre gauche	on your left
sur, sous	on, under
devant, derrière	in front of, behind
dans	in, inside
entre	between
il faut combien de temps?	how long does it take?
il faut environ 25 minutes	you need about 25 minutes

▶ Numbers over 90

quatre-vingt-dix	90	cent	100
quatre-vingt-onze	91	cent un	101
quatre-vingt-douze	92	cent deux	102
quatre-vingt-treize	93	cent vingt trois	123
quatre-vingt-quatorze	94	cinq cent trente-quatre	534
quatre-vingt-quinze	95	mille	1000
quatre-vingt-seize	96	mille neuf cent quinze	1915
quatre-vingt-dix-sept	97	deux mille	2000
quatre-vingt-dix-huit	98		
quatre-vingt-dix-neuf	99		

▶ Dialogue

Jane passe la journée chez les Durand. L'après-midi, elle décide d'aller au centre ville de Chatou.

Jane is spending the day with the Durands. She decides to go to the town centre in the afternoon.

*While you listen to the recording, look at the street map (**le plan de ville**) of Chatou on page 54. How do you get from M. Durand's house to the park and how long does it take to walk there?*

Jane	M. Durand, avez-vous un plan de Chatou? Je voudrais aller **d'abord** au parc et puis, **si j'ai le temps**, dans les magasins ...
M. Durand	**Voici** le plan. Vous pouvez **le garder** car j'en_ai deux.
Jane	Merci beaucoup. Où est le parc de Chatou?
M. Durand	**Voyons**, nous sommes_ici sur le plan. Vous tournez à gauche **en sortant de la maison**, vous_allez jusqu'au bout de la rue Vaugirard, vous tournez à droite dans la rue Vincennes et puis c'est sur votre gauche à 200 mètres.
Jane	Bon, alors, à gauche en sortant puis je tourne à droite et c'est sur ma gauche ... C'est loin à pied?
M. Durand	Non, pas très loin; il faut environ 25 minutes.
Jane	Oh là là, c'est **trop loin** pour moi. Euh, on peut y aller en_autobus?
M. Durand	Oui, oui. L'arrêt d'autobus est situé juste au coin de la rue Vaugirard. C'est très pratique et il y a un autobus toutes les dix minutes.
Jane	Je voudrais aussi **faire des_achats** pour moi et acheter quelques souvenirs pour ma famille en Grande-Bretagne et au Canada.
M. Durand	Eh bien, vous pouvez aller au **centre commercial**. Il est sur la place du marché à côté de la gare. Vous_avez un_autobus direct. Il va du parc au centre commercial.
Jane	Bon, je pars tout de suite ... j'ai beaucoup de choses à acheter et ... je voudrais rentrer vers 19 heures.

d'abord	*firstly*
si j'ai le temps	*if I have the time*
voici	*here is ...*
le garder	*keep it*
voyons	*let's see*
en sortant de la maison	*as you leave the house*
trop loin	*too far*
faire des_achats	*to do some shopping*
le centre commercial	*the shopping centre*

Grammar

1 Asking the way and giving directions

Pour_aller à (*to get to*) is a very useful structure to remember. Used in a questioning tone it means *How do I/we get to ...?*

Pardon, Monsieur, pour_aller à Gordes?	*Excuse me, Sir, how do we get to Gordes?*
Pour_aller à Gordes, prenez la route pour St. Saturnin.	*To get to Gordes, take the road to St Saturnin.*

2 *Aller* to go *partir* to leave

Here are two very useful verbs. Both verbs are irregular, and **aller** is particularly useful as it is used when speaking about the future (explained in Unit 10):

aller *to go*	**partir** *to leave*
je vais	**je pars**
tu vas	**tu pars**
il/elle/on va	**il/elle/on part**
nous allons	**nous partons**
vous allez	**vous partez**
ils/elles vont	**ils/elles partent**

Vous_allez jusqu'au bout de la rue.	*You go to the end of the road.*
Je voudrais aller à la banque.	*I would like to go to the bank.*
Je pars tout de suite.	*I'm leaving immediately.*

3 Understanding directions

Understanding directions can be more tricky than asking the way as the directions can sound complicated, so it is important to pick out the essential words:

a As an answer to your question, you'll probably hear one of the following constructions:

prenez	**descendez**	**tournez à**	**allez**	**montez**
take	*go down*	*turn*	*go*	*go up*

Il faut prendre ...	You have to (lit. it's necessary to) take ...
Il faut descendre ...	You have to go down ...
Il faut tourner ...	You have to turn ...
Il faut aller ...	You have to go ...
Il faut monter ...	You have to go up ...

b The t in **droite** *right* is sounded but it is not in **droit** *straight*. **Droit** is usually preceded by **tout**: **tout droit** *straight on*. **Droite** is preceded by à or **sur la**: **à droite, sur la droite**:

| Il faut aller **tout droit**. | You have to go straight on. |
| La gare est **sur la droite**. | The station is on the right. |

c You may be unlucky when asking directions and find that you are asking a tourist! His answer would be **je ne sais pas** (*I don't know*), or **je ne suis pas d'ici** (*I am not from here*).

d If you don't understand the information, e.g. the address, the street name, or the number of the building you are given, use the structure **c'est quel(le) ...?** (Unit 3) to have the information repeated:

C'est quelle rue?	*Which street is it?*
C'est quel numéro?	*Which number is it?*
C'est quelle adresse?	*Which address is it?*

4 When to use à; when to use *en*

To say that you are in town or you are going / want to go to a town always use **à** (with an accent to differentiate it from **a** *has*). Study the examples below:

| Je suis à Bordeaux. | *I'm in Bordeaux.* |
| Nous_allons à Bordeaux. | *We're going to Bordeaux.* |

To say that you are in a country or you're going to a country, use **en** with feminine countries (often finishing with an -e) and au/aux with the others.

Je suis en_Australie.	*I am in Australia.*
Je vais en_Angleterre.	*I'm going to England.*
Vous_allez au Canada.	*You're going to Canada.*

i The country is preceded by its article in sentences such as:

| Je connais bien la Suisse. | *I know Switzerland, quite well.* |
| J'aime beaucoup le Portugal. | *I like Portugal a lot.* |

5 When *à* (at, to, in, on) is followed by *le, la, l', les* ...

The preposition à followed by a definite article (le, la, l', les) changes its form in the following way:

à + le	becomes	**au**
à + la	remains	**à la**
à + l'	remains	**à l'**
à + les	becomes	**aux**

Pour_aller **au musée** du Louvre, s'il vous plaît? *Which way to the Louvre Museum please?*

Nous_allons **à l'église** St. Paul. *We are going to St Paul's Church.*

Il arrive **à la gare** à huit heures du matin. *He arrives at the station at eight o'clock in the morning.*

Il va **aux_États-Unis** deux fois par mois. *He goes to the United States twice a month.*

6 Locating the exact spot

Remember that when **de** is used in a combination with **le, la, l', les** in expressions such as **en face de** *opposite*, **à côté de** *next to*, **au coin de** *at the corner of*, **près de** *near*, you need to change its form (Unit 2):

au coin **du parc** *at the corner of the park*
près **des grands magasins** *near the department stores*
en face **de la piscine** *opposite the swimming pool*
à côté **de l'office** du tourisme *next to the tourist office*

7 *Premier, deuxième, troisième* first, second, third

If you are directed to the 3rd floor, the 2nd street and so on, the numbers end in -**ième**:

deuxième	*second*	**quatrième**	*fourth*
troisième	*third*	**dixième**	*tenth*

But, first is **premier** before all masculine nouns, and **première** before all feminine nouns:

Vous montez au **premier** étage. *You go up to the first floor.*

C'est la **première** porte.	*It is the first door.*
Vous prenez la **deuxième** à gauche.	*You take the second on the left.*
C'est le **troisième** bâtiment.	*It's the third building.*

ℹ Self-evaluation

- How well are you doing with speaking French? The revision of the last six dialogues, at the end of this unit, will give you the opportunity to test your overall speaking performance. If you experience some difficulties, look back at the last five units. They give advice on how to organize the study of vocabulary and grammar and how to create opportunities to practise your French.

- How well are you doing with understanding: are you listening to some French every day? Look at page 87 and read about the various ways in which you can improve your understanding. If you have the recording, listen to the dialogues again and again pausing and repeating until you feel familiar with the passages. When listening to a passage, pick out the most important key words.

Activities

1 You are Jane, visiting Chatou for the first time. How would you ask a passer-by the way to:

a la piscine

b la gare   **c** l'église St. Paul

d le musée   **e** l'office du tourisme

▶ 2 Now listen to the replies of the passers-by on the recording and work out which letter on the map represents each of these places. If you haven't got the recording, read the replies below:

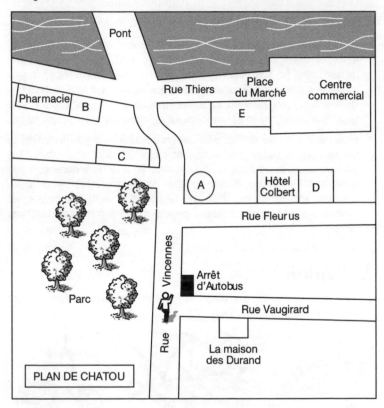

a C'est très facile. Vous montez la rue Vincennes et vous prenez la première à gauche. La piscine se trouve sur votre droite, en face du parc.

b Bon, pour la gare, continuez tout droit, toujours tout droit. Juste avant le pont, tournez à droite et vous_êtes dans la rue Thiers. La gare_est à côté du centre commercial.

c L'église St. Paul? Eh bien, c'est tout droit, à 100 mètres d'ici, sur votre droite, au coin de la rue Fleurus.

d Euh – attendez voir – il faut tourner tout de suite à droite puis descendez la rue Fleurus et le musée est_à 10 minutes à pied sur votre gauche à côté de l'Hôtel Colbert.

e Vous_allez tout droit jusqu'au pont. Juste avant le pont tournez à gauche et l'office du tourisme se trouve à côté d'une pharmacie.

3 Now it's your turn to practise giving directions. Use the text above as a model but you don't have to answer exactly like it; for example instead of **vous montez/descendez la rue** you can say **(vous) allez/continuez tout droit**. (The answers are not given in **Key to the exercises**.) Here are the questions:

a Pardon Monsieur, pour_aller à la piscine?

b S'il vous plaît Madame, je voudrais aller au musée; pouvez-vous me dire où il se trouve?

c Pardon Monsieur, savez-vous où est l'office du tourisme?

d Pardon Mademoiselle, je ne suis pas d'ici ... euh, il y a un centre commercial à Chatou?

4 Choose the right answer.

Jane habite   à Brighton?
               en Brighton?
               de Brighton?

Elle et son petit_ami passent leurs vacances en France
                                         au France
                                         France

mais_ils préfèrent Allemagne.
                     l'Allemagne.
                     en Allemagne.

Jane est restée une semaine à Berlin et trois jours Bonn.
                             Berlin   au Bonn
                             en Berlin   à Bonn.

Cet_été (*this summer*) elle va au Danemark   où elle a des_amis.
                                 Danemark
                                 en Danemark

Son petit_ami va souvent en États-Unis   et au Japon.
                                aux_États-Unis   en Japon.
                                les_États-Units   Japon.

Il est_homme d'affaires (*businessman*) et travaille en Londres.
à Londres.
Londres.

5 Look at the **centre commercial de Chatou** and fill in the blanks using the words from the list below.

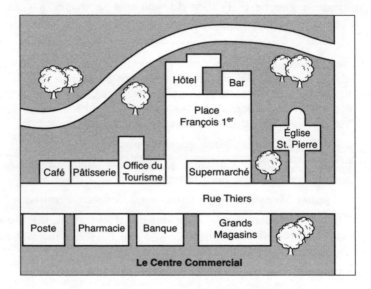

a La poste est .... café.
b Le café est .... pâtisserie.
c L'office du tourisme est ....
la place François 1er.
d La pharmacie est .... la
poste et la banque.
e L'église est .... la rue
Thiers.
f Les .... sont en face du
supermarché.
g Le .... est à côté de
l'hôtel.
h La .... est entre le café et
l'office du tourisme.
i La pharmacie est ....
Thiers.
j Le supermarché est ....
François 1er.

à côté de la

en face du

dans la rue

entre

grands
magasins

pâtisserie

sur la place

au coin de

au bout de

bar

6 Numbers

Test yourself. Pick numbers from the box below and say them aloud in French. Check your answers at the back of the book where all the numbers are listed. Repeat the exercise over a number of days and see if you can improve your performance.

```
    72   24   80   92   65   43   75   61
76    68    15   66    17   96    87    70
    19   21   49   55   65   56   13   77
```

▶ 7 Rôle-play

You are in the shopping centre in Chatou. A French passer-by stops you and asks about the shops. Look at the street map and answer her.

Test

In this unit, **Mini-Test** is replaced by a revision of the last six dialogues: try translating the dialogues from Units 1 to 6 into English and then from English retranslate them orally into French. Check your answers with the book. You might like to record yourself, imagining that you're French. If you have the original recording, compare your own recording with it. How different is yours from the original? Try in your recording to match the speed, the accent and intonations on the original recording.

07

c'est comment?
what is it like?

In this unit you will learn
- how to describe things and people
- how to say precisely what you want
- how to compare people and objects
- colours

Before you start

In Unit 2 you've already seen how to ask for things using just a few words. Getting precisely what you need may involve giving a few more details. This unit will provide you with some of the keywords you'll need to describe what you are looking for, specifying colours, materials, quantities, prices, etc. There is a lot of new vocabulary in this unit, appearing in the sections **Key words and phrases**, **Grammar** and **Activities**. It will be useful to you when doing Unit 11 which concentrates on the topic of shopping in France.

Essayez! **Have a go!** Fill in the blanks in the sentences below with some of the prepositions you met in the last unit.

1 Les fleurs sont .... (*in*) le vase.
2 Le croissant est .... (*on*) l'assiette.
3 Le journal est .... (*between*) le vase et l'assiette.
4 Le jus d'orange est .... (*next to the*) journal.
5 La carte postale est .... (*under*) l'assiette.
6 Les clefs sont .... (*in front of*) le jus de fruit.
7 Les aspirines sont .... (*behind*) le vase.

Key words and phrases

For you to say

faire des achats, des courses, du shopping	*to do some shopping*
dépenser	*to spend*
qu'est-ce que vous_avez comme ... souvenirs/cadeaux?	*what do you have in the way of ... souvenirs/presents?*
qu'est-ce que c'est?	*what is it?*
vous_avez autre chose?	*do you have anything else?*
ça coûte/ça fait combien?	*how much is it?*
c'est de quelle couleur?	*what colour is it?*
je cherche quelque chose ...	*I'm looking for something ...*
grand/moyen/petit	*big/medium/small*
un peu plus grand	*a little bigger*
un peu moins cher	*a little less expensive*
meilleur marché	*cheaper*
spécial/différent	*special/different*
pour réparer, ouvrir	*to repair, open*
je vais prendre le plus petit	*I'll take the smallest*
rouge, blanc, vert, marron/brun, bleu, jaune	*red, white, green, brown, blue, yellow*
faire un paquet-cadeau	*to gift-wrap*
qui est-ce?	*who is it?*
c'est_une personne sympathique	*he/she is a nice person*
c'est_un jeune homme français	*he's a young Frenchman*
c'est_une jeune fille anglaise	*she's a young English girl*
c'est quelqu'un de grand/petit/ gros/mince	*it's someone tall/small/ big/thin*
il porte des lunettes de soleil	*he wears/is wearing sunglasses*
il a les cheveux noirs et raides	*he has black, straight hair*
elle porte une chemise unie	*she wears/is wearing a plain shirt*
elle a les yeux marron	*she has brown eyes*

For you to understand

je vais vous montrer	*I'll show you*
il vaut mieux prendre	*you should take* (lit. *it is better to take*)
si vous voulez bien me suivre	*would you come this way*
payez à la caisse	*pay at the till*

▶ Dialogue

Jane fait des courses dans un grand magasin de Chatou.

Jane is shopping in a department store in Chatou. She is looking for something special to take back to her mother in the UK.

Listen to the recording or read the dialogue in the book: Why does Jane buy the small scarf? She asks for it to be gift-wrapped. What does she say in French?

Vendeuse	Vous désirez?
Jane	Je cherche un souvenir pour ma mère ... euh quelque chose de spécial pour **ramener** en Angleterre.
Vendeuse	Bon, très bien. Alors si c'est pour votre mère, je peux vous montrer des **foulards en soie** avec des scènes typiquement françaises.
Jane	Oh, ils sont très **jolis** et leurs couleurs sont vraiment superbes. C'est combien?
Vendeuse	Alors, les grands coûtent 68€50 et 53€ et les petits 46€.
Jane	Je peux voir **ceux qui** sont à 46€?
Vendeuse	Mais bien sûr. Ils représentent les monuments **célèbres** de Paris. **Certains** sont rouges et bleus, **d'autres** verts et jaunes.
Jane	Je préfère les grands, mais_ils sont trop chers et je ne veux pas trop dépenser.
Vendeuse	Alors, il vaut mieux prendre un petit à 46€.
Jane	Oui, je vais prendre **ce petit** qui représente l'Arc de Triomphe. Ses couleurs bleues et rouges sont superbes et il n'est pas trop cher. **Je crois que** ma mère **sera** très **contente**. Vous pouvez me faire un paquet-cadeau, s'il vous plaît?
Vendeuse	Oui, un instant ... si vous voulez bien me suivre? (*The shop assistant wraps the present up*.) Et maintenant vous payez_à la caisse.
Jane	Ah bon, merci bien, Madame.

ramener	to bring back
foulard (m)	*scarf*
en soie	*made of silk*
joli(e)	*pretty*
ceux qui ...	*the ones which ...*
célèbres	*famous*
certains ... d'autres	*some ... others*

	ce petit	*this small one*
	je crois que	*I believe that*
	sera contente	*will be pleased*

Grammar

1 *Ce, cet, cette, ces* this, that, these, those

Ce, cet, cette all mean *this* or *that*; ces means *these* or *those*. Ce comes before masculine singular nouns, cet before masculine singular nouns beginning with a vowel or silent h, cette before feminine singular nouns and ces before plural nouns:

	masculine	*masc. (before a vowel or silent h)*	*feminine*
singular	ce	cet	cette
plural	ces	ces	ces

ce foulard	*this/that scarf*
cet_homme	*this/that man*
cette femme	*this/that woman* (**femme**, *pronounced 'fam', also means 'wife'*)
ces_enfants	*these/those children*

2 Saying precisely what you want

You already know how to ask for something (Unit 5), e.g. **je voudrais cette bouteille**. This is the most general way of asking for things, but you may want to give more information.

a How much? Expressions of quantity are linked with **de**:

Combien d'enfants?	*How many children?*
beaucoup d'enfants?	*lots of children*
un verre de vin	*a glass of wine*
une boîte de haricots	*a tin of beans*

b Made of what? You can use **de** or **en** to say what things are made of:

une chemise de coton	*a cotton shirt*
une robe en soie	*a silk dress*

c What kind? Add adjectives to describe in more detail:

un verre de vin **rouge**	*a glass of red wine*
une boîte de **petits** pois français	*a tin of French peas*
un kilo de raisins **noirs**	*a kilo of black grapes*

d What's in/on it? Special features such as patterns, flavours or key ingredients are linked with **à**:

un yaourt à l'abricot	*an apricot yoghurt*
un sandwich **au** fromage	*a cheese sandwich*
une glace **à la** vanille	*a vanilla ice cream*
une tarte **aux** pommes	*an apple pie*

Don't forget to change the **à** to **au** or to **aux** if the following noun is masculine or plural.

e With/without. Put **avec** (*with*) or **sans** (*without*) in front of what you want or don't want:

une chambre **avec** télévision	*a room with (a) television*
un hôtel **sans** parking	*a hotel without car park*

3 How adjectives work

As explained in Unit 3 adjectives change according to what they are describing; they may take masculine, feminine or plural forms:

	masculine	feminine
singular	petit	petite
plural	petits	petites

ce **petit** foulard	*this little scarf*
c'est_une **bonne** école	*it's a good school*
les **petits** pois sont verts	*peas are green*
avec des scènes françaises	*with French scenes*

a Adding an **-e** to the masculine (if it has not already got an **-e**) to form the feminine, often changes the pronunciation as in **petit** (m), **petite** (f), but not always, e.g. **noir** (m), **noire** (f), **bleu** (m), **bleue** (f). The **-s** in the plural is not sounded.

b **Brun** is used almost exclusively to refer to the colour of someone's hair, complexion or brown ale (**bière brune**). For most brown objects, use **marron**, which is an invariable form.

c A few adjectives have two masculine forms: the second one is used in front of nouns beginning with a vowel or silent **h**:

le **nouveau** garçon	*the new boy*
le **nouvel**_élève	*the new pupil*
le **vieux** port	*the old harbour*
le **vieil**_hôtel	*the old hotel*

d Here are some common adjectives with irregular endings. You will pick up others as you go along:

masc. masc. 1 masc. 2	*fem.*	*masc. pl.*	*fem. pl.*
beau bel	belle	beaux	belles
nouveau nouvel	nouvelle	nouveaux	nouvelles
vieux vieil	vieille	vieux	vieilles

e Adjectives are usually placed after the noun:

un café **noir**	*a black coffee*
une bière **brune**	*brown ale*

except with common ones such as: **petit** (*small*), **bon(ne)** (*good*), **beau** (*beautiful*), **grand** (*tall*), **jeune** (*young*), **vieux** (*old*), **mauvais** (*bad*), **joli** (*beautiful*), **tout** (*all*):

un **grand** café	*a large coffee*
une **bonne** bière	*a good beer*

f If there are two or more adjectives they are placed after the noun and linked with **et,** or they are placed either side of the noun:

des cheveux **blonds et longs**	*long, blond hair*
un **grand** homme **mince**	*a tall, slim man*

4 Making comparisons

To say that something is *more ... than* or *less ... than* use:

plus ... que	*more ... than*
moins ... que	*less ... than*

Le train est **plus rapide que** la voiture.
The train is faster than the car.

Il est **moins grand que** moi.
He's less tall than I.

i The -s of **plus** is not pronounced except in the following cases:

- before a vowel or silent **h**, **-s** is sounded **z**: **plus_âgé**

- whenever the word means *plus* (+), **-s** is sounded **s**:

  Il y a du beurre **plus** du lait dans la recette.
  There is some butter plus some milk in the recipe.

- when it is followed directly by **que** to produce **plus que** *more than*, (**-s** is sounded **s**):

  Il travaille **plus que** moi.
  He works more than I.

Saying 'better'

To say that something/someone is *better*, use **meilleur (e)**; to say that you do something *better* use **mieux**:

> Le film est meilleur que le livre.
> *The film is better than the book.*

> Elle parle français mieux que moi.
> *She speaks French better than I.*

i Learning to cope with uncertainty

- **Don't over-use your dictionary.**
  When reading a text in the foreign language, don't be tempted to look up every word you don't know. Underline the words you do not understand and read the passage several times, concentrating on trying to get the gist of the passage. If after the third time there are still words which prevent you from getting the general meaning of the passage, look them up in the dictionary.

- **Don't panic if you don't understand.**
  If at some point you feel you don't understand what you are told, don't panic or give up listening. Either try and guess what is being said and keep following the conversation or, if you cannot, isolate the expression or words you haven't understood and have them explained to you. The speaker might paraphrase them and the conversation will carry on.

- **Keep talking.**
  The best way to improve your fluency in the foreign language is to talk every time you have the opportunity to do so: keep the conversation flowing and don't worry about the mistakes. If you get stuck for a particular word, don't let the conversation stop; paraphrase or replace the unknown word with one you do know, even if you have to simplify what you want to say. As a last resort use the word from your own language and pronounce it in the foreign accent.

Activities

1 **A la gare routière:** fill in the blanks with **ce, cet, cette** or **ces**. To check if the words are masculine or feminine look at the **French–English vocabulary**.

Touriste   Pardon Monsieur, ... autobus va à Quimper?

Homme   Oui, Madame, tous ..... autobus vont à Quimper.

Touriste   Je voudrais partir ..... matin. A quelle heure partent les_autobus?

Homme   Bon, ... deux_autobus partent pour Quimper ..... matin. Le premier part à 8.30 et arrive à 12.00 et le deuxième part à 9.15 et arrive à 13.15 ..... après-midi.

Touriste   Très bien. Je veux rentrer ..... nuit. A quelle heure rentre le dernier_autobus de Quimper?

Homme   Alors ..... semaine, le dernier bus quitte Quimper à 20.30.

▶ 2 Using the grid below and M. Durand's description as a model, write down in a few sentences what Mme Durand and Jane look like. Make sure that the adjectives agree with the nouns they describe. Check the vocabulary with the drawings below or in the vocabulary list at the back of the book. Then write a few sentences describing yourself.

	M. Durand	**Mme Durand**	**Jane**
sexe	homme	femme	femme
âge	40 ans	35 ans	23 ans
cheveux	noirs/raides	blonds/longs	bruns/courts
yeux	marron	verts	bleus
taille	1,78 mètre	1,70 mètre	1,62 mètre
poids	79 kg	65 kg	55 kg
signes particuliers	moustache	lunettes rondes	–
vêtements	costume bleu marine, cravate jaune, chaussures noires	ensemble vert uni, chemise blanche, chaussures légères	jean bleu pâle, pull- over blanc, bottes noires

Monsieur Durand a 40 ans. Il a les cheveux noirs et raides et les yeux marron; il fait 1 mètre 78 et pèse 79 kg. Il a une moustache. Il porte un costume bleu marine, une cravate jaune et des chaussures noires.

Look in the **Key** at the back of the book and check that what you've written is correct. Using as a model **M. Durand's** description on the recording, read aloud what you've written.

3 How would you ask for all the items on the list? The words in the box will help, though they aren't all there!

baba (m) vanille (f) petits pois (m) vin (m) pommes (f) fromage (m) citron (m) sucre (m) sandwich (m) poulet (m) verre (m) lait (m) tarte (f) rhum (m) glace (f) café (m) sorbet (m) boîte (f) bouteille (f)	**a** *a tin of French peas* **b** *an apple tart* **c** *a rhum baba* **d** *a vanilla ice cream* **e** *a lemon sorbet* **f** *a big glass of red wine* **g** *a white coffee without sugar* **h** *a chicken at 6€80* **i** *a small black coffee* **j** *a cheese sandwich* **k** *a bottle of milk*

4 Sally is spending Christmas and New Year in France with a French family. She writes to her friend Isabelle. Can you fill the gaps with the words from the box overleaf? You may have to look up some of the words in the **Vocabulary** at the back of the book.

(a) .... Isabelle,

Je suis depuis une semaine avec la (b) .... Guise. Ici
(c) .... le monde est très (d) .... et je passe de très
(e) .... vacances. La maison est (f) .... et (g) .... Je
fais de (h) .... promenades presque tous les (i) .... La
cuisine française est (j) .... que la cuisine (k) .... et je
mange trop. Je parle (l) .... le français maintenant. Je
retourne chez moi la semaine (m) ....

Joyeux Noël et Bonne Année
Sally

> meilleure   longues   tout   jours   confortable
>
> prochaine   famille   bonnes   grande   anglaise   mieux
>
> Chère   sympathique

5 You are in a **café** with four of your friends. The waiter arrives
and you order (**vous commandez**):

Garçon	Bonjour, Messieurs-Dames. Qu'est-ce que vous désirez?
a *You*	*A large black coffee.*
Garçon	Un grand café, oui…
b *You*	*Two draught beers*
Garçon	Oui.
c *You*	*And a small white coffee.*
Garçon	Alors un grand crème, deux limonades et un petit café noir, c'est ça?
d *You*	*No. Two draught beers, a small white coffee and a large black coffee.*
Garçon	Bon très bien. Excusez-moi.
e *You*	*Have you got some croissants?*
Garçon	Vous_en voulez combien?
f *You*	*Say you want four.*
Garçon	Très bien, Monsieur.

▶ 6 Rôle-play

You have organized a trip to Paris to meet your French pen-
friend whom you have never met. He has offered to meet you
at the station. He phones you to find out about your arrival.
Take part in the conversation.

Mini-test

Now test yourself and see how well you remember the information in Units 6 and 7.

1 How would you say:
  a at the end of the street
  b take the road to Lille

2 **Il faut prendre** means:
  a you can take
  b you must take
  c you take

3 **Vous_allez tout droit** means:
  a you go straight on
  b you turn right
  c you take the second on the left

4 How would you say:
  Do you have anything else?
  What colour is it?
  I'll take the smallest.

Before going on to Unit 8, do the **Self-assessment test 1** (Units 4–7). As in Unit 3, record your score below. If your score is between 40 and 50 points, you can go straight on to Unit 8. If it is between 20 and 40 points, revise the points and areas which require more work. Below 20 points, you need to go back over Units 4, 5, 6 and 7, and take the test again to see how much you have improved.

Self-assessment score (Units 4–7)

Points: _____/50

08

vous aimez le sport?

do you like sport?

In this unit you will learn how to
- ask and talk about likes and dislikes
- say what you and others do as a hobby
- talk about the weather

Before you start

Once you know a French person well enough you'll find yourself wanting to express your likes and dislikes and talk about your hobbies; here are the structures you'll need:

j'adore	*I adore, I love*
j'aime beaucoup	*I like very much*
je n'aime pas	*I don't like*
je déteste	*I hate*
je joue	*I play*
je fais	*I do*

Talking about the weather is a particularly important aspect of the British way of life; you may find it useful to enquire about the weather forecast if you are planning some kind of outdoor activity.

Essayez! **Have a go!** You are in a shop in France looking for a corkscrew. However, you don't know the French word for it. How would you say that you're looking for something to open bottles of wine?

You ....

Shopkeeper Ah! **Vous voulez un tire-bouchon** (a corkscrew)?

Key words and phrases

For you to say

qu'est-ce que vous faites/ pratiquez comme sport?	*what sport do you do?*
vous faites quoi pendant vos loisirs?	*what hobbies do you have?*
vous aimez faire du sport?	*do you like doing sport?*
quelle est votre opinion préférée?	*which evening do you prefer?*
j'adore aller au restaurant	*I love going to the restaurant*
mon sport préféré est la natation	*swimming is my favourite sport*
j'aime (beaucoup) ...	*I like (very much) ...*
jouer au squash	*playing squash*
la cuisine française	*French cooking*
écouter de la musique	*listening to music*
regarder la télévision	*watching television*

je n'aime pas ...	*I don't like ...*
la planche à voile	*windsurfing*
la musique classique	*classicial music*
me promener à pied	*going for a walk*
je déteste faire la cuisine	*I hate cooking*
je joue au tennis	*I play tennis*
je joue du piano	*I play the piano*
je préfère l'équitation	*I prefer riding*

For you to understand

moi, ce que j'aime c'est	*what I really like is going out*
sortir avec mes_amis	*with my friends*
moi, ce que je déteste c'est	*what I really dislike is*
la viande saignante	*rare meat*

Le temps *The weather*

quel temps fait-il?	*what's the weather like?*
il fait beau, mauvais	*the weather is fine, bad*
il fait chaud, froid	*it is hot, cold*
le soleil brille	*the sun shines*
il pleut	*it's raining*
il neige	*it's snowing*

▶ Dialogue

Jane parle de sports et de loisirs avec les Durand.

Jane and the Durands are talking about sport and hobbies.

Listen to the recording or read the dialogue and then answer the following questions: What's Mrs Durand's favourite hobby? What sports does Mr Durand do?

Jane	Mme Durand, qu'est-ce que vous faites pendant vos loisirs?
Mme Durand	Moi, j'adore faire la cuisine, **surtout** la cuisine française.
Jane	Et dans la cuisine française, quels sont vos **plats favoris**?
Mme Durand	Eh bien, j'aime beaucoup faire tous les plats en sauce, en particulier **le boeuf bourguignon** ou **le**

coq au vin. Vous savez, mon mari aime bien manger et bien **boire**; c'est un gourmet et **il apprécie** ma cuisine … alors **ça fait plaisir**!

Jane Et vous, Monsieur Durand, vous_aimez faire la cuisine?

M. Durand Moi, **je laisse la cuisine** à ma femme. Elle la fait très bien. Je préfère le sport.

Jane Quels sports **pratiquez**-vous?

M. Durand Je joue au squash deux fois par semaine après mon travail et **quand j'ai le temps**, je fais de la natation avec les_enfants le samedi, à la piscine de Chatou.

Mme Durand Tu aimes bien aussi faire de la planche à voile **en_été**.

M. Durand Oui, **c'est vrai**. J'aime beaucoup la planche à voile surtout quand_il y a du **vent**, mais je déteste en faire quand_il fait froid ou quand_il pleut.

Mme Durand Et vous Jane, qu'est-ce que vous faites comme sport?

Jane Oh moi, je pratique un peu tous les sports: le badminton, le tennis et quelquefois l'équitation, mais je n'ai pas beaucoup de temps pour faire du sport.

surtout	*mainly*
plats favoris	*favourite dishes*
le boeuf bourguignon	*beef stew with wine*
le coq au vin	*chicken cooked in wine*
vous savez	*you know*
boire	*to drink*
il apprécie	*he appreciates*
ça fait plaisir	*it is a pleasure*
je laisse la cuisine	*I leave the cooking*
pratiquer	*to do*
quand j'ai le temps	*when I have the time*
en_été	*in summer*
c'est vrai	*it's true*
le vent	*the wind*

Grammar

1 Asking and saying what you do as a hobby

In French to answer questions such as **qu'est-ce vous faites comme sport?** *what do you do in the way of sport?* or **qu'est-ce que vous faites pendant vos loisirs?** *what are your hobbies?* use **je fais de ...** or **je joue à ...** if it is a game. If you play a musical instrument use **je joue de.**

Je fais **de la** natation et **du** surf.
I swim and I surf.
Je joue **au** tennis et **à la** pétanque.
I play tennis and petanque (kind of bowls played in the South of France).
Je joue **du** piano et **de la** trompette.
I play the piano and the trumpet.

2 Likes and dislikes

To express your tastes and feelings, you can use **aimer** (*to like, to love*) or the two extremes **adorer** and **détester**:

j'adore	aller au restaurant
j'aime (beaucoup)	jouer au squash
	cuisiner
	écouter des disques
	regarder la télé
je n'aime pas	la planche à voile
	la musique classique
	me promener à pied
je déteste	faire la cuisine

To say what you like/dislike doing, add the infinitive after **j'aime, j'adore, je déteste, je préfère: je déteste faire de la bicyclette:** *I hate cycling.*

Include the article **le, la, les** when making generalizations:

J'aime **les** fromages français. *I like French cheese.*
L'histoire est plus_intéressante *History is more interesting*
que **la** géographie. *than geography.*

When stating likes/dislikes you will often hear French people use the following structures:

Moi, ce que j'aime c'est sortir avec mes_amis.
Moi, ce que je déteste c'est la viande saignante.

3 Pronouns: *le, la, les* it, him, her, them

The pronouns **le** (*it, him*), **la** (*it, her*), **les** (*them*) are used to avoid unnecessary repetitions of nouns; they are placed before the verb to which they refer:

Vous connaissez M. Durand?	*Do you know Mr Durand?*
Oui, je **le** connais.	*Yes, I know **him**.*
Vous prenez la carte postale?	*Are you taking the postcard?*
Oui, je **la** prends.	*Yes, I'm taking **it**.*
Vous_achetez ces foulards?	*Are you buying these scarves?*
Oui, je **les**_achète.	*Yes, I'm buying **them**.*
Vous_aimez le thé?	*Do you like tea?*
Oui, je **l'**aime.	*Yes, I like it.*

i **L'** replaces **le** or **la** when the next word starts with a vowel or silent **h**. In a negative sentence, **l'**, **le**, **la**, **les** come between the **ne** or **n'** and the verb:

Vous préférez le tennis?	*Do you prefer tennis?*
Non, **je ne le préfère pas.**	*No, I don't prefer it.*

4 More negatives

You saw in Unit 3 how to make a statement negative in French, using **ne ... pas**:

Je **n'**ai **pas** d'enfants.	*I have no children.*

There are other negatives you can use:

ne ... plus	*no more/no longer*
ne ... rien	*nothing*
ne ... jamais	*never*
ne ... que	*only*

Je **n'**ai **plus** de vin.	*I have no more wine.*
Il **ne** veut **rien**.	*He wants nothing.*
Il **n'**a **jamais** d'argent.	*He never has any money.*
Je n'ai que dix euros.	*I've only got ten Euros.*

5 'To know': when to use *savoir*, when to use *connaître*

There are two verbs for *knowing*: **savoir** and **connaître**.

a Use **savoir** (on its own) to say that you *know* or *don't know* a fact:

Je **sais** à quelle heure part le train.	*I know when the train leaves.*

| Je ne sais pas où est l'arrêt d'autobus. | *I don't know where the bus stop is.* |

b Use **savoir** followed by the infinitive to say that you *know how to do* something:

| Je sais faire la cuisine. | *I know how to cook.* |
| Vous savez faire du ski? | *Do you know how to ski?* |

c Connaître is used to say that you *know people and places*:

| Je connais Paris. | *I know Paris.* |
| Depuis combien de temps est-ce que vous le connaissez? | *How long have you known him?* |

6 *Quel temps fait-il?* What's the weather like?

The easiest way to talk about the weather is to start with **il fait**:

il fait beau, mauvais	*it's fine, the weather is bad*
il fait froid, chaud	*it's cold, hot*
il fait du vent	*it's windy*
il fait du brouillard	*it's foggy*
il pleut	*it's raining*
il neige	*it's snowing*
le soleil brille	*the sun is shining*

Pratiquez! Practise!

How would you answer the question:
Quel temps fait-il aujourd'hui? **Aujourd'hui il ...**

i Learn from your errors

- Don't let errors interfere with getting your message across. Making errors is part of any normal learning process, but some people get so worried that they won't say anything unless they are sure it is correct. This leads to a vicious circle as the less they say, the less practice they get and the more mistakes they make.

- Note the seriousness of errors. Many errors are not serious as they do not affect the meaning; for example if you use the wrong article (**le** or **la**), wrong pronoun (**je l'achète** for **je les achète**) or wrong adjective ending (**blanc** or **blanche**). So concentrate on getting your message across and learn from your mistakes.

Activities

▶ 1 Roger Burru has agreed to take part in a survey and is ready to talk about himself. Can you ask him in French the questions on the right? Then listen to the whole survey on the recording and check your answers (or check them in the **Key to the exercises**).

a	Nom	Roger Burru	*What's your name?*
b	Âge	35	*How old are you?*
c	Marié(e)	oui	*Are you married?*
d	Enfant(s)	non	*Have you any children?*
e	Profession	professeur	*What's your job?*
f	Depuis ...	10 ans	*Since when?*
g	Adresse	Lille	*Where do you live?*
h	Sport	natation	*What sport do you do?*
i	Loisir	faire la cuisine	*What are your hobbies?*

Now it's your turn to take part in a survey. Can you answer in French the same questions? (the answers are not included in **Key to the exercises**).

▶ 2 On the recording you will hear Cloé talk about her likes and dislikes. Listen carefully and put a tick in the appropriate box below:

	adore	aime beaucoup	n'aime pas	déteste
a Playing volleyball	☐	☐	☐	☐
b Working on Sundays	☐	☐	☐	☐
c Going out in the evenings	☐	☐	☐	☐
d Watching TV	☐	☐	☐	☐
e Listening to music	☐	☐	☐	☐
f Shopping	☐	☐	☐	☐
g Eating out	☐	☐	☐	☐
h Cooking	☐	☐	☐	☐

Now it's your turn to tell Cloé what you like and dislike. Can you think of any more likes/dislikes you could add to the list?

3 Answer the following questions using the example as a model. You may have to revise the verbs ending in -er (page 21), -ir and -re (page 40), prendre (page 42) and faire (page 42).

a Vous_achetez les_oranges?   Oui nous les_achetons.
b Vous prenez le train?   Oui, je ...
c Je connais M. Durand?   Oui, vous ...
d Elle a les timbres?   Oui, elle ...
e Vous_avez l'adresse de Claude?   Oui, je ...
f Ils_aiment le coq au vin?   Oui, ils ...
g Vous faites la cuisine?   Oui, je ...
h Vous_attendez l'autobus?   Oui, nous ...
i Il regarde la télé?   Oui, il ...
j Vous_écoutez les disques?   Oui, nous ...

4 Find the right ending for each sentence:

a Il ne va ...   i jamais de sport.
b Il n'écoute ...   ii plus de viande. Il est
c Elle ne veut ...   végétarien.
d Il ne mange ...   iii pas du piano.
e Elle ne boit ...   iv rien faire.
f Je ne regarde ...   v qu'une fille.
g Il ne joue ...   vi plus comme secrétaire.
h Elle ne travaille ...   vii jamais de musique.
i Il n'a ...   viii pas dans les musées.
j Elle ne fait ...   ix que de l'eau.
                            x plus la télé.

▶ 5 Listen to the weather report while looking at the map; some of the statements below are true (vrai), others are false (faux). Put an x in the appropriate boxes.

	vrai	faux
a Il fait beau à Newcastle.	☐	☐
b A Brighton, il pleut.	☐	☐
c Il pleut à Calais.	☐	☐
d Le soleil brille à Nice.	☐	☐
e Il pleut à Strasbourg.	☐	☐
f Il fait froid en Espagne.	☐	☐
g Il fait du vent à Malaga.	☐	☐
h Il fait très chaud en Italie.	☐	☐
i Il fait du vent à Rome.	☐	☐
j En Suisse il fait chaud.	☐	☐

k Il neige à Ostende.   □   □
l Le soleil brille à Bruxelles.   □   □

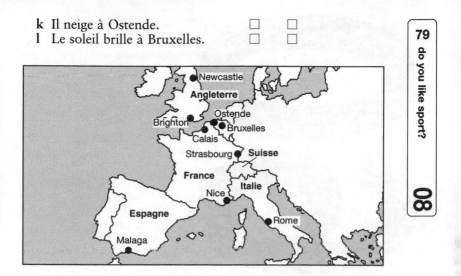

▶ 6 Rôle-play

You take part in a phone-in radio programme. The interviewer asks you questions on your likes and dislikes and those of your partner.

Mini-test

Check how well you've understood and remembered Units 7 and 8 with this test. How would you say:

1 I play squash better than Fabrice.
2 France is bigger than England.
3 She has glasses and long hair.
4 I'm looking for something to mend my car.
5 I like squash but I prefer playing tennis
6 I like French cooking very much.

ℹ Remember that French people talk about **le** squash, **la** France, l'Angleterre, **la** cuisine française, while the English do not use the article.

09

qu'est-ce qu'il faut faire?

what should I do?

In this unit you will learn
- a few useful linking words
- how to ask for assistance
- how to use **pouvoir** and **vouloir**
- how to give and understand instructions

Before you start

This unit prepares you to cope with difficulties you may encounter in France. It gives you the few structures you need to let people know that you're having a problem: **je suis perdu, je ne comprends pas, la machine ne marche pas,** and also to ask for help: **vous pouvez me montrer? qu'est-ce qu'il faut faire?** (see **Key words and phrases**).

Essayez! Have a go!

1 How would you ask someone politely to:
   a repeat
   b speak more slowly
2 How would you answer the question:
   Quel temps fait-il aujourd'hui?

Key words and phrases

For you to say

pardon Monsieur, Madame ...	*excuse me*
je suis perdu	*I'm lost*
je ne sais pas ...	*I don't know ...*
je ne comprends pas ...	*I don't understand ...*
vous pouvez m'aider, s'il vous plaît?	*can you help me please?*
qu'est-ce qu'il faut faire?	*what must I/we do?*
la machine ne marche pas	*the machine does not work*
utiliser l'Internet	*to use the Internet*
excusez-moi de vous déranger	*sorry to disturb you*
d'abord	*firstly*
et puis	*and then*
après ça	*after that*
finalement	*finally*

For you to understand

il faut_introduire ...	*you must insert ...*
il faut vérifier le niveau d'huile	*you have to check the oil level*
vous devez composter le billet	*you must date-stamp the ticket*
je vais m'en_occuper	*I'll attend to it*
ne pas déranger	*do not disturb*
en dérangement/en panne	*out of order (machine, telephone)*
hors de service	*out of order*

▶ Dialogues

Jane est au garage. Elle demande au mécanicien de vérifier le moteur de son auto qui fait un drôle de bruit.

Jane is at the garage, asking the mechanic to check the engine of her car which is making a strange noise.

Jane	Ah, bonjour Monsieur. Voilà … Depuis ce matin il y a un drôle de bruit dans le moteur de ma voiture. Je ne sais pas ce que c'est. Je ne comprends pas, la voiture marche bien mais …
Mécanicien	Oui, bien sûr! Avez-vous vérifié le niveau d'huile? Le niveau d'eau? Il fait très chaud aujourd'hui et peut-être que **le moteur chauffe trop**.
Jane	Euh … non. Je ne sais pas ce qu'il faut faire. Vous pouvez vérifier tout ça, s'il vous plaît?
Mécanicien	Bon, allez … d'accord, **repassez** dans trois_heures, je m'en_occupe.

le moteur chauffe trop	*the engine is heating up too much*
repassez	*come back*

Jane est sur le quai de la gare. Elle essaie de composter son billet pour le valider mais sans succès. Elle arrête une passante.

Jane is on the platform at the station. She is trying to date-stamp her ticket but she is having difficulties. She stops a passer-by:

Jane	Pardon, Madame, je ne sais pas comment marche cette machine. Vous pouvez m'aider, s'il vous plaît?
Passante	Mais oui, Mademoiselle, c'est très facile; il faut introduire votre billet sous **la flèche verte**.
Jane	**C'est ce que j'ai fait** et ça ne marche pas.
Passante	Alors il faut peut-être tourner le billet **dans l'autre sens**?
Jane	(*she hears a click*) Ah, bien, le billet est maintenant composté. Merci, Madame, et excusez-moi de vous avoir dérangée.
Passante	**De rien**, Mademoiselle.

la flèche verte	*the green arrow*
c'est ce que j'ai fait	*that's what I've done*
dans l'autre sens	*the other way round*
de rien	*don't mention it* (lit. *for nothing*)

Grammar

1 Asking for assistance

There are several ways of asking a favour, depending on how polite you want to be and how well you know the person.

The easiest but perhaps least polite way of asking is to use the verb in the 2nd person plural (i.e. **vous** person) deleting the **vous**:

Faites le plein, s'il vous plaît.   *Fill the car up with petrol, please* (lit. make the full, please).

A more polite way of asking is to start with **vous pouvez** (*can you*) and raise the voice on the last word:

Vous pouvez me montrer, s'il vous plaît?   *Can you show me, please?*

Some likely answers:

Oui, avec plaisir   *Yes, with pleasure*
Certainement   *Certainly*
D'accord   *OK*
Bien sûr   *Of course*

Like the verbs **aimer, détester, adorer** (Unit 8), **vous pouvez** is followed by a verb in the infinitive:

Vous pouvez vérifier le niveau d'huile, s'il vous plaît?   *Can you check the oil level, please?*

2 Two very useful verbs: *pouvoir* to be able to, *vouloir* to want

Pouvoir and **vouloir** are two verbs used very frequently in French:

pouvoir *to be able to, can*	vouloir *to want*
je peux	**je veux**
tu peux	**tu veux**
il/elle/on peut	**il/elle/on veut**
nous pouvons	**nous voulons**
vous pouvez	**vous voulez**
ils/elles peuvent	**ils/elles veulent**

3 Giving and understanding instructions

a The simplest and most commonly used way to give instructions is to use the **vous** or **tu** forms of the present tense:

Pour téléphoner en Angleterre,
vous composez le 00,
vous attendez la tonalité,
vous faites le 44 puis l'indicatif
de la ville sans le 0.

To phone England,
dial 00, wait for the
dialling tone, dial 44 then
the local code without
the zero.

b In written instruction a verb is often in the infinitive:

Introduire votre billet sous
la flèche verte, le **glisser** vers
la gauche jusqu'au déclic;
si la mention 'tournez votre
billet' apparaît, **présenter**
l'autre extrémité.

Insert your ticket under the
green arrow and slide it to
the left until there is a click;
if the sign 'turn your ticket'
appears, insert the
other end.

c **Qu'est-ce qu'il faut...?** To find out what needs to be done use **qu'est-ce qu'il faut** followed by the appropriate verb in the infinitive:

Qu'est-ce qu'il faut faire
pour composter son billet?

What do you have to do to
date-stamp your ticket?

d **Il faut + a verb.** Followed by a verb in the infinitive, **il faut** (which is only used in the 3rd person) means any of the following, depending on the context: *it is necessary, I/we/you have to, must, one has to, must*:

Il faut décrocher l'appareil.
Il faut attendre la tonalité.

You must lift the receiver.
One must wait for the
dialling tone.

Il faut composter le billet.

You must date-stamp
your ticket.

e **Il faut + a noun.** Followed by a noun, **il faut** means *you need/one needs/I need*. The pronouns **me** (*to me*), **lui** (*to him, to her*), **nous** (*to us*) can be inserted to make it more personal:

Il lui faut une télécarte
pour téléphoner.
Il me faut_un passeport
pour aller en France.

He needs a phone card
to phone.
I need a passport to go
to France.

Activities

1 Using the words in the box, say what is needed in each case. Practise the questions and answers aloud:

Qu'est-ce qu'il faut

a pour ouvrir une bouteille?
b pour prendre le train?
c pour envoyer une lettre?
d pour faire une omelette?
e pour jouer au tennis?
f pour jouer de la musique?
g pour apprendre le français?
h pour aller en France?
i pour acheter de l'essence?

i une station-service
ii le livre *Teach Yourself Beginner's French*
iii une raquette et des balles
iv un passeport
v un tire-bouchon
vi des_oeufs
vii un billet
viii un_instrument
ix un timbre

2 Below is a list of things you need to do to keep fit **pour être en pleine forme**. Match them up with the appropriate verbs on the left. You may need to look up some of the words in the vocabulary list at the back of the book.

Pour être en pleine forme **il faut**

a boire
b manger
c pratiquer
d dormir
e diminuer

f aimer

i un sport
ii les sucreries et le sel
iii son travail
iv peu d'alcool
v beaucoup de légumes et de fruits
vi huit heures par jour

3 Here is a recipe from a children's cookery book. Match the instructions with the corresponding drawings overleaf then answer the questions:

L'omelette

(pour quatre personnes)

a D'abord tu bats sept oeufs dans un grand bol.

b Puis tu poivres et tu sales.

c Ensuite tu fais fondre dans la poële 30 grammes de beurre.

d Quand le beurre est chaud, tu verses les oeufs.

e *Après trois ou quatre minutes, tu mélanges avec une fourchette.*

f *Finalement, quand l'omelette est cuite, tu sers immédiatement.*

A   B   C

D   E   F

   i   How many eggs are needed?
  ii What do you do after beating the eggs?
 iii What do you melt in the frying pan?
  iv When is the egg mixture poured into the bowl?
   v What do you use to mix the mixture?

4 To understand what to do in a French cybercafé you need to know some key words. Match the French words in the left-hand column with the correct English translation on the right.

a	l'ordinateur	i	mouse
b	mettre en marche	ii	click
c	appuyer	iii	keyboard
d	le bouton	iv	start
e	la souris	v	computer
f	cliquer	vi	switch
g	le clavier	vii	press

▶ **5 Rôle-play**

You are now ready to check your emails using a computer in a French cybercafé. Follow the prompts.

ℹ️ Learn to guess the meaning

Here are three tips to help your general listening and reading comprehension:

- **Imagine the situation.**
  When listening to the recording try to imagine where the scene is taking place and who the main characters are. Let your experience of the world help you guess the meaning of the conversation, e.g. if a dialogue takes place in a snack bar you can predict the kind of vocabulary that is being used.

- **Concentrate on the main part.**
  When watching a foreign film you usually get the meaning of the whole story from a few individual shots. Understanding a foreign conversation or article is similar. Concentrate on the main parts to get the message and don't worry about individual words. When conversing with French speakers look out for clues given by facial expressions and body language; they can tell you a lot about the mood and atmosphere of the conversation.

- **Guess the key words; if you cannot, ask.**
  When there are key words you don't understand, try to guess what they mean from the context. If you're listening to a French speaker and cannot get the gist of a whole passage because of one word or phrase, try to repeat that word with a questioning tone; the speaker will probably paraphrase it, giving you the chance to understand it. If for example you wanted to find out the meaning of the word **voyager** (*to travel*) you would ask **Que veut dire voyager?**

Pratiquez! **Practise!** The notice below is situated in the grounds of a museum of sculptures in Paris. There are strict rules about what you can and cannot do! What are they? (Check your answers with the translation in **Key to the exercises and tests.**)

IL EST EXPRESSÉMENT DÉFENDU:

- de dégrader les sculptures, vases
- de cueillir des fleurs ou des fruits
- d'escalader les sculptures
- de marcher sur le gazon et de monter sur les bancs
- de déjeuner hors de la zone réservée à la cafétéria
- d'introduire des animaux
- de circuler à bicyclette
- de jouer avec des balles et ballons
- de déposer ou de jeter des ordures ailleurs que dans des corbeilles à papier

Mini-test

1 Say in French: Today it is cold but it's not raining.
2 How would you ask for what needs to be done?
3 How would you say that you need a phone card to phone?
4 Imagine that you are in Paris. Ask someone to help you with three things starting with:

   a Vous pouvez me montrer ...?
   b Vous pouvez me dire ...?
   c Vous pouvez me donner ...?

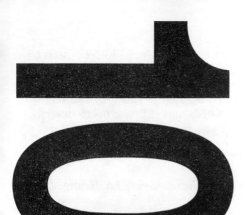

10

à l'avenir
in the future

In this unit you will learn

- how to say what you usually do
- how to say what you need
- how to talk about your future plans
- how to use the pronoun **y**
- two useful verbs **sortir** and **venir**

Before you start

Talking about the future is very easy in French. All you need to do is to use **je vais** followed by the infinitive form of whatever you're going to do. For example to say that you intend to play tennis tomorrow you would say: **demain je vais jouer au tennis**. In this unit you'll learn useful words and expressions to describe your typical day and say what you intend to do in the future.

Essayez! Have a go!

1 If you see on a telephone box a notice saying **En dérangement** what does it mean?

2 You want to use the Internet from a post office in France. How would you ask: *What must I do to use the Internet?*

Key words and phrases

demain	*tomorrow*
à l'avenir	*in the future*
qu'est-ce que vous_allez faire?	*what are you going to do?*
je vais ...	*I'm going to ...*
visiter les monuments historiques	*visit old buildings*
rendre visite à mes_amis	*visit my friends*
voyager	*to travel*
marcher, se promener	*to walk, to go for walks*
faire de longues promenades	*to go for long walks*
faire du tourisme	*to do some sightseeing*
passer quelques jours ...	*spend a few days ...*
partir pour une semaine ...	*go for a week ...*
au bord de la mer	*to the seaside*
à la campagne	*to the countryside*
à la montagne	*to the mountains*
en_été, en_automne, en_hiver	*in summer, in autumn, in winter*
au printemps	*in spring*
l'année prochaine	*next year*
en mars	*in March*
pendant le mois d'août	*during the month of August*
j'ai besoin de ...	*I need ...*
j'ai chaud, froid	*I'm hot, cold*
j'ai soif, faim	*I'm thirsty, hungry*
comment passez-vous votre journée?	*how do you spend your day?*

généralement	*generally*
je me lève	*I get up*
je m'habille	*I get dressed*
je me lave	*I wash*
je prends le petit-déjeuner	*I have breakfast*
je pars de la maison	*I leave the house*
j'emmène les_enfants à l'école	*I take the children to school*
je vais chez mes_amis	*I go to my friends' house*
je fais des courses	*I do some shopping*
je prépare le déjeuner	*I prepare lunch*
je vais chercher Jean à la gare	*I go and fetch John from the station*
le soir, je vais au cinéma	*in the evening I go to the cinema*
je me couche/je vais au lit	*I go to bed*
louer	*to rent*
se baigner	*to go for a swim*
surtout	*mainly*
se reposer	*to rest*
lire	*to read*
sortir (en boîte)	*to go out* (to a nightclub/ private membership club)
à la maison	*at home*

▶ Dialogue

Les Durand parlent de leurs projets pour les vacances d'été.

The Durands talk about their summer holiday plans.

Listen or read at least twice. How long are they going on holiday for? Where are they going? Note down at least three things M. and Mme Durand intend to do. Does their daughter Rosine enjoy sightseeing?

Jane	Monsieur et Madame Durand, qu'est-ce que vous_allez faire pour vos vacances cet_été?
M. Durand	Nous_allons prendre quatre semaines de vacances: une semaine au bord de la mer au mois de juillet et trois semaines à la montagne en_août.
Jane	Vous_allez rester à l'hôtel ou vous_allez louer une maison?
Mme Durand	Nous_allons d'abord passer quelques jours chez nos_amis au bord de la mer. Ils_habitent à 50 km de Nice. Après ça nous_allons dans notre maison de campagne dans le petit village de Puy-St.-Pierre près de Briançon.

Jane	Et comment_allez-vous passer vos vacances?
Mme Durand	Au bord de la mer, je vais me baigner tous les jours. A Puy-St.-Pierre, je voudrais jouer au tennis, faire de longues promenades et visiter les monuments historiques de la région.
M. Durand	Moi, je vais surtout me reposer, lire et faire un peu de sport comme le tennis ou jouer à la pétanque avec les_enfants. Le soir, j'espère sortir quelquefois pour voir un bon film ou même aller au restaurant.
Rosine	Moi, cette année je ne veux pas faire de tourisme **parce que** c'est **ennuyeux**. Je préfère rester à la maison ou sortir avec mes_amis en boîte.

> **parce que** *because*
> **ennuyeux** *boring*

Grammar

1 Saying what you usually do using some reflexive verbs

When describing your typical day you can't avoid using reflexive verbs, i.e. verbs describing things you do to or for yourself such as **se lever** (*to get oneself up*), **s'habiller** (*to get dressed*). While in English the *myself, yourself, himself,* etc... is often dropped, in French the **me, te, se,** etc ... must be kept. Here is the pattern followed by all reflexive verbs in the present:

> **se laver** *to wash (oneself)*
>
> | **je me lave** | *I wash (myself)* |
> |---|---|
> | **tu te laves** | *you wash (yourself)* |
> | **il/elle/on se lave** | *he/she/it/one washes (himself, etc...)* |
> | **nous nous lavons** | *we wash (ourselves)* |
> | **vous vous lavez** | *you wash (yourself/selves)* |
> | **ils/elles se lavent** | *they wash (themselves)* |

i Perhaps the most useful reflexive verbs is **s'appeler** (lit. to call oneself).

Comment vous_appelez-vous? Je m'appelle ...
Comment t'appelles-tu? (friendly form) Je m'appelle ...
Comment s'appellent-ils? Ils s'appellent ...

The letter **e** before a single **l** as in **appeler** is always sounded as **e**.

The letter **e** before a double **ll** as in **appellent** is always sounded as **è**.

Pratiquez! **Practise!** To check that you understand reflexive verbs: try to write out **s'habiller** (*to get dressed*). The **me, te, se,** will be shortened to **m', t', s'** as **habiller** starts with an h.

2 Saying what you need: *j'ai besoin de ...*

To say what item you need, use **j'ai besoin de (d')** followed by a noun:

J'ai besoin d'un passeport pour la France.	*I need a passport for France.*
Il a besoin d'un timbre de 50 centimes pour envoyer sa lettre.	*He needs a 0€50 stamp to send his letter.*

To say what you need to do, use **j'ai besoin de (d')** followed by a verb in the infinitive:

J'ai chaud; **j'ai besoin de boire** un verre d'eau.	*I'm hot; I need to drink a glass of water.*
Elle n'a plus d'argent. **Elle a besoin d'aller** à la banque.	*She has no money left. She needs to go to the bank.*

i • **J'ai chaud/froid/faim/soif** use **avoir** (not **être!**).

  • **Pour** is used before verbs in the infinitive to translate the idea of *in order to*: **Pour** envoyer sa lettre il a besoin d'un timbre.

3 Stating your intentions

Just as you use **je voudrais** to say what you would like to do, use **je vais** to say what you are going to do followed by the verb in the infinitive:

Je vais	**me lever** à huit heures.
I'm going	*to get up at eight o'clock.*
Tu vas	**prendre** le petit-déjeuner à neuf heures.
You're going	*to have breakfast at nine o'clock.*
Il/Elle va	**partir** de la maison.
He/She is going	*to leave the house.*
Nous_allons	**faire** des courses à midi.
We're going	*to do some shopping at lunchtime.*
Vous_allez	**chercher** Jean à la gare.
You're going	*to fetch John from the station.*
Ils/Elles vont	**se coucher** vers 11 heures.
They're going	*to go to bed around 11 o'clock.*

4 The pronoun *y*

To replace an expression of place preceded by **à,** use the pronoun y (*there*):

Vous_allez à **Paris?**
  Oui, j'y vais.
Il va travailler à **la pharmacie?**
  Oui, il va y travailler.

Are you going to Paris?
  Yes, I'm going there.
Is he going to work at
  the chemist's? Yes, he's
  going to work there.

i Like other pronouns, e.g. **en, le, la, les,** etc. (Unit 8), **y** is placed just before the verb to which it refers, e.g. **il faut y aller** *we must go there.*

5 *Sortir* to go out, *venir* to come

Here are two useful verbs to describe daily activities:

sortir *to go out*	**venir** *to come*
je sors	**je viens**
tu sors	**tu viens**
il/elle/on sort	**il/elle/on vient**
nous sortons	**nous venons**
vous sortez	**vous venez**
ils/elles sortent	**ils/elles viennent**

6 Using capital letters

The months, seasons and days of the week do not take a capital letter in French unless they begin a sentence (Unit 3): **en juillet, en_été, le mardi.**

7 When to use *visiter* (to visit) in French

French people talk about visiting museums, old buildings or interesting places but they do not visit the cinema or their relations! They **go** to the cinema or the pub and they **pay a visit** or **see** their relations or friends:

Je vais_aller **visiter** le
  Louvre l'été prochain.

I'm going to visit the
  Louvre next summer.

Ce week-end je vais **rendre visite**
  à ma grand-mère.

This weekend I'm going to
  visit my grandmother.

Ils vont **voir** leurs_amis dans
le sud de la France.

*They are going to visit
their friends in the south
of France.*

ℹ️ Assess yourself and keep up with grammar

Having reached the end of the Grammar section it may be useful to
find out how well you're doing with grammar, ways to practise it and,
in Units 11–20 of the book, how to build on what you already know.

* **How well are you doing with grammar?**
  Look at the **Index** with grammar terms and decide which
  functions you feel are particularly important. Test yourself on two
  or three of these at a time using the **Activities** of Units 1–10. If you
  find the exercises difficult, revise the **Grammar** carefully studying
  the examples.

* **Test yourself in a practice activity.**
  Once you've completed successfully all the activities in Units 1–10
  of *Teach Yourself Beginner's French* you may feel that you need to
  test yourself with another book of grammar exercises with the
  answers at the back. To test yourself you can read the
  explanations first and do the exercises or try the questions first,
  check the answers and work out the rule.

* **Build up a 'pattern bank'.**
  Using the material from Units 11–20 of the book and any other
  French material, collect examples that can be listed under the
  structures you've already met. Seeing the structures in various
  contexts will help you assimilate them.

Activities

1 Imagine you're the man or woman whose typical day is
  illustrated overleaf. Write underneath the pictures what you
  do during the day but first have a go at saying it aloud.

2 Repeat Exercise 1. This time pretend that you are describing
  your friend's, brother's or sister's typical day. Start the
  sentences with **il ...** or **elle ...** .

a D'abord je … **b** puis je … **c** ensuite …

d A 8h.30 j'… **e** ensuite … **f** à midi …

g L'après-midi … **h** ou je … **i** ou je …

j Le soir je … **k** ou j' … **l** enfin …

3 Your friends Robert and Jeanine have just planned their holidays for this summer. You ask them about it:

a What does Robert say?
b What does Jeanine tell you?

	Robert	Jeanine
Tu va partir quand?	in August	on 21st June
Pour combien de temps?	three weeks	ten days
Où vas-tu aller?	to Oxford in England	to Anglet near Biarritz in the South of France
Comment vas tu passer tes vacances?	• learn English • visit old buildings • see some friends • go out in the evening • play tennis	• go swimming • read a lot • watch a bit (**un peu**) of TV • go for long walks • go to bed early (**tôt**)

Practise the exercise several times and try memorizing the questions.

4 What questions would you ask Robert and Jeanine if you said **vous** to them?

5 Jane has received a letter from a French friend who is about to visit her in Brighton. Fill in the gaps using each of the words in the box overleaf.

Chère Jane,

Merci (a)............ pour ta gentille lettre.

Oui, mon (b)........, mon fils et moi allons bientôt te rendre visite en (c)........ . Marc (d)........ l'école le 27 juin donc nous pensons quitter Paris le (e)........ 30 juin à midi pour arriver à Gatwick à deux heures de (f) l' ....

Nous pensons (g)........ avec toi quelques (h)........, puis nous voulons faire un peu de tourisme à Londres pour (i)........ les monuments historiques. Ensuite nous voulons aller à

Oxford où (j)........ nos amis Green. Tu n'as pas (k)........
d'aller nous chercher à Gatwick. Nous pouvons très bien
(l)........ le train jusqu'à Brighton et puis un taxi jusqu'à chez
toi. A très bientôt. Amicalement.

prendre	jours	mari	Grande-Bretagne

finit   habitent   samedi   rester   visiter

beaucoup   besoin   après-midi

▶ 6 Michel has a lot of things planned for tomorrow. Listen
to the recording and try to find out what's he's going to do.
He has a list of nine things. If you haven't got the recording,
look at the answers in the **Key to the exercises and tests** to
find out about Michel's plans.

▶ 7 **Rôle-play**

Now it is your turn to speak about your next holiday. Listen
to Michel and use his prompts to answer.

Mini-test

1 You cannot date-stamp your ticket at the machine.
   a Ask someone to help you?
   b You are told what to do but you don't understand. What
   do you say?
2 Finish the following sentences with an appropriate ending
following the example:
   Tu vas en France? Tu as besoin d'un passeport.
   a Il a soif? Il a besoin de _____
   b Nous n'avons pas d'argent. Nous _____
   c Ils ont faim? Ils _____
   d Je suis malade. J'_____
3 Fill in the blanks with the right endings of the verb **aller**:
   M. et Mme Durand (**a**) .... prendre quatre semaines de
   vacances. M. Durand (**b**) .... lire et faire du sport. Mme
   Durand et Rosine (**c**) .... se baigner tous les jours. Et toi
   qu'est-ce que tu (**d**) .... faire? Moi? Je (**e**) .... rester chez
   moi. Mais le samedi après-midi moi et mon petit_ami (**f**)
   .... regarder un match de football à la télé.

You have finished the first part of the book with the basic structures and grammatical points. Before going on to the second part of the course which deals with everyday situations, do the **Self-assessment test 1** (Units 8–10). Check your written answers in the **Key to the exercises and tests** and record your score underneath. If your score is between 40 and 50 points go straight on to Unit 11. Between 20 and 40 points, revise the points and areas which require more work. Below 20 points, go back over Units 8, 9 and 10, and take the test again to see how much you have improved.

Self-assessment score (Units 8–10)

Points: _____/50

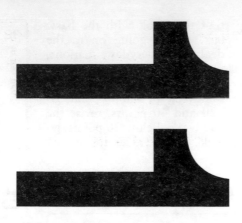

11

shopping

les courses

In this unit you will
- find out about shops in France
- practise buying groceries
- practise buying something to wear

Before you start, revise

- numbers (page 233)
- asking what's available (page 13)
- *some* and *any* (page 13)
- asking the price (page 14)
- saying precisely what you want (page 62)
- *less ..., more ...* (page 64)
- colours (page 60)

Les magasins en France Shops in France

To find out about French shops read the passage below. Answering the questions in **Activity 1** will help you to understand it.

i Les magasins, en France, restent ouverts en général jusqu'à 19 heures ou 20 heures. Beaucoup ferment entre 12 heures et 14 heures. Le lundi ils sont souvent fermés dans les petites villes.

La boulangerie ouvre très tôt, vers sept heures du matin, et ferme tard car beaucoup de Français achètent leur pain deux fois par jour. Le dimanche matin, beaucoup de magasins comme les pâtisseries et les charcuteries restent ouverts. Les supermarchés (Monoprix) et hypermarchés (Auchan, Mammouth et Leclerc) sont encore généralement fermés le dimanche.

Dans toutes les grandes villes il y a un marché presque tous les jours et souvent le dimanche. Dans les petites villes ou villages il y a un marché une fois par semaine: le jour du marché. Au marché, on peut acheter **des légumes**, des fruits, **du poisson**, **de la viande** et même **des vêtements**.

les légumes	*vegetables*	**la viande**	*meat*
le poisson	*fish*	**les vêtements**	*clothes*

Activity 1

a Until what time do shops generally stay open during the week?
b Are they usually open or shut at lunchtime?
c What day of the week do they often shut?
d Which shops are often open on Sunday morning?
e Are supermarkets generally open on Sundays?

Activity 2

Now read the passage several times and then, without looking at it, try to say out loud in French what you know about French shops. Check back with the passage.

- The **-s** at the end of the plural nouns is not pronounced.

- The **-nt** at the end of the verbs such as **ferment**, **restent** is not pronounced so **ferment** sounds like 'fairm' and **restent** like 'rest'.

Key words and phrases

With the key words below you should be able to cope with most buying situations. A good way to test yourself once you've learnt the **Mots-clés** is to hide the left side of the page, look at the English and say the French out loud.

For you to say

où est la boulangerie la plus proche s'il vous plaît?	*where is the nearest bakery please?*
où est le supermarché le plus proche?	*where is the nearest supermarket?*
où est-ce que je peux acheter/ trouver un/une/des ...	*where can I buy/find a/some ...*
je voudrais/il me faut un/une/des ...	*I would like/I need a/some ...*
un paquet/une plaquette de ...	*a pack of ...*
une tranche de ...	*a slice of ...*
un morceau de ...	*a piece of ...*
vous avez autre chose?	*do you have anything else?*
c'est trop grand/petit/cher	*it's too big/small/expensive*
je cherche quelque chose de différent	*I'm looking for something different*
vous avez quelque chose de plus grand/petit/moins cher?	*have you got anything bigger/smaller/cheaper?*
je vais prendre une tranche/ un kilo/une livre de plus/ 500 grammes de moins	*I'll take a slice/ a kilo/a pound more/ 500 grams less*
un demi-kilo	*half a kilo*
c'est combien?	*how much is it?*
c'est tout, merci	*that's all, thank you*

For you to understand

on s'occupe de vous?	*are you being served?*
et avec ceci (ça)?	*is that all? (lit. and with this?)*

Acheter des provisions Food shopping

À la boucherie (*butcher's*), on achète:

du veau	veal
du boeuf	beef
du porc	pork
des saucisses	sausages
un poulet	chicken

À la charcuterie (*delicatessen*), on achète:

du jambon	ham
du saucisson	salami-type sausage

À la boulangerie/pâtisserie (*baker's*), on achète:

une baguette	French 'stick'
un pain complet	wholemeal loaf
des petits pains	soft bread rolls
une tarte aux fraises	strawberry tart
des croissants	croissants

À l'épicerie (*grocer's*), à l'alimentation (*foodstore*), au supermarché (*supermarket*) on achète:

du thé	tea
du café	coffee
du beurre	butter
du lait	milk
des oeufs (rhyming with deux)	eggs
du fromage (de chèvre)	(goat's) cheese
de la lessive	washing powder
des pommes	apples
des pommes de terre	potatoes
une laitue	lettuce
des yaourts à la fraise	strawberry yoghurts
des boissons (jus de fruit, vins, etc.)	drinks (fruit juice, wine, etc.)

Activity 3

There is no supermarket around; say in French which shops sell:

a chicken
b bread rolls
c pork
d washing powder

e milk
f salami
g wine

Activity 4

Below is a dialogue between a grocer and a client. See if you can put the lines in their correct order starting with **Bonjour Madame.**

a Une douzaine (*a dozen*), s'il vous plaît.
b Voilà, Madame, ça fait 6€85.
c **Bonjour Madame.**
d Non, il me faut aussi du jus de fruit.
e Oui ... voilà une douzaine d'oeufs, c'est tout?
f Bonjour Monsieur, je voudrais des oeufs, s'il vous plaît.
g Qu'est-ce que je vous donne: jus de pomme, orange ou ananas (*pineapple*)?
h Vous en voulez combien?
i Je vais prendre le jus d'orange.

▶ Dialogue 1: *Au marché* At the market

Un client achète des provisions pour un pique-nique.

At the market a customer buys some food for a picnic.

Listen to the recording (read the dialogue if you haven't got the recording) then without looking back at the text try Activity 5.

Client	Bonjour, mademoiselle. Je voudrais du beurre, s'il vous plaît?
Vendeuse	Une plaquette comme ça?
Client	Non, quelque chose de plus petit. Et qu'est-ce que vous avez comme fromages?
Vendeuse	Brie, fromage de chèvre, gruyère. Qu'est-ce que je vous donne?
Client	Du gruyère.

Vendeuse	Un morceau comme ça?
Client	Ah non … ça c'est un peu trop gros. Vous pouvez m'en donner un peu moins, s'il vous plaît? C'est pour notre pique-nique.
Vendeuse	Ah bon, d'accord. Voilà … 300 grammes. Et avec ça? Qu'est-ce qu'il vous faut? Des fruits, des yaourts, des biscuits?
Client	Euh, je vais prendre aussi des fruits.
Vendeuse	Alors nous avons des fraises, des bananes, des pommes, des pêches et du melon.
Client	Elles sont bonnes les fraises?
Vendeuse	Délicieuses. Je vous en mets un demi-kilo?
Client	500 grammes! Non, c'est un peu trop. Une demi-livre c'est assez. Ah oui, je voudrais aussi deux grandes bouteilles d'eau minérale … Voilà, c'est tout, c'est combien?
Vendeuse	Alors, ça vous fait 19€83.
Client	Et pour acheter du pain?
Vendeuse	Vous trouverez une boulangerie à 200 mètres sur votre gauche. Et … bon pique-nique Monsieur.

Activity 5

Look at the three columns below. Can you pick out four items bought by the customer?

a du poulet
b du beurre
c du saucisson
d du fromage

e des pommes
f du melon
g des fraises
h des pêches

i du lait
j du vin
k de la bière
l de l'eau minérale

Activity 6

Pretend that you're a customer. Using the dialogue above and the **Key words and phrases** on pages 102–3 practise buying a small packet of butter, 300 grams of cheese and half a pound of strawberries. Don't forget to find out where you can buy some bread. (The answers are not given in the **Key to the exercises and tests**.)

Acheter autre chose Shopping for other things

Les grands magasins de Paris (*department stores*): **www.paris.org/shops**

Saviez-vous que l'on trouve des plans de Paris gratuits dans les grands magasins? Profitez-en *(take advantage of it)* pour en demander un: «Vous avez un plan de Paris, s'il vous plaît?»

Activity 7

Here is a list of some shops and services in the town of Cauterets.

Alimentation Générale – Primeurs – Ets. Vaud
Bijouterie – **Angélique**
Brasserie – *«Au bon accueil»*
Boucherie – Charcuterie – Bon et fils
Cave – Marchand de Vin – *Veuve de Bonnet*
Chaussures – *Saint-Etienne*
Confection – MariSol
Droguerie – *Sans souci*
Généraliste – Dr LeGrand
Informatique – **infocom**
Librairie – *Blanchard*
Lingerie – Vêtements – «Chez Madame»
Pressing – *A votre service*
Traiteur – bonne bouche

Can you identify the French words for:

a Fashion boutique
b Dry-cleaner's
c General practitioner
d Book shop/store
e IT
f Jewellery
g Shoe shop/store
h Ladies' wear
i Delicatessen
j Off-licence/liquor store

À la droguerie (*hardware shop*)

une brosse à dent	*toothbrush*
un savon	*soap*
un peigne	*comb*
de l'huile pour bronzer	*suntan lotion*
des kleenex	*tissues*
un ouvre-boîte	*tin opener*
un tire-bouchon	*corkscrew*

Au bureau de tabac (*newsagent's*)

un carnet de timbres	*book of stamps*
des journaux	*newspapers*
du chewing gum	*chewing gum*
une carte postale	*postcard*
des magazines	*magazines*

Au magasin de vêtements (*clothes shop*)

un pull-over	*pullover*
un pantalon	*trousers*
une chemise	*a shirt*
une paire de chaussures	*shoes*
un maillot de bain	*swimming costume*
une robe	*dress*
une jupe	*skirt*
un jean/des jeans	*jeans*

Activity 8

To make the most of French sales (**les soldes**) read the following paragraph and do the activity. For each word in bold find its English meaning in the box. Then read the rest of the text and say whether the statements are **vrai** or **faux**. Correct the false ones.

Deux fois par an, c'est le rendez-vous tant attendu des (a) **amateurs de bonnes affaires** et des victimes de la mode, quand les prix (b) **baissent**. Il y a alors beaucoup de (c) **remises** importantes et de (d) **promotion**.

come down   reductions   special offers   bargain lovers

Les soldes concernent principalement la mode (vêtements, chaussures, accessoires), mais aussi le linge de maison et des milliers d'autres articles. Généralement il s'agit des invendus de la collection précédente. Chaque période de soldes ne peut excéder six semaines. A Paris, elles durent un mois chacune et se déroulent en hiver (janvier/février) et en été (juin/juillet). En période de soldes, les magasins peuvent ouvrir le dimanche.

	vrai	faux
e The sales are only for household linen.	☐	☐
f The new season's collection is sold in the sales.	☐	☐
g The sales last up to eight weeks.	☐	☐
h During the sales, shops sometimes open on Sundays.	☐	☐

▶ Dialogue 2: *Dans un magasin de vêtements* In a clothes shop

For this dialogue, you need to understand two new questions:

1 Quelle taille? (*What size?*) when you're buying clothes. (42 is the European equivalent to the woman's size 14 in Britain and 12 in America, 44 is equivalent to size 16 in Britain and 14 in America, etc.). **Quelle pointure?** means *What size shoes?* Size 5 in Britain or 7 in America = 38, size 6 in Britain and 8 in America = 39, etc.

2 Je peux essayer? (*Can I try?*) when you want to try something on.

Cliente	Bonjour, Madame, je cherche une jupe noire.
Vendeuse	Noire … euh oui d'accord. **Vous faites quelle taille?**
Cliente	40 … 40/42, **ça dépend du modèle**.
Vendeuse	J'ai ce modèle-ci en 40 et 42. C'est une jupe en coton. En 40, je n'ai pas de noir; j'ai du rouge, du gris mais pas de noir.
Cliente	Elles font combien ces jupes?
Vendeuse	63€.
Cliente	Vous n'avez pas quelque chose de moins cher?
Vendeuse	Euh non, sauf ces jupes **en solde** à 47€ mais elles sont grises.
Cliente	Non, il me faut du noir. Bon, eh bien, je vais essayer la jupe à 63€.
Vendeuse	(*pointing to a changing room*) Vous avez **la cabine d'essayage** là-bas.

(after a while)

Vendeuse Elle vous va bien?

Cliente Ça va; elle est un peu large mais je crois que je vais la prendre car j'en ai besoin pour ce soir. Vous acceptez les cartes de crédit?

Vendeuse Mais bien sûr, Madame.

vous faites quelle taille?	*what size are you?*
ça dépend du modèle	*it depends on the style*
en solde	*on sale*
la cabine d'essayage	*changing room*
là-bas	*over there*

▶ Activity 9

Listen to the recording again and try to spot the French version of the following phrases, then write them down:

a I'm looking for a black skirt ....

b What's your size? ....

c something cheaper ....

d I shall try ....

e the skirt at 63€...€

f How does it fit? ....

Activity 10

You're at the **bureau de tabac** (the c in **tabac** is not sounded) and wish to buy a newspaper, stamps, cards and a magazine for your wife.

Vendeur Bonjour, Monsieur, vous désirez?

a You *Say you would like a newspaper. Ask him what English newspapers he's got.*

Vendeur Comme journaux anglais? Nous avons *le Times*, le *Guardian* et le *Daily Telegraph*

b You *Say that you will take* The Times *and these three postcards. Ask how much a stamp for England is.*

Vendeur Un timbre pour l'Angleterre? C'est 54 centimes.

c You *Say that you will take eight stamps.*

Vendeur Voilà, Monsieur; huit timbres à 54 centimes. C'est tout?

d You *Say that you'll also buy the magazine* Elle *for your wife.*

Vendeur Très bien, Monsieur. Ça vous fait 13€27.

▶ **Activity 11**

On the recording you will hear Michel shopping. Listen to the conversation several times and then answer the questions below, in English.

a What does he want to buy?
b What colours does he ask for?
c What's wrong with the first garment?
d What's wrong with the second garment?
e How much is the one he buys?
f Where is he likely to get a street map?

Mini-test

How do you say in French:

1 I need some tissues.
2 I would like something bigger, please.
3 Do you have anything else?
4 That's all.
5 Do you accept credit cards?

12

se reposer, dormir

resting, sleeping

In this unit you will

- find out about accommodation in France
- find out how to ask for information at the tourist office
- practise booking into a hotel and a campsite
- complain about things missing/not working
- learn to spell your name
- book accommodation online

Before you start, revise

- saying what you want (page 62)
- asking what you can do (page 39)
- different ways to ask a question (page 39)
- asking the price (page 14)
- recognizing 'first', 'second', 'third', etc. (page 52)
- saying that there isn't any (page 31)
- dates (page 41)

Key words and phrases

je cherche ...	*I'm looking for ...*
à louer	*to rent*
un logement	*accommodation*
un appartement	*a flat/apartment*
un gîte rural	*a self-catering cottage*
meublé et équipé	*furnished and fully equipped*
rester chez l'habitant	*to stay as a paying guest*
le mobil-home	*mobile home*
le terrain de camping	*campsite*
vous avez ... ?	*have you ... ?*
une chambre de libre	*a vacancy*
une chambre d'hôte	*a room in a guest house*
je voudrais réserver	*I would like to book*
une chambre simple/double	*a single/double room*
à deux lits	*with two single beds*
avec un grand lit	*with a double bed*
avec douche et WC	*with shower and WC*
avec salle de bains	*with bathroom*
avec pension complète	*with full board*
avec demi-pension	*with half board*
pour ... personne(s)	*for ... person(s)*
pour ... nuit(s)	*for ... night(s)*
du ... au	*from ... to*
le petit déjeuner est compris?	*is breakfast included?*
c'est en supplément/ en plus/en sus	*it's extra*
c'est à quel nom?	*in whose name?*
l'acompte (m), les arrhes	*deposit*
c'est complet	*it's full up*

Choisir son logement Choosing one's accommodation

Les offices du tourisme et syndicats d'initiative:

- Maison de la France: **www.franceguide.com**
- L'office du tourisme à Paris: **www.paris-touristoffice.com**
- FNOTSI (Fédération Nationale des Offices de Tourisme et Syndicats d'Initiative): **www.tourisme.fr**

Pour louer des logements touristiques:

- Syndicat National des Résidences de Tourisme: **www.snrt.fr**
- CléVacances: **www.clevacances.com/FR**

i A l'hôtel

Les hôtels sont **homologués** par le gouvernement d'une **étoile** *(hôtel simple) à quatre étoiles luxe ****L (très grand confort, palace). Tous doivent **afficher** leurs prix TTC (toutes taxes comprises) à l'extérieur de l'hôtel et dans les chambres. Les chambres proposent en général un lit deux personnes ou deux lits une personne. On a le choix entre pension complète et demi-pension. Il faut demander si le petit-déjeuner est compris dans le prix de la chambre. Il est souvent en supplément. La **taxe de séjour** est toujours en sus. Pour réserver votre chambre, **renseignez-vous** dans les offices de tourisme/syndicats d'initiative ou **auprès des** centrales de réservation sur l'Internet.

Autres logements

Pour des séjours généralement plus longs (une semaine, un mois ou plus), il existe plusieurs formules:

- la résidence de tourisme/hôtelière. Cette formule propose des logements meublés et équipés avec toutes les prestations d'un bon hôtel. Ces résidences sont habituellement situées dans des **lieux** touristiques.
- la location en meublé qui propose des villas, appartements, studios, chalets, meublés et tout équipés.
- gîte ou la chambre. En louant chez l'habitant (à la nuit ou à la semaine, avec petit-déjeuner et, parfois, table d'hôte), le touriste a l'occasion de mieux connaître et **partager** la façon de vivre des Français.

homologué	classified
une étoile	star
afficher	display
la taxe de séjour	tourism tax
renseignez-vous auprès de	ask for information
la prestation	service
le lieu, l'endroit	place
partager	share

Activity 1

The following visitors are looking for accommodation in France. Look at their requirements and decide which of the types of accommodation listed in the box best suits their needs:

a Une famille canadienne veut passer plusieurs semaines calmes dans un joli coin rural de la France.

b Un anglais a un rendez-vous d'affaires à Paris.

c Un couple de personnes âgées cherche un appartement pour un mois au bord de la mer et près d'un golf. Ils n'aiment pas faire la cuisine.

d Un couple américain désire visiter la France. Ils veulent pratiquer leur français et goûter à la cuisine traditionnelle.

hôtel	résidence de tourisme	chambre d'hôte
	villa meublée et équipée	

Activity 2

Study the icons below. They describe the type of services you are likely to find in a four-star hotel and room. Find the matching explanation for each icon then listen to the recording to check your answers.

a   i Climatisation

b   ii Accès handicapé

c   iii Mini-bar

d		iv Bureau de change dans l'hôtel
e		v Service en chambre
f		vi Bagagiste
g		vii Sèche-cheveux
h		viii Navette aéroport
i		ix Coffre-fort
j		x Chambre non-fumeur
k		xi Piscine
l		xii Ascenseur
m		xiii Télévision via satellite
n		xiv Animaux acceptés
o		xv Bar
p		xvi WiFi
q		xvii Parking privé

▶ Dialogue 1: À *la recherche d'un hôtel* Looking for a hotel

À l'office du tourisme une touriste accompagnée de son mari se renseigne sur les hôtels à Paris.

At the tourist office, a tourist accompanied by her husband enquires about hotels in Paris.

What's the tourist's concern regarding the hotel?

Touriste	Bonjour Madame. Je viens d'arriver à Paris et je cherche une chambre. Vous avez une liste d'hôtels, s'il vous plaît?
Hôtesse	Oui Madame, voilà.
	(the tourists look at the brochure)
Touriste	Vous pouvez me réserver une chambre, s'il vous plaît?
Hôtesse	Oui, bien sûr. Vous choisissez quel hôtel?
Touriste	Un hôtel à trois étoiles, l'Hôtel Victor Hugo, dans le 16ème arrondissement. Mais c'est où le 16ème arrondissement?
Hôtesse	Paris est divisé en 20 arrondissements. Le 16ème se trouve au nord-ouest de Paris. C'est un quartier très résidentiel et très calme, et le Bois de Boulogne est tout près.
Touriste	Ah bon, alors c'est d'accord.
Hôtesse	C'est pour combien de personnes?
Touriste	Euh, pour mon mari et moi.
Hôtesse	Et pour combien de nuits?
Touriste	Pour deux nuits.
Hôtesse	Bien. Une chambre à deux lits ou un grand lit?
Touriste	Un grand lit. Nous voulons aussi une douche ou une salle de bains dans la chambre.
Hôtesse	Bon, alors une chambre pour deux nuits, pour deux personnes avec un grand lit et douche ou salle de bains. Très bien, je vais téléphoner et je vous réserve ça tout de suite.
Touriste	J'espère que l'hôtel n'est pas complet!
Hôtesse	Je crois qu'en cette saison, il y a des chambres de libre.

Activity 3

Listen to the dialogue as often as you need and spot the French version of the following phrases:

a I have just arrived. ....
b Can you book me a room? ....
c Where is the 16th district? ....

d We also want a shower or a bathroom. . . . .
e I hope the hotel is not full! . . . .
f There are some vacancies. . . . .

▶ Dialogue 2: *À l'hôtel* In the hotel

À la réception: les Wilson arrivent à leur hôtel.

At reception: the Wilsons arrive at their hotel. Does the hotel serve meals other than breakfast?

Touriste	Bonjour, Monsieur. Nous avons une réservation au nom de Wilson.
Réceptionniste	Ah oui, vous êtes les Anglais qui ont téléphoné cet après-midi!
Touriste	Oui, c'est ça.
Réceptionniste	Bon, vous avez la chambre 43 au deuxième étage. C'est une chambre très agréable avec grand lit, douche et WC.
Touriste	Le petit-déjeuner est compris dans le prix de la chambre?
Réceptionniste	Ah non, Madame, c'est en plus : sept euros par personne.
Touriste	Et à quelle heure servez-vous le petit-déjeuner?
Réceptionniste	À partir de 7.30 heures jusqu'à 10 heures.
Touriste	Vous servez le petit déjeuner dans la chambre?
Réceptionniste	Mais oui, Madame, bien sûr.
Touriste	Très bien. Pouvez-vous nous apporter demain matin le petit-déjeuner à 8.30, s'il vous plaît?
Réceptionniste	C'est entendu, Madame.
Touriste	Et est-ce qu'il y a un ascenseur dans l'hôtel? Nos valises sont très lourdes.
Réceptionniste	Oui, au fond du couloir à droite.
Touriste	On peut prendre un repas dans l'hôtel?
Réceptionniste	Non, je regrette, nous ne servons que le petit-déjeuner mais il y a beaucoup de bons restaurants tout près d'ici.

Activity 4

Answer the following statements with **vrai** or **faux**:

	vrai	faux
a Room 43 is on the third floor.	☐	☐
b Breakfast is included in the price.	☐	☐

c Breakfast is served from eight o'clock. □ □
d Their suitcases are heavy. □ □
e The lift is at the end of the corridor on the left. □ □
f They serve only breakfast. □ □
g There are a lot of restaurants nearby. □ □

Activity 5

By surfing the Internet you found a central hotel in the 5th district. Judging from its description, it seems quiet and comfortable, which is just what you are looking for. You make your way there to book a room for two.

HOTELS URIS
de Paris

Hôtel Relais
Saint-Jacques

★★★★

3, rue de l'Abbé de l'Epée, 75005 Paris
Metro: Saint-Michel (4)
Luxembourg (RER B)
Tél: 33 (0) 1 43 40 77 79   Fax: 33 (0) 1 70 60 11 30

HOTELS URIS
de Paris

À deux pas des Jardins du Luxembourg,
de la Sorbonne, du Panthéon, et de la
rue Mouffetard, sur une petite place calme,
cet hôtel de pur style Haussmannien fréquenté
jadis par le célèbre écrivain autrichien
Rilke, conjugue harmonieusement: luxe, confort,
raffinement, spiritualité.

Vous	*Say 'good evening' and ask if they have a room.*
Réceptionniste	Oui, qu'est-ce que vous voulez comme chambre? Une chambre pour une personne?
Vous	*Say 'no, a double room with two beds and a bathroom'.*
Réceptionniste	C'est pour combien de nuits?
Vous	*It's for four nights.*
Réceptionniste	Oui, j'ai une chambre avec salle de bains.
Vous	*How much is it?*

Réceptionniste	Alors, pour quatre nuits, nous faisons une promotion.
Vous	*Ask what 'promotion' is.*
Réceptionniste	Une promotion? C'est une offre spéciale. Vous restez chez nous quatre nuits, mais vous ne payez que trois nuits. Donc 140€ par nuit multipliés par trois, ça vous fait un total de 420€ au lieu de 560€.
Vous	*Ask if breakfast is included.*
Réceptionniste	Oui, le petit-déjeuner est compris.
Vous	*Ask what time breakfast is served.*
Réceptionniste	Entre huit heures et dix heures.
Vous	*Ask if you can have a meal in the hotel.*
Réceptionniste	Mais oui, bien sûr. Le restaurant est au premier étage.
Vous	*Ask who Haussmann is.*
Réceptionniste	Le Baron Haussman a modernisé Paris au 19ème siècle. C'est lui qui a crée les grandes avenues.

Se plaindre Complaining

Things aren't always as they ought to be and you may have to complain about things not working ... **ne marche(ent) pas** or things that are missing **il n'y a pas de ....** If the situation is really bad you can always ask to speak to the **directeur** (manager).

Activity 6

Use the words in the box overleaf and explain to the **directeur** that some objects in your room are not working (those in the square boxes) and some are missing (those in the circles).

l'eau chaude   le savon   les couvertures

le radiateur   la douche

la lampe   la télévision

les serviettes

Au camping-caravaning At the caravan-campsite

Camping en France: **www.campingfrance.com/**

Fédération Française de Camping-Caravaning: **www.ffcc.fr**)

i En France, il y a 9000 terrains de camping aménagés classés de 0 à 4* et 2300 terrains à la ferme. Les offices du tourisme ont la liste des campings; ils peuvent vous aider à réserver un emplacement pour votre tente ou votre caravane.

Le camping sauvage (*camping on unauthorized sites*) est permis avec l'autorisation du propriétaire du terrain, mais interdit sur les plages, au bord des routes ou dans les sites classés. Renseignez-vous auprès des offices du tourisme ou à la gendarmerie.

Activity 7

Michael Price, his wife and two children, aged eight and six, are on their way to the Pyrénées in the south of France. They stop in a tourist office and enquire about caravan sites. Michael is given a leaflet on 'Le Cabaliros'. Study it and help Michael decide whether or not it is suitable for the family.

a Mr Price wants to know which services for his caravan are provided by Le Cabaliros?

b Mrs Price wants an easy and relaxed holiday. What facilities are there to help housewives and mothers?

c What sporting activities are available for the family?

d What fun activities can Mr and Mrs Price do while the children are occupied?

100 emplacements, dont 88 tourisme

LE CABALIROS
65110 CAUTERETS
E-mail: chantal.boyrie@wanadoo.fr
Tel: 05 62 92 55 36
Tel: 05 62 92 55 38 (H.S.)
Fax: 05 62 92 55 36

GCC Emplacement avec branchement électrique.
Alimentation en eau.
Evacuation toutes eaux usées.

Ouverture: 1.06/30.09

CAUTERETS 16km S. Argelès-Gazost. Altitude : 1000 m 1113 habitants

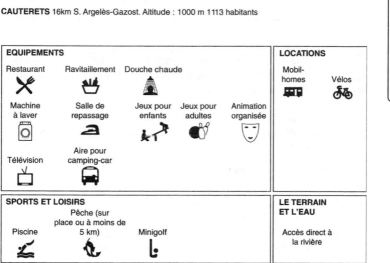

EQUIPEMENTS					LOCATIONS	
Restaurant	Ravitaillement	Douche chaude			Mobil-homes	Vélos
Machine à laver	Salle de repassage	Jeux pour enfants	Jeux pour adultes	Animation organisée		
Télévision	Aire pour camping-car					

SPORTS ET LOISIRS			LE TERRAIN ET L'EAU
Piscine	Pêche (sur place ou à moins de 5 km)	Minigolf	Accès direct à la rivière

▶ Dialogue 3

Monsieur Price vient d'arriver à l'accueil du Cabaliros.

Mr Price has just arrived at the reception of 'Le Cabaliros'. Is electricity included in the price?

Mr Price Bonjour Madame. **Avez-vous** un emplacement pour une voiture et une caravane ... pour huit jours?

Femme Pour huit jours? Oui, c'est possible.

Mr Price Il nous faut **un branchement électrique**.

Femme Oui, sans problème.

Mr Price C'est combien la nuit?

Femme Alors pour le forfait emplacement, c'est 20€60 la nuit.

Mr Price	Forfait emplacement?
Femme	Oui, **c'est-à-dire** le prix pour l'emplacement de 90 m²; donc pour une voiture, une caravane et deux personnes.
Mr Price	Il faut payer pour l'électricité?
Femme	Oui, c'est en plus: 3€70 par nuit. Mais **par contre** pas de supplément pour l'eau chaude … **ni** pour les douches.
Mr Price	Ah bon … On peut voir l'emplacement?
Femme	Bien sûr. **Il me reste** un **emplacement à l'ombre**, vous le voulez?
Mr Price	Avec plaisir.
Femme	Mais avant, j'ai besoin de noter la plaque d'immatriculation de votre véhicule. Vous la connaissez?
Mr Price	Euh, oui. GY53 FKB.
Femme	Merci bien, Monsieur Price. On peut aller voir l'emplacement maintenant.

---

branchement électrique	*electric connection*
c'est-à-dire	*which means*
par contre	*on the other hand*
(ni…) ni	*(neither…) nor*
il me reste …	*I have got … left*
l'emplacement à l'ombre	*pitch in the shade*
la plaque d'immatriculation	*number plate*

L'alphabet français The French alphabet

Knowing the French alphabet is useful. As in Mr Price's case, you may be asked to give the numberplate of your car, or more simply your name, when booking accommodation or tickets: **votre nom?** You may also be asked to spell it: **vous pouvez épeler?** or **ça s'écrit comment?**

Activity 8

Read the alphabet below several times and practise spelling your name and your address.

A	B	C	D	E	F	G
ah	bé	cé	dé	eux	eff	j'ai
H	I	J	K	L	M	N
ahsh	ee	j'y	kah	elle	emm	enne
O	P	Q	R	S	T	U
oh	pé	ku	erre	ess	té	u*
V	W	X	Y	Z		
vé	doubl'vé	eeks	ee grec	zed		

*as in **du**

i • To spell double consonants the French will say **deux** .... For example, to spell **mallet** they'll say: emm - ah - *deux* - *elle* - eux - té; and to spell **poussin**: pé - oh - u - *deux ess* - ee - enne
• Be particularly careful when spelling the French letters **e, i, g** and **j** as they can be confusing for English speakers.

Réserver en ligne, envoyer un courriel
Booking online, sending an email

i Si vous avez l'intention de faire du camping ou de réserver un hôtel en France, il vaut mieux (*it's better*) réserver longtemps à l'avance surtout pendant les périodes de vacances. Lorsque la réservation est faite en ligne ou par courriel, il est généralement demandé de l'accompagner d'un versement d'arrhes ou d'un acompte *(an advance)*.

Activity 9

John Osborne decides to book a mobile home online. For his reservation to be accepted, he needs to download it (**télécharger**), sign the contract, add the words **Lu et approuvé** next to his signature and return it to the campsite owner with **les arrhes**.

Read the contract and help John make sense of it by choosing for each highlighted word in the text its equivalent in English:

CONTRAT de RÉSERVATION de MOBIL-HOME

* Réserver un mobil-home au CAMPING LE GLACIER du _____ au _____ à partir de 16h ou avant 10h

* Nombre de personnes: _____

* Au prix net de: _____

* Montant des arrhes 25% de la location:_____

* Taxe de séjour en supplément: 0.22€ p/jour par adulte ____

_____

_____

• **Draps et linge** non fournis.
• Pour tout **retard** supérieur à 24h, le client s'engage à en **aviser** le camping.
• En cas de départ anticipé, il n'y aura aucun **remboursement**.
• Une **caution** de 200€ sera demandée à l'arrivée et restituée au départ si l'entretien du Mobil-home a été effectué correctement.

Signature du client précédée de _____

Lu et approuvé en manuscrit _____

i   cleaning
ii refund
iii deposit
iv delay
v   sheets and towels
vi inform

Activity 10

John wrote an email (**un courriel**) to the **directeur du camping Le Glacier** in which he asked several questions. He has received the following reply. Read it and write in French the four questions that John is likely to have asked in his email.

To: **Josborne@hotmail.com**

Cc:

Subject: Réservation mobil-home

Cher Monsieur Osborne,

J'ai le plaisir de confirmer votre réservation du mobil-home du 15 au 22 août.

Je réponds à vos questions:

a) Entre quatre et six personnes peuvent dormir dans le mobil-home.

b) Oui, il faut amener les draps et les serviettes car nous ne les fournissons pas.

c) Oui, nous acceptons les chiens sans supplément.

d) Il faut payer une caution de 200 à votre arrivée.

À très bientôt le plaisir de vous voir.

Le Directeur du Camping Le Glacier

Mini-test

How do you say in French:

1 I'm looking for a two-star hotel.
2 Can you book a room for me?
3 Is breakfast included?
4 There's no telephone in the room.
5 How much is a pitch for a car, two people and caravan for eight days?

13

bien manger, bien boire

eating and drinking well

In this unit you will
- find out where to eat
- practise ordering a snack
- choose a menu and order a meal

Before you start, revise

- saying what you want (page 62)
- the verb **prendre** (page 42)
- some, any (page 13)
- asking questions (page 39)
- likes and dislikes (page 74)

Bien manger Eating well

i La cuisine en France est très variée, chaque région offrant ses produits et spécialités gastronomiques. Grâce à sa population importante d'immigrés, la France a une cuisine ethnique riche et relativement bon marché. On peut également acheter un peu partout du fast-food et **des plats à emporter** dans des McDonald's, Pizza Hut etc. Par contre, les restaurants végétariens sont rares, ainsi que les menus qui incluent des plats végétariens.

On peut très bien manger en France dans des restaurants modestes appelés **les petits restaurants du coin**. Au menu ils ont souvent des plats simples mais appétissants comme un pâté maison et **un plat garni**.

On peut aussi manger dans **une brasserie** et commander un plat unique comme **la choucroute** avec de la bière; ou encore dans **un bistrot** où on choisira entre un bifteck-frites, une excellente spécialité et **le plat du jour**; ou pour pas cher dans une **crêperie**, un bar ou un café.

Les restaurants proposent en général plusieurs **menus**, du plus cher, 'le menu gastronomique', au plus modeste, 'le menu touristique' et **la carte**.

Le pourboire est toujours inclus (15 %) dans l'addition. Si vous êtes satisfait, vous pouvez laisser quelques euros à la personne qui vous a servi.

le plat à emporter	take-away food
le petit restaurant du coin	local restaurant offering good but cheap food
le plat garni	dish with meat and vegetable or salad
la brasserie	cross between a café and a restaurant

la choucroute	cabbage, bacon, sausages, potatoes
le bistrot	cheap restaurant
le plat du jour	today's special
la crêperie	pancake house
le menu	list of dishes served at a fixed price for the whole meal
la carte	list of dishes individually priced
le pourboire	tip

Activity 1

Without looking at the passage above, choose the correct phrase to complete the sentences below then check your answers in the **Key to the exercises** at the end of the book.

a French cuisine consists only of *regional specialities/a variety of cuisines.*

b Fast-food and take-away food *can easily/cannot be found.*

c **Les petits restaurants du coin** are usually *cheap/expensive.*

d **Un plat garni** is a dish with *meat only/meat, vegetables or noodles.*

e In a **brasserie** one can eat *pancakes/a limited range of dishes.*

f **Le plat du jour** is *'today's special'/a dish with cold food.*

g If you want a pancake you go to a *crêperie/bar.*

h If you want the cheapest menu, you choose the *menu gastronomique/le menu touristique.*

Key words and phrases

vous désirez?	what will you have?
vous avez choisi?	have you made a choice?
qu'est-ce que vous avez à manger?	what do you have to eat?
à boire?	to drink?
qu'est-ce que vous avez comme boissons/snacks?	what do you have in the way of drinks/snack?
comme parfums?	of flavours?
il ne reste plus de ...	there is no ... left
il n'y a plus de ...	there is no more
des sandwiches au jambon/ au fromage	ham/cheese sandwiches

une glace à la vanille	vanilla ice-cream
de la bière en bouteille	bottled beer
de la pression	draught beer
un café	a black coffee
un café crème	a white coffee (with milk not cream)
un thé au citron	lemon tea
un thé nature	tea (without milk, etc...)
un thé avec du lait froid	tea with cold milk
une orange pressée	freshly-squeezed orange
un jus de fruit	fruit juice
un jus de pomme/d'ananas/ de pamplemousse	apple/pineapple/ grapefruit juice
qu'est-ce que c'est le/la/les ...?	what's the ...?
c'est quoi le/la/les ...?	what's the ...?
je vais en prendre un (une)	I'll take one
pour commencer ...	to start with ...
comme entrée	as a starter
comme plat principal	as a main course
ensuite ...	then ...
comme dessert ...	for dessert ...
le plat	dish, course
le plat cuisiné	ready-cooked meal
plats à emporter	take-away food
saignant/bleu	rare (lit. bleeding/blue)
à point	medium
bien cuit	well done
l'addition (f)	the bill

▶ Dialogue 1: *Commander un snack* Ordering a snack

À la terrasse d'un café deux touristes sont prêts à commander.

Two tourists sitting outside a café are ready to order.

*The man asks the waiter what a **croque-monsieur** is. Listen to or read the waiter's explanations: how would you explain to someone English what a **croque-monsieur** is? What is the woman ordering? What drinks are they having?*

Garçon Bonjour, Messieurs-dames. Qu'est-ce que vous désirez?
Homme Qu'est-ce que vous avez à manger?
Garçon À manger, nous avons des sandwiches au jambon blanc, **rillettes**, pâté de campagne, saucisson sec, hot-dogs,

Homme	omelettes, croque-monsieur … Qu'est-ce que c'est un croque-monsieur?
Garçon	Un croque-monsieur? C'est deux **tranches de pain grillé** avec jambon et fromage **au milieu**.
Homme	**Ça a l'air** délicieux … je vais en prendre un.
Garçon	Et pour vous Madame?
Femme	Moi, je crois que je vais prendre une omelette … qu'est-ce que vous avez comme omelettes?
Garçon	Omelettes au fromage, aux **champignons**, aux herbes …
Femme	Une omelette aux champignons.
Garçon	Et comme boissons, Messieurs-dames?
Homme	Vous avez de la bière?
Garçon	Oui … nous avons de la bière pression et de la Kronenbourg en bouteille.
Homme	Bon, une pression s'il vous plaît.
Garçon	Je vous sers **un demi**?
Homme	Oui, c'est ça.
Femme	Moi, je vais prendre un café crème.
Garçon	Bon, alors une pression, un café crème, une omelette aux champignons et un croque-monsieur.
Homme	Merci bien, Monsieur.

rillettes	*type of potted meat, usually pork, similar to pâté*
tranche de pain grillé	*slice of toasted bread*
au milieu	*in the middle*
ça a l'air	*it seems*
les champignons	*mushrooms*
un demi	*half* (usually half a pint, but sometimes half a litre)

Activity 2

See if you can unscramble the dialogue below, starting with the sentence in bold:

a Je vais prendre une pression.
b À manger nous avons des sandwiches, des croque-monsieur, des pizzas …
c **Bonjour Monsieur, qu'est-ce que vous désirez?**
d De la pression et de la Kronenbourg en bouteille.
e Qu'est-ce que vous avez à manger?
f Je vais prendre une pizza; et comme bières, qu'est-ce que vous avez?

Activity 3

You're hungry and decide to go to a café for a snack. Here comes the waiter ... be prepared to order:

Garçon Qu'est-ce que vous désirez?
a Vous *Say that you would like a croque-monsieur.*
Garçon Je suis désolé, Monsieur, mais il n'y en a plus.
b Vous *Ask him if he has any omelettes.*
Garçon Oui, nous avons omelettes nature, jambon et Parmentier.
c Vous *Ask what Parmentier is.*
Garçon Omelette Parmentier? C'est une omelette avec des pommes de terre.
d Vous *Say that you'll take the potato omelette.*
Garçon Bien, alors une omelette Parmentier; et à boire, Monsieur, qu'est-ce que je vous sers?
e Vous *Ask him what he has in the way of fruit juice (the e of juice is not pronounced).*
Garçon Comme jus de fruit nous avons du jus d'orange, du jus d'ananas, du jus de pamplemousse ...
f Vous *Say that you would like a pineapple juice and the bill, please.*

Activity 4

Using the menu below and dialogue in Activity 3 as a guide, act out similar situations varying the dishes and drinks. (The answers are not given in the **Key to the exercises and tests**.)

Salades composées

Salade mixte 7,00
Tomates, salade, oeuf

Chef salade 9,00
Tomates, pommes à l'huile, jambon, gruyère, salade, oeuf dur

Salade végétarienne 7,80
Tomates, poivron, maïs, carotte concombre, salade

Salade niçoise 12,00
Tomates, oeuf, thon, poivrons, concombre, olives, salade, anchois

Buffet chaud

Croque monsieur 5,00
Croque madame......................5,50
Croque niçois 5,80
Croque-monsieur avec tomate et anchois

Buffet froid

Poulet froid mayonnaise.............8,50
Assiette charcuterie 9,30
Assiette anglaise................9,30
Assiette de viande froide............9,30

Buffet chaud

Omelette nature (3 pièces) 5,50
Omelette jambon 6,50
Omelette fromage 6,50
Omelette savoyarde. 7,10
Omelette parmentier 7,10

Sandwiches

Jambon de paris 3,70
Paté ou rillettes 4,00
Camembert ou gruyère 4,00
Saucisson sec ou à l'ail 4,00

Boissons

Café express 2,60
Thé au citron 3,60
Jus de fruit 3,60
Bière pression 3,60
Bière bouteille 3,60
Eau minérale 3,60
Soda 3,60
Apéritif anisé 5,00

▶ Dialogue 2: *Au restaurant* At the restaurant

Menu à 33€

En entrée

L'oeuf cocotte au foie gras,

La soupe gratinée à l'oignon,

Le Crottin de chèvre chaud et salade

En plat

Le confit de canard

La poule au pot d'Henry IV garnie maison

Le steak au poivre avec sa garniture

Dessert

La crème brûlée à l'ancienne

Les profiteroles au chocolat

La tarte des demoiselles Tatin à la crème

Browsing on the Internet, a tourist finds 'La Poule au Pot', an authentically Art Deco bistro in the centre of Paris. He likes the menu and decides to try it out. Read the menu and listen to the conversation between the tourist and the waiter:

Customer	Vous avez une table pour une personne?
Garçon	Oui, monsieur, il nous en reste juste une près de la fenêtre.
	(*later*) Alors, qu'est-ce que ce **sera** pour vous, le menu à 33€ ou la carte?
Customer	Je vais prendre le menu.
Garçon	Qu'est-ce que je vous sers comme entrée?
Customer	C'est quoi 'L'oeuf cocotte au foie gras'?
Garçon	C'est une spécialité bien française. C'est deux oeufs **cuits au four** dans un ramequin. On y ajoute une tranche de foie gras et de la crème en fin de cuisson.
Customer	Je crois que je préfère la soupe à l'oignon.
Garçon	Une soupe gratinée, alors. Bien et ensuite?
Customer	Le steak au poivre.
Garçon	Vous le voulez comment? Saignant, à point ou bien cuit?
Customer	À point. Vous le servez avec quoi le steak?
Garçon	Avec une garniture de légumes de saison, **haricots verts**, carottes et une salade verte. Vous prendrez quelque chose à boire?
Customer	Oui, de l'eau minérale et puis une bouteille de Bordeaux. Vous pouvez **me conseiller** pour le vin?
Garçon	Oui, d'accord, je vous **apporte** un bon Bordeaux.
	(*later*) **C'était bon?**
Customer	Très bon, merci.
Garçon	Vous avez choisi un dessert?
Customer	Comme dessert, je vais prendre la tarte des demoiselles Tatin à la crème.
Garçon	Je vous la recommande ... elle est délicieuse et faite maison.
Customer	Vous pouvez expliquer le nom de la tarte?
Garçon	C'est une histoire célèbre. Les demoiselles Tatin avaient un hôtel familial dans la vallée de la Loire. Stéphanie Tatin était spécialiste de la tarte aux pommes. Un jour, **étourdie**, elle cuit la tarte et la servit à l'envers ...
Customer	**À l'envers?**
Garçon	Euh oui ... la tarte était complètement renversée ... comme ça ... Eh bien c'était un tel succès que ce plat est entré dans notre gastronomie nationale. Et voilà, vous prendrez bien un café après la tarte?
Customer	Non merci, et amenez l'addition après le dessert, s'il vous plaît.

sera	*will be*
cuit au four	*cooked in the oven*
haricots verts	*green beans*
me conseiller	*advise me*
apporter/amener	*bring along*
c'était bon?	*was it good?*
étourdi	*absent-minded*
à l'envers	*upside down*

Listen to the dialogue again and spot the French version of the following phrases:

a   What is 'L'oeuf cocotte au foie gras'?
b   It is two eggs cooked in the oven.
c   I think that I prefer ...
d   How do you serve the steak?
e   Can you advise me about the wine?
f   Can you explain the name of the tart?
g   Bring the bill after dessert.

Activity 6

Now it's your turn to order a meal. When you check your answers in the **Key to the exercises and tests**, remember that there are variations to the answers given.

Serveuse Bonjour, Monsieur/Madame, vous avez choisi?
a *You* *Say that to start with you'll have a **filet de hareng**.*
Serveuse Je regrette, il n'y a plus de filet de hareng.
b *You* *Say that you'll have an **avocat à la vinaigrette**.*
Serveuse Bien, un avocat à la vinaigrette, et ensuite ...
c *You* *Ask what is **cassoulet**.*
Serveuse C'est une spécialité française avec de la viande de porc et haricots blancs.
d *You* *Say that you don't like beans. Say you prefer the **grillade du jour** with **frites**.*
Serveuse Vous la voulez comment, votre viande?
e *You* *Say medium and say that you would also like a bottle of Sauvignon.*
Serveuse (*after the starter*) Voilà. Une grillade avec frites.
f *You* Ask what she has in the way of desserts.
Serveuse Fromage, glaces, crème au caramel.
g *You* *Say that you'll have a vanilla ice-cream.*
Serveuse Ah, je regrette mais nous n'avons plus de vanille.

h *You*   *Ask what other flavours they have.*
Serveuse Citron, café, chocolat, fraise.
i *You*   *Say that you will have a strawberry ice-cream.*

Activity 7

You are on holiday in 'Les Landes' with your friend and her three children. You want to take them out on Friday for a nice meal. Look at the restaurants below. Which one will you choose? Obviously, price needs to be considered plus the fact the children are boisterous. Luckily they eat any type of food!

BAR – TABACS - AUBERGE
LE PLATANE
Place de la République, 40300 PEYREHORADE
TÉL. 05 57 37 66 54

Service de 12 h à 14.30 et de 19 h à 22 h
MENU du jour 14€
Dimanche menus du jour de 18€30 à 26€ + CARTE

Traiteur – Cuisine régionale
et traditionnelle. Plats à emporter.
Banquets, mariages, séminaires, Groupe.

L'AUBERGE AU BON COIN
40230 SAUBRIGUES
TÉL. 05 58 94 71 33

Service de 12 h à 14 h et de 19 h 30 à 22 h
MENUS: 13€ – 18€ – 23€ – 28€
CARTE: 14€ à 25€
MENU ENFANT: 8€

Fermeture hors saison lundi soir et mardi

Cuisine traditionnelle,
spécialités régionales, dans un cadre typique
et familial au calme de la campagne landaise. Grande
capacité d'accueil, service en terrasse l'été. Grand parking.

Mini-test

You can now test yourself on Units 11, 12 and 13.

1 How would you say:
   a Where is the nearest restaurant?
   b I'm looking for something cheaper.
   c Do you have anything else?

2 You are asked to spell your name. Choose the French equivalent:
   a **Ça s'écrit comment?**
   b **C'est à quel nom?**
   c **Est-ce qu'il reste encore des chambres?**

3 How would you say:
   a There are no more cheese sandwiches.
   b For dessert, I'll have a vanilla ice cream.
   c What drinks do you have?

Before going on to Unit 14 take the **Self-assessment test 2** (Units 11–13). Once you have done it, check your answers in the **Key to the exercises and tests** and write your score in the box below. If you score between 40 and 50 points, you can go straight on to Unit 14. If your score is between 20 and 40 points, you need to spend more time revising the **Dialogues** and **Key words and phrases**. Below 20 points, go back over Units 11, 12 and 13 and take the test again to see how much you have improved.

Self-assessment score (Units 11–13)

Points: _____/50

14

les transports publics
public transport

In this unit you will
- find out about public transport in France
- learn key expressions to make travelling by bus, taxi, train and underground easier
- find out how to ask for information

Before you start, revise

- finding out what's available (page 13)
- asking for and understanding directions (page 50)
- expressions of time, days of the week **Key words and phrases** (page 36)
- numbers (page 233)

Key words and phrases

où est-ce que je peux ...?	*where can I ...?*
où est-ce qu'il faut ...?	*where do you have to ...?*
il faut monter, descendre	*you have to get on, get off*
arriver, quitter	*arrive, leave*
changer	*change*
composter le billet	*date-stamp the ticket*
réserver une couchette	*book a sleeper*
le billet/ticket	*ticket*
le carnet (de tickets)	*set of ten tickets*
c'est quelle direction?	*which line* (lit. 'direction') *is it?*
c'est direct?	*is it direct?*
le trajet, le voyage	*travel, journey*
voyager de jour, de nuit	*travel in the daytime, overnight*
dans la matinée, soirée	*in the morning, evening*
le métro	*the underground*
le RER (réseau express régional)	*fast extension of the métro to the suburbs of Paris*
la banlieue	*the suburbs*
desservir	*to serve*
la station de métro	*tube station*
la correspondance	*connection*
manquer la sortie	*miss the exit*
le taxi	*taxi*
la station de taxis	*taxi rank*
l'autobus (m) (bus)	*town bus*
l'autocar (m) (car)	*coach/long distance bus*
la gare routière	*bus station*
l'arrêt (m) d'autobus	*bus stop*
c'est quelle ligne?	*what number (bus) is it?*
la SNCF (Société Nationale des Chemins de Fer)	*French railways*
la gare	*station (train)*
le guichet	*ticket office*

une place	*a seat (also square,* *as in place du Marché)*
un aller (simple)	*single ticket*
un aller-retour	*return ticket*
le plein tarif	*full fare*
le bureau de renseignements	*information office*
la consigne	*left luggage*
consigne automatique	*left luggage lockers*
un horaire	*timetable*
la période de pointe	*peak times*
le prochain/dernier train	*the next/last train*
en première/seconde classe	*first/second class*
dans le train	*on the train*
le quai	*platform*
la voie	*track (often used for 'platform'* *instead of* **quai***)*
au-delà	*beyond*

Le Métro et tramway parisiens The Paris underground and tramway

RATP: **www.ratp.fr**

i Le métro parisien est très pratique et économique. Avec un seul ticket (1€50), vous pouvez aller n'importe où (*anywhere*) dans Paris pour une durée de deux heures. Si vous achetez les tickets par carnet ils coûtent moins cher (dix tickets pour 11€10).

Pour découvrir Paris et sa région d'Île-de-France en métro, tramway, bus, RER et trains SNCF, achetez 'Paris Visite', un forfait transport (*travel pass*), valable un, deux, trois ou cinq jours consécutifs. Il permet également de bénéficier de réductions sur l'entrée de nombreux sites touristiques de la capitale.

Le métro a 14 lignes identifiables par leur numéro et leurs directions (les deux stations terminus). Pour changer d'une ligne à l'autre, suivez les panneaux oranges 'Correspondance' et le nom de la ligne que vous désirez prendre. Du métro vous pouvez passer facilement au RER. C'est un métro ultra-rapide avec cinq lignes (A, B, C, D et E) qui dessert Paris et sa banlieue. Il faut payer un supplément si vous prenez le RER, au-delà de la zone 2.

Après avoir déserté Paris il y a presque 70 ans, la capitale a retrouvé son métro le 16 décembre 2006! La ligne T3 traverse les 15ème, 14ème et 13ème arrondissements de Paris du sud-ouest au sud-est sur un parcours de 7,9 km ponctué de 17 stations.

Activity 1

Answer the following assertions with **vrai** or **faux**:

		vrai	faux
a	There is a flat rate in central Paris.	☐	☐
b	A set of ten tickets is more expensive than ten single tickets.	☐	☐
c	One can buy a tourist pass for ten days.	☐	☐
d	Each line is known by one name.	☐	☐
e	**Correspondance** is the sign to look for to change line.	☐	☐
f	To go on the RER you may pay more.	☐	☐
g	The tramway stops every 7.9 km.	☐	☐

Activity 2

A tourist has just arrived at Charles de Gaulle airport. He needs to go to Orly-Sud to catch an internal flight. Look at the diagram below then complete the dialogue, filling the blank spaces with the words in the box.

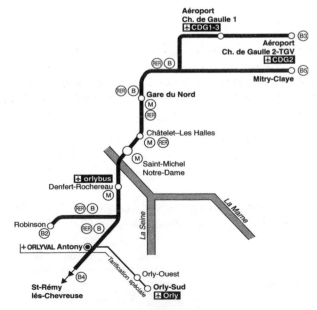

Touriste	Pardon Monsieur, c'est quelle a _____ pour l'Aéroport Orly-Sud?
Homme	Orly? Vous b _____ la ligne B du RER direction St-Rémy lès-Chevreuse.
Touriste	C'est direct?
Homme	Non, il faut c _____ à la station Antony.
Touriste	Bon, je change à Antony et puis?
Homme	Là, vous avez la liaison Orlyval. C'est un métro automatique qui va vous d _____ aux aéroports d'Orly.
Touriste	C'est pas compliqué.
Homme	Non, mais faites bien attention de prendre direction B4 St-Rémy-lès-Chevreuse. Si vous prenez la direction B2, vous e _____ la station d'Antony.
Touriste	Ah, merci, Monsieur.

manquerez   mener (*take to*)   changer   prenez   direction

▶ Activity 3

An American cannot understand the directions he's given to get from the **Orly-Sud** to the **Gare du Nord**. Listen to the recording (if you haven't got it look at the diagram on page 140) and tell him in English what to do.

Prendre un taxi Taking a taxi

À Paris, il y a 5300 taxis qui sont jour et nuit à la disposition de la clientèle. Le numéro unique d'appel des stations est le **01 45 30 30 30**!

ℹ️ Dans les grandes villes, on peut prendre un taxi à une station de taxi, en le hélant (*hailing*) dans la rue, si son lumineux (*light on the roof*) est éclairé, ou en téléphonant à l'une des principales compagnies.

Il y a un supplément à payer pour le transport d'une quatrième personne adulte ou d'un deuxième bagage dans le coffre.

▶ Dialogue 1: *La station de taxis* The taxi rank

Listen carefully to the recordings, or read below, then answer the following questions:

The tourist doesn't get any information from the first passer-by: why? How far is the taxi rank? At the crossroads does he have to go right or straight on?

Touriste	Pardon, Monsieur, où est la station de taxis la plus proche?
Homme	Je ne sais pas, je ne suis pas d'ici …
	(*Later* …)
Touriste	S'il vous plaît, Madame, savez-vous où il y a une station de taxis?
Femme	Mais oui, c'est très simple, vous en avez une, à 500 mètres, à côté de la Gare du Nord.
Touriste	La gare du Nord, c'est où exactement?
Femme	Bon, il faut d'abord monter le boulevard Magenta. Au carrefour, vous allez continuer tout droit et prendre le boulevard Denain et à droite de la Gare du Nord vous allez trouver la station de taxis.

Activity 4

Would you be able to find the taxi rank? Choose the correct word:

a **Il faut monter** means
  i turn ii go up iii cross

b **Un carrefour** is
  i crossroads ii traffics light iii sign post

c **Vous continuez tout droit** means
  i turn left ii turn right iii carry straight on

Voyager en autobus Travelling by bus

RATP: **www.ratp.fr**

Information on Eurolines: **www.eurolines.fr**

Gare routière internationale de Paris: 28 Avenue du Général de Gaulle, 93170 Bagnolet, tél: 08 92 90 91 (Métro: Gallieni)

i À Paris, on utilise les mêmes tickets pour le métro et pour l'autobus. On peut acheter un billet simple dans l'autobus, mais avec un carnet de tickets, c'est plus économique. Les carnets sont vendus dans certaines stations de métro ou d'autobus. Ils se trouvent aussi dans certains magasins de livres (FNAC) ou de tabac. Avec un ticket d'autobus vous pouvez aller jusqu'au bout de la ligne. Avec deux tickets, vous pouvez aller n'importe où (*anywhere*) dans la ville de Paris.

▶ Dialogue 2: *À la gare routière* At the bus station

A tourist is finding out about buses and tickets. What is she advised to do?

Touriste	Pardon, Monsieur, c'est quelle ligne pour aller à la Gare d'Austerlitz?
Homme	Alors pour la Gare d'Austerlitz le plus simple c'est de prendre la ligne 57 …
Touriste	C'est direct?
Homme	Non, il faut changer au deuxième arrêt, puis vous prenez la ligne 24.
Touriste	C'est loin à pied?
Homme	D'ici? Ah oui, vous ne pouvez pas y aller à pied.
Touriste	Le prochain bus part à quelle heure?
Homme	Dans dix minutes.
Touriste	Et … où est-ce que je peux acheter un ticket?
Homme	Au guichet là-bas …
Touriste	(*later*) Je voudrais acheter un ticket aller-retour pour la Gare d'Austerlitz.
Femme	Il n'y a pas de tickets aller-retour. Achetez deux tickets ou bien alors un carnet, c'est plus pratique et moins cher.
Touriste	Un carnet, qu'est-ce que c'est?
Femme	C'est dix tickets pour le prix de sept.
Touriste	Très bien. Je vais prendre un carnet.

▶ Dialogue 3: *Être dans le bon autobus* On the right bus

The same tourist asks the driver when she should get off. Can you understand where?

Touriste Ce bus va bien à la Gare d'Austerlitz?

Chauffeur Oui, c'est bien ça.

Touriste Vous pouvez me dire où il faut descendre?

Chauffeur Oui, bien sûr. C'est très facile. C'est le premier arrêt une fois que vous avez traversé la Seine.

Touriste Euh ... oui mais je ne connais pas Paris. Il faut combien de temps pour arriver à la gare?

Chauffeur Oh, une bonne demi-heure. Dans trente minutes vous allez passer sur le pont et juste après vous descendrez.

Activity 5

How would you say:

a What bus number goes to the Gare d'Austerlitz?
b Is it direct?
c Is it far on foot?
d At what time does the next bus leave?
e Where can I buy a ticket?
f I would like to buy a return ticket to les Invalides.
g I'll take a set of tickets.
h How long does it take to get to the station?

La SNCF French railways

> www.sncf.fr
>
> www.voyages-sncf.com/leisure/fr/launch/home/

ℹ️ In France, tickets must be stamped by each passenger at the point of departure using one of the **composteurs** (machine in which you have to insert your ticket). You will be fined if you board a train without having done so.

When travelling on TGV (**train grande vitesse**) or Eurostar, you need to reserve a seat; when travelling on the other SNCF lines you are advised to do so, particularly at the beginning and the end of school holidays.

▶ Dialogue 4: *Au bureau de renseignements* At the information office

*We are in the information office in **la Gare de Lyon** in Paris. A man enquires about trains. Listen to the recording or read the dialogue. Try to answer the following questions: Where does the man want to go? Which train does he want to catch? Where does he want to sit?*

Homme   Bonjour, Madame, je voudrais un aller pour Marseille.
Hôtesse   Marseille … bon. Vous voyagez quel jour?
Homme   Le 10 juin … un samedi.
Hôtesse   À quelle heure voulez-vous quitter Paris?
Homme   Dans la matinée.
Hôtesse   Bon, vous avez quatre TGV : le premier part à 8.20, le deuxième à 9.20, le troisième à 10.20, le quatrième à 11.20.
Homme   **Celui de** 10.20 **me convient** très bien.
Hôtesse   Il quitte Paris Gare de Lyon à 10.20 et arrive à Marseille St Charles à 13.29. La réservation est obligatoire.
Homme   D'accord, bon alors, **il met un peu plus de** trois heures?
Hôtesse   Oui, c'est bien ça.
Homme   C'est combien l'aller simple?
Hôtesse   Vous avez une réduction?
Homme   Non, je n'ai pas de carte.
Hôtesse   OK, alors en 1ère ou en 2ème classe?
Homme   En 2ème classe.
Hôtesse   Alors en seconde classe, l'aller tarif normal coûte 94€, la réservation est incluse dans le prix.
Homme   Oh, c'est un peu cher. Il y a moins cher?
Hôtesse   Le train qui quitte Paris à 9.20 est moins cher. C'est un billet «Découverte Séjour» et l'aller coûte 57€60. Ça vous va?
Homme   Oui, c'est **beaucoup mieux**. Mais, il y a des restrictions?
Hôtesse   Oui, c'est un billet **ni échangeable ni remboursable**
Homme   Donc je ne peux pas le changer une fois pris.
Hôtesse   Oui, c'est tout à fait ça.
Homme   On peut manger dans le train?
Hôtesse   Oui, bien sûr, vous avez une voiture-bar où vous pourrez acheter des sandwiches, des salades ou des **plats cuisinés** ainsi que des boissons chaudes et fraîches.
Homme   Ah bon, et pour ma place?
Hôtesse   Vous avez le choix entre un siège côté fenêtre ou côté couloir?
Homme   Je préfère côté fenêtre.

celui de ... me convient	the one at ... suits me
il met un peu plus de ...	it takes a bit more than ...
beaucoup mièux	much better
ni échangeable	neither exchangeable
ni remboursale	or refundable
une fois pris	once taken
plats cuisinés	hot food

Activity 6

Aller le Lundi 08/10 entre 12h12 et 19h29
MARSEILLE St CHARLES–PARIS
prix total pour 1 passager

Départ à	12h12	12h27	13h29	14h31	15h29	19h29
Meilleur prix	77.20€	94.00€	94.00€	94.00€	94.00€	38.90€
Durée	10h37	03h14	03h12	03h00	03h16	03h12

voir les trains suivants

Before taking the part of the traveller in this conversation, look at the Marseille–Paris timetable accessible on the SNCF website. How many TGVs are leaving Marseille in the afternoon?

a Vous   Ask for a return to Paris.

Employé   Vous voulez partir quel jour?

b Vous   Say on the 8th October in the afternoon.

Employé   Alors vous avez plusieurs trains qui quittent Marseille St Charles l'après-midi. Il y a un train toutes les heures.

c Vous   Ask how long the journey lasts?

Employé   Environ trois heures, trois heures et quart.

d Vous   Say that you do not want to arrive in Paris after 19.00.

Employé   Alors dans ce cas vous pouvez prendre le train qui quitte St Charles à 13.29, ou à 14.31 ou même à 15.29.

e Vous   Say that the 15.29 train suits you and ask for the price of the ticket in second class.

Employé   Le billet en 2ème classe tarif plein coûte 94€00.

f Vous   Say that it is a little expensive. Ask if there is something cheaper.

Employé   Alors, un instant ... Le train de 12.12 est moins cher. Le prix du billet aller-retour ne coûte que 77€20.

g Vous   Ask if you can change the ticket?

Employé Oui, oui tout à fait. Le billet est remboursable et échangeable.

h Vous *Ask at what time the train arrives in Paris?*

Employé Le train met 10.37 pour arriver à Paris.

i Vous *Say that it is too long and that you will take the 15.20 train.*

Employé D'accord ...

Le Vélib

> Pour tout savoir sur le Vélib et son utilisation dans Paris: **www.velib.paris.fr/**

Le Vélib est un système de **location** de vélos en libre service très simple à utiliser. Vous prenez un vélo dans une station et vous le déposez dans n'importe quelle autre station Vélib. Disponibles 24h/24 et 7j/7, les stations Vélib sont distantes de 300 mètres environ et constituées de **bornes** et de **points d'attache** pour les vélos. **www.velib.paris.fr/comment_ca_marche/plan_des_stations**

Pour prendre un vélo, rien de plus simple! Il faut vous identifier sur la borne, accéder au menu, et choisir votre vélo **parmi ceux** qui seront proposés à **l'écran**. Vous pouvez **souscrire un abonnement** courte durée par carte bancaire (Ticket Vélib 1 jour et Ticket Vélib 7 jours). En plus Vélib vous offre gratuitement les 30 premières minutes de chaque trajet.

la location	hiring/renting
la borne	terminal
le point d'attache	stand for parking
parmi ceux	among those
l'écran	screen
souscrire un abonnement	subscribe for an account

Activity 7

Answer the following statements with **vrai** or **faux**:

	vrai	faux
a Il faut ramener le vélo à la station où on l'a pris.	☐	☐
b Les stations sont ouvertes jour et nuit et tous les jours de l'année.	☐	☐
c Tout se fait à partir de la borne.	☐	☐
d On ne peut pas prendre un abonnement d'un jour.	☐	☐
e On ne paie pas pour la première demi-heure de chaque trajet.	☐	☐

Mini-test

Test yourself to find out how much you can remember from Units 13 and 14.

How would you say:

1 I would like a cheese sandwich?
2 What do you have to drink?
3 I would like a set of ten tickets?
4 At what time does the next train to Paris leave?

15 faire du tourisme

sightseeing

In this unit you will

- learn how to ask for a town map
- find out about visiting interesting places
- practise buying admission tickets
- find out about museums in France
- book an excursion

Before you start, revise

- saying what you want (page 62)
- asking and understanding directions (page 50)
- asking what you can do (page 39)
- expressions of time, days of the week **Key words and phrases** (page 36)

Key words and phrases

le plan de la ville	*town map*
des renseignements	*information*
les environs	*surroundings*
qu'est-ce qu'il y a à faire?	*what is there to do?*
qu'est-ce qu'il y a à voir?	*what is there to see?*
une visite guidée	*guided tour*
faire une promenade/	*to go for a walk*
balade à pied	
les jours fériés/les jours de fête	*public holidays*
l'entrée	*way in, admission charge*
en pleine saison	*in high season*
le tarif réduit, plein tarif	*reduced rate, full rate*
accès (m) gratuit	*free entry*
nocturne	*late-night opening*
hors saison	*out of season*
le musée	*museum*
faire une excursion	*to go on an excursion*
pique-niquer	*to picnic*
l'aire de jeux	*children's playground*
une agence de voyages	*travel agency*

Se renseigner sur les choses à voir
Getting information on things to see

- Fédération Nationale des Offices de Tourisme et Syndicats d'Initiative: **www.tourisme.fr**
- Office de Tourisme à Paris: **www.parisinfo.com**

- Visites guidées en autocar ou en minibus à Paris: **www.touringscope.com**
- Croisières sur la Seine: **www.vedettesdeparis.com**
- Croisières sur les canaux: **www.pariscanal.com**
- D'autres sites utiles:
  www.paris.org
  www.franceguide.com
  www.guideweb.com (sur les régions françaises)
  www.skifrance.fr (informations sur les stations de ski, etc.)

i Dès votre arrivée dans une ville ou une région, rendez-vous à l'office de tourisme le plus proche pour demander un plan ainsi que des brochures sur la ville et ses environs. Son personnel multilingue répondra à toutes vos questions sur les hébergements, visites, musées, loisirs, manifestations culturelles, circuits touristiques …

En France, il y a de nombreux jours fériés (*public holidays*). Il est prudent de les connaître car les magasins, musées et monument historiques sont souvent fermés ces jours-là.

Activity 1

French public holidays are listed in the right-hand column. Match the dates with the corresponding holidays:

a	1 janvier	**i**	Toussaint
b	entre le 2 mars et le 25 avril	**ii**	Noël
c	1er mai	**iii**	Assomption
d	8 mai	**iv**	Jour de l'An
e	20 mai	**v**	Fête du travail
f	le 7ème lundi après Pâques	**vi**	Victoire 1945
g	14 juillet	**vii**	Ascension (40 jours après Pâques)
h	15 août		
i	1er novembre	**viii**	Lundi de Pentecôte
j	11 novembre	**ix**	Armistice 1918
k	25 décembre	**x**	Lundi de Pâques
		xi	Fête Nationale

▶ Dialogue 1: *À l'office du tourisme*
At the tourist office

Listen to the recording or read the dialogue below. Can you name at least three things the tourist could see or do?

Touriste	Bonjour, Madame, je voudrais un plan de la ville, s'il vous plaît.
Hôtesse	Oui, voilà.
Touriste	Nous ne sommes pas d'ici. Qu'est-ce qu'il y a à voir à Orléans?
Hôtesse	Il y a beaucoup de monuments historiques, surtout dans la vieille ville, comme la maison de Jeanne d'Arc, au numéro 52 sur le plan, à côté de la cathédrale Sainte-Croix; et puis il y a une belle promenade à pied à faire le long de la Loire. Du pont George V, vous avez une vue magnifique sur la Loire.
Touriste	Et qu'est-ce qu'il y a à faire pour les enfants?
Hôtesse	Près d'ici, il y a une piscine couverte ou même le Musée des sciences naturelles qui se trouve rue Emile Zola. Un peu plus loin, vous avez le Parc Floral.
Touriste	Et pour aller au Parc Floral ... il y a un bus?
Hôtesse	Oui, vous avez un autobus toutes les 30 minutes. Il part du centre ville, place du Martroi.

Activity 2

a How would you ask for a town map?
b Ask what there is to see.
c Ask what there is to do for the children.
d Ask if there is an indoor swimming pool.
e Ask if there is a bus to go to the *Parc Floral*.

Activity 3

The Wilsons want to visit the *Parc Floral*, a 35 hectare designed landscape garden near Orléans, on their way to the South of France. Read the brochure opposite and answer the questions.

a Would the visit be enjoyable for their seven-year-old boy?
b Can they eat there?
c They intend to visit the park in the summer months. What will they be able to see besides the gardens?

LES RENDEZ-VOUS DE L'ANNÉE

- PETIT TRAIN
- PARC ANIMALIER
- AIRE DE JEUX
- GOLF MINIATURE
- BOUTIQUES
- AIRE DE PIQUE-NIQUE

TOUT LE MOIS D'AVRIL
Renaissance du sous-bois !
Floraison exceptionnelle de 200 000 tulipes,
narcisses, jacinthes, muscaris...

DIMANCHE 23 AVRIL
"A la recherche des œufs de Pâques"

- ANIMATIONS
  PÉDAGOGIQUES
- VISITES GUIDÉES
  (sur réservation) :
  15 personnes
  minimum

DE MI MAI À DÉBUT JUIN
Floraison de la Collection Nationale d'iris
(900 variétés), rassemblée dans un jardin
contemporain

SAMEDI 20 ET DIMANCHE 21 MAI
Fête de l'iris - Conseils, vente

DIMANCHE 18 JUIN
La Saint-Fiacre et les Peintres au Jardin

- JARDIN
  DE LA SOURCE

SAMEDI 9 ET DIMANCHE 10 SEPTEMBRE
Journées de découverte du nouveau potager
Conseils, vente

DIMANCHE 17 SEPTEMBRE
Concert par la Musique Municipale d'Orléans

DU 28 OCTOBRE AU 12 NOVEMBRE
31ᵉ Salon du Chrysanthème

DU 1ᵉʳ AVRIL AU 12 NOVEMBRE
La serre aux papillons - Découverte du monde
coloré des papillons exotiques dans un jardin
tropical de 250 m².
Exposition : l'univers fascinant des couleurs
chez les insectes. Insectes en 3D

www.parcfloral-lasource.fr

DÉPARTEMENT DU LOIRET, VILLE D'ORLÉANS

45072 Orléans cedex 2 • Tél: 02 38 49 30 17

▶ Dialogue 2: *On visite* Let's visit

Mrs Wilson phones the Parc Floral to find out about opening hours, prices, etc. Listen to the recording or read the dialogue twice and answer the following question: How much would the family pay to visit the park and the butterfly glasshouse?

Touriste Allô, je voudrais savoir à quelle heure ouvre le parc, s'il vous plaît?

Hôtesse Le parc est ouvert tous les jours de 10 heures à 19 heures, même les jours fériés! Quant à la serre aux papillons, elle n'ouvre que les après-midi, et les mercredi et dimanche matin.

Touriste Ah merci. Euh, la serre, c'est quoi?

Hôtesse C'est un jardin tropical où vivent des papillons exotiques. Nous y avons aussi des projections de films et des expositions thématiques.

Touriste Et c'est combien l'entrée?

Hôtesse Alors pour le parc seul, c'est 4€. Pour le parc et la serre, c'est 6€80. C'est pour combien de personnes?

Touriste Trois, deux adultes et un enfant de 7 ans.

Hôtesse Pour l'enfant, c'est 4€50 pour le parc et la serre.

Touriste Ah bon. Et le parc est facile à trouver en voiture?

Hôtesse Oui, très. Si vous prenez la A71, c'est sortie Orléans – la Source. Vous avez accès à l'Internet?

Touriste Euh, oui, oui.

Hôtesse Alors c'est encore plus facile, tapez www.parcfloral-lasource (en un seul mot).fr. Vous y trouverez le plan d'accès au Parc Floral et autres renseignements pratiques.

Touriste Vous pouvez répéter plus lentement, s'il vous plaît?

Hôtesse Oui, bien sûr, alors pour le site vous tapez www.parcfloral-lasource.fr. Et voilà!

Hôtesse Merci beaucoup madame, et au revoir.

Activity 4

Now it is your turn to buy some tickets for the park. You are accompanied by your daughter, who is 12. She wants to go on the **petit train** and play **mini golf**.

a *You*   *Ask how much the admission charge is.*

Hôtesse L'entrée coûte 4€ par personne, 6€80 avec la serre.

b *You*   *Ask what the 'serre' is.*

Hôtesse C'est pour l'exposition des papillons. Votre fille a quel âge?

c *You*   *Say her age. Ask if you need to pay for the 'petit train' and the mini golf.*

Hôtesse	Oui, pour le 'petit train' c'est 1€60 pour elle et 2€ pour vous. Le golf miniature est gratuit.
d *You*	*Ask if you can have a picnic.*
Hôtesse	Oui, bien sûr. Je vais vous montrer l'aire de pique-nique sur le plan.
e *You*	*Thank her and ask what time the park closes.*
Hôtesse	Nous fermons à 19 heures.

Les musées Museums

 Les musées et monuments sont généralement ouverts tous les jours, sauf le lundi ou le mardi, de 10 à 12h et de 14 à 18h en été. Ces horaires peuvent varier. La plupart sont fermés les jours fériés. L'entrée est généralement gratuite pour les enfants de moins de 18 ans. Les étudiants, personnes âgées et enseignants actifs ont droit à une réduction (entre 30 % et 50 %) sur présentation d'un justificatif, et quelquefois l'entrée est gratuite un jour par semaine.

Carte musées–monuments

> Musées et monuments en Ile-de-France: **www.intermusees.com**
> Musées et monuments en France: **www.monuments-france.fr**
> Paris Museum Pass: **www.parismuseumpass.com**

Valable deux, quatre ou six jours, la carte musées-monuments permet de visiter librement et sans attente 60 musées et monuments de Paris et d'Île-de-France. Elle est en vente dans les musées et monuments, principales stations de métro, office de tourisme de Paris, **magasins FNAC**. Le forfait pour un jour est de 30€, pour quatre jours consécutifs: 45€ et six jours consécutifs: 60€.

> **FNAC**: the largest French retailer of books, CDs and DVDs, computer software and hardware, television sets, cameras and video-games.

Activity 5

Look at the following information – this is the kind of information you may find on places of interest – then answer the questions:

A

Art Moderne (Musée National d')
Centre Georges-Pompidou
Place Georges Pompidou – 75004 Paris
Tél. 01 44 78 12 33   Métro : Hôtel-de-ville, Rambuteau
www.centrepompidou.fr   RER A : Châtelet-Les Halles

Ouvert tous les jours de 11h à 21h sauf mardi (avec possibilité de nocturnes pour les expositions). Plein tarif: 10€ – Tarif réduit: 8€.

Ce billet est valable le jour même pour toutes les expositions en cours, le Musée et l'Atelier Brancusi. Accès gratuit le 1er dimanche de chaque mois.

Collection d'oeuvres d'artistes modernes et d'artistes contemporains, sans oublier les architectes, les designers, les photographes ainsi que les cinéastes.

B

Cité des Sciences et de l'Industrie – la Villette
Centre Parc de la Villette
30, avenue Corentin-Cariou – 75019 Paris
Tél. 01 40 05 80 00   Métro: Porte-de-la-Villette
www.cite-sciences.fr

De 10h à 18h. Le dimanche de 10h à 19h. Fermé le lundi. Plein tarif: 15€ Cité des enfants : 13€ Planétarium: 11€ Tarif réduit : 11€ et 8€

Située dans le parc de la Villette, la cité présente un panorama complet des sciences et techniques à travers des expositions, des spectacles, des maquettes, des conférences et des jeux interactifs.

C

Louvre (Musée du)
Entrée principale par la Pyramide
Cour napoléon – 75001 Paris
Tél. 01 40 20 51 51   Métro : Palais-Royal-Musée-du-Louvre
www.louvre.fr

Ouvert tous les jours de 9h à 18h, sauf le mardi et certains jours fériés. Nocturnes les mercredi et vendredi jusqu'à 22h.

Plein tarif : 9€ – Tarif réduit : 6€ (de 18h à 21.45). Gratuité appliquée aux moins de 18 ans demandeurs d'emploi, enseignants en histoire, handicapés et le 1er dimanche de chaque mois.

Le Musée du Louvre, ancienne demeure des rois de France, et l'un des plus grands musées du monde.

D

Picasso (Musée National)
Hôtel Salé
5, rue de Thorigny – 75003 Paris
Tél. 01 42 71 25 21
Métro : Saint-Paul/Saint-Sébastien Froissart/Chemin Vert
Bus : 29 – 96 – 69 – 75 www.musee-picasso.fr

Été: 9h30–18h – Hiver: 9h30–17h30.
Nocturne le jeudi jusqu'à 20h.
Plein tarif : 7€70. Tarif réduit (de 18 ans à 25 ans inclus) : 5€70
Gratuit pour les moins de 18 ans et le premier dimanche de chaque
mois.
Fermé le mardi, le 1er janvier et le 25 décembre.

Installé dans l'Hôtel Salé (XVIIe siècle), le musée rassemble une
importante collection des oeuvres de l'artiste.

a If you were in Paris on a Tuesday, what could you visit?
b If you did not have much money, which day would you
   choose to visit the attractions above?
c What could you visit late in the evening and when?
d Which museum would most interest a child?

Faire une excursion Going on an excursion

Activity 6

You're interested in French wines, so you've decided to go with
your partner on a coach excursion following **la route des vins de
Bourgogne**. Look at the information and answer the questions:

a At what time should you be at the bus stop in the morning?
b How long do you stop at Vezelay?
c Name at least two things you could do from lunchtime until
   4 p.m.
d How much is the excursion for two people?

LA ROUTE DES VINS DE BOURGOGNE

EXCURSION EN CAR

1 JOUR

13 mai
3/17 juin
22 juillet
20 oct
11 nov

Aller/retour....92€

Rendez-vous 7h15.
Départ 7h30.

Arrivée à Vezelay vers 10h.
Arrêt d'une heure pour visiter
la basilique Sainte-Madeleine.
Continuation vers Beaune. Arrêt
pour déjeuner et temps libre

pour visiter les Hospices et
le Musée du vin. Visite d'une
cave avec dégustation.

Départ à 16h par la route des vins.
(Nuits-Saint-Georges, Gevrey-
Chambertin).
Retour à Paris vers 23h.

Activity 7

You and your friend decide to book the trip to Beaune. Speak for both of you.

a	*You*	*Say you would like to go on the excursion of **la route des vins de Bourgogne.***
	Employé	Vous voulez réserver des places pour quel jour?
b	*You*	*Say you'd like two places for the 22nd July.*
	Employé	Le 22 juillet? Bon... ça va, il y a de la place ... ça fait 184€.
c	*You*	*Ask if the coach leaves from here.*
	Employé	Non, le car part de la place Denfert-Rochereau, devant le café de Belfort.
d	*You*	*Ask him to repeat.*
	Employé	Oui, place Denfert-Rochereau devant le café de Belfort; mais je vais vous donner tous ces renseignements par écrit.
e	*You*	*Thank him; ask what time the coach leaves.*
	Employé	Le car part à 7.30 mais il faut être là à 7.15.
f	*You*	*Ask if you can buy some wine in the wine cellar.*
	Employé	Oui, vous pouvez déguster et acheter des vins de Bourgogne à un prix spécial.

▶ Activity 8

Listen to Michel discussing the possibility of going on a coach excursion to Versailles and Trianon with his friend Agnès. If you haven't got the recording, read the tour description, then answer the questions. You will need to listen to the recording to be able to answer all the questions.

a Jour de l'exclusion choisi par Michel et Agnès
b Heure du départ de Paris
c Durée du tour
d Programme de la visite
e Prix de l'entrée de la visite
f Qui paie pour l'excursion et pourquoi

Journée Royale à Versailles 102 €

- *Visite guidée des Appartements Royaux.*
- *Eté: Bosquets*
- *Hiver: Promenade en petit train.*
- *Déjeuner face au Grand Canal.*
- *Trianon.*
- *Hameau de la Reine.*

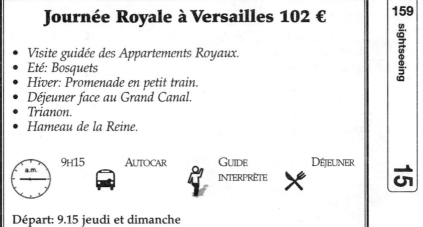

9H15   AUTOCAR   GUIDE   DÉJEUNER
                   INTERPRÈTE

Départ: 9.15 jeudi et dimanche
Retour approximatif: 16.15
À partir d'Avril à Septembre

Nous vous proposons de commencer votre journée à Versailles par la visite guidée des Grands Appartements Royaux puis par la visite des jardins (été) ou une promenade en petit train dans le parc (hiver). Le déjeuner sera servi au restaurant 'la Flotille' dans le parc du château en face du Grand Canal.

L'après-midi se poursuivra par la visite guidée des Trianon (vastes pavillons dans lesquels Louis XV et Louis XVI aimaient travailler et séjourner en retrait de la cour) et par la découverte du Hameau de la Reine Marie-Antoinette construit pour son divertissement.

Entrées incluses.

Mini-test

How would you ask:

1 for a town map and information on the cathedral?
2 if the museum closes between 12.00 and 14.00?
3 if there is a guided tour?

16

sortir
going out

In this unit you will
- practise finding out what's on
- book tickets for a concert
- find out where you can play tennis and other sports

Before you start, revise

- finding out what's on and where (page 150)
- saying what you want (page 62)
- asking what you can do (page 39)
- talking about your likes and dislikes (page 74)
- expressions of time, days of the week **Key words and phrases** (page 36)

Key words and phrases

qu'est-ce qu'il y a comme ...?	what sort of ... is/are there?
qu'est-ce qu'on peut faire?	what can I/we/one do?
un spectacle	a show
une soirée	evening entertainment, party
un dîner-dansant	dinner dance
l'ambiance (f)	atmosphere
la salle	room, hall, auditorium
une boîte (de nuit)	nightclub
un piano-bar	all night restaurant with small band
louer	to book, to hire
la location	hiring
le prêt	lending
le bureau de location	booking office
la place	seat
une séance	performance, film showing
entrée (f) libre	free admission
il/elle doit payer?	he/she must pay?
c'est combien l'heure?	how much is it an hour?
c'est combien la journée?	how much is it a day?
une carte d'abonnement	season ticket
un court de tennis	tennis court
un cours particulier	private lesson
l'inscription (f)	enrolment
faire une randonnée	to go for a walk/hike
faire du vélo	to go cycling
le jeu de société	board game

Où aller? Where to go?

> Everything you want to know about Parisian outings (theatre, cinema, restaurants, arts, music, visits and walks): **www.premiere.fr**

i Pour connaître le programme des spectacles, adressez-vous à l'office du tourisme – qui vous réservera des places, si vous le leur demandez. Si vous êtes à Paris, achetez un journal spécialisé comme *Pariscope*, *l'Officiel des Spectacles* ou alors *Zurban*.

▶ Dialogue 1: *Sortir le soir* Going out in the evening

At the tourist office two tourists enquire about activities in the evening.

Touriste Je passe quelques jours dans la région. Qu'est-ce qu'on peut faire ici le soir?

Hôtesse Il y a beaucoup de choses à faire mais ça dépend, qu'est-ce que vous aimez? Le jazz? La danse?

Touriste Oui, nous aimons danser mais surtout … bien manger.

Hôtesse Eh bien pourquoi n'allez-vous pas à un dîner-dansant ou dans un restaurant piano-bar?

Touriste Un restaurant piano-bar, qu'est-ce que c'est?

Hôtesse C'est un restaurant où il y a de la musique avec orchestre. En général, il y a une très bonne ambiance et ça reste ouvert toute la nuit. Mais … si vous aimez danser, vous avez le restaurant 'Raspoutine' tout près d'ici qui organise des soirées dansantes avec repas et orchestre tzigane.

Touriste C'est combien pour la soirée dansante?

Hôtesse C'est 100€ par personne, tout compris, avec spectacle.

Touriste Je peux acheter les billets ici?

Hôtesse Non, il faut aller au restaurant qui se trouve au bout du boulevard Victor Hugo; mais … attendez un instant, je vais vous chercher le programme des spectacles de la semaine avec la liste des restaurants et des bars.

Activity 1

Without looking back at the text say if the following assertions are **vrai** or **faux** and correct the false answers:

	vrai	faux
a The tourist wants to know what's on in the daytime.	☐	☐
b They like going to concerts.	☐	☐
c A piano-bar is a place that is open only at lunchtime.	☐	☐
d At 'Raspoutine' you can eat and dance.	☐	☐
e The price for everything including the meal is 100€ per person.	☐	☐
f The hostess gives the tourist the programme of the week.	☐	☐

Activity 2

Here are the kinds of night attractions described in a brochure that you can find at the tourist office. Read what is on at each night-spot and say who would enjoy which one most:

a A single lady who likes disco dancing – particularly older tunes – and would love to meet a male friend.

b A couple who like playing bowls with their friends on Sundays.

c A single person who likes betting and socializing on a regular basis.

d A group of students who enjoy Latin music and dancing.

e A man who enjoys tasting different types of beer, has a sweet tooth and likes music.

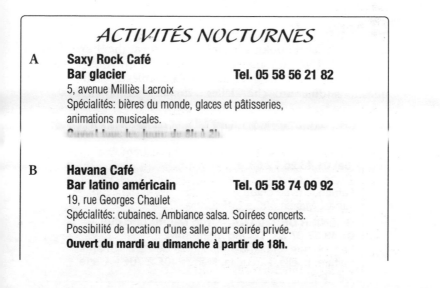

ACTIVITÉS NOCTURNES

A **Saxy Rock Café**
Bar glacier   Tel. 05 58 56 21 82
5, avenue Milliès Lacroix
Spécialités: bières du monde, glaces et pâtisseries, animations musicales.
Ouvert tous les jours du 8h à 2h.

B **Havana Café**
Bar latino américain   Tel. 05 58 74 09 92
19, rue Georges Chaulet
Spécialités: cubaines. Ambiance salsa. Soirées concerts.
Possibilité de location d'une salle pour soirée privée.
Ouvert du mardi au dimanche à partir de 18h.

C   **Casino de Dax**   **Tel. 05 58 56 86 86**
Avenue Milliès Lacroix
Roulette, Black-jack, animations (spectacles, Calas),
arts et culture, restaurant, bar.
Ouvert tous les jours à partir de 15h.

D   **César Palace**
        Casino   **Tel. 05 58 91 52 72**
Lac de Christus,
40990 Saint-Paul-lès-Dax – 3 km Ouest
**Boule le dimanche de 16h à 19h et tous les soirs
de 22h à 4h. Machines à sous de 12h à 4h.**

E   **Club rétro**
        Le Richelieu – Club   **Tel. 05 58 90 20 53**
                                 ou 05 58 58 49 49

Rue Sainte-Eutrope
Pour danser sur les souvenirs du temps passé.
Entrée + consommation: 11€. Samedi: 13€
(autres consommations: 8€).
Ouvert du mercredi au dimanche à partir de 21h 30.
Le mercredi entrée gratuite pour tous jusqu'à minuit.
Le jeudi entrée gratuite pour les dames jusqu'à minuit.

▶ Activity 3

Listen to Michel booking a table by phone at the 'Burro Blanco'
restaurant. Can you answer the following questions? You will
need to listen to the recording to be able to answer all the
questions (**dîner aux chandelles** = *dinner by candlelight*).

Espagnoles

**BURRO BLANCO. 79, rue Cardinale Lemoine
(5e) 01 43 25 72 53.**
Tlj jsq 5h du mat. F. Lun. A la Contrescarpe, véritable
flamenco avec chanteurs, guitaristes et danseurs.
Tapas. Menus 50€ à 60€. Carte.

**GRENIER DE TRIANA, 7, rue Mouffetard (5e)
01 43 57 97 33. Tls jsq 4h du mat.**
La meilleure ambiance espagnole de Paris. Chants,
guitare, paëlla, zarzuella. Menus 40€ à 70€ + Carte.
Groupes.

a Which day is the restaurant shut?
b What special occasion is Michel celebrating?
c What does he ask for?
d What type of cooking is served?
e At what time does the show finish?
f What is included in the price?

▶ Dialogue 2: *Réserver une place* Booking a ticket

A student is booking seats for a guitar recital. Why does she get a cheaper ticket?

Jeune fille	Pardon Monsieur, je voudrais des places pour le récital de guitare, samedi prochain.
Employé	Je regrette, samedi c'est complet mais il reste encore des places pour jeudi et vendredi.
Jeune fille	Bon, eh bien je vais prendre deux places pour jeudi. Ça finit à quelle heure le concert?
Employé	Le concert commence à 19.45 donc je pense qu'il finira vers 22h.
Jeune fille	Bon, ça va, ce n'est pas trop tard. C'est combien la place, j'ai une carte étudiant?
Employé	Alors avec une carte étudiant, c'est tarif réduit à 20€60.
Jeune fille	Ma soeur a 15 ans. Elle doit payer?
Employé	C'est entrée libre jusqu'à 16 ans.

Activity 4

How do you say:

a I would like some seats for next Sunday.
b At what time does the concert finish?
c How much is it for a ticket?
d It is reduced rate.
e Does my sister have to pay?

Activity 5

Using the Internet may be a useful way to find out what's on in the cinemas but the information can be a little confusing. Look at the example overleaf and try to work out the address of the cinema, who is entitled to a reduced rate, and on which days? If you find it puzzling, look at the upside-down clues overleaf, then check with the **Key to the exercises and tests.**

▶ Dialogue 3: *Réserver un court de tennis* Booking a tennis court

Une touriste veut jouer au tennis. Elle se renseigne à l'office du tourisme.

A tourist wants to play tennis. She enquires at the tourist office. She asks five questions; try to note at least three of them.

Touriste Où est-ce qu'on peut jouer au tennis?

Hôtesse Vous avez à Anglet le Club de Chiberta avec 15 courts.

Touriste Ah très bien, et où est-ce qu'on réserve les courts?

Hôtesse Vous réservez les courts au club.

Touriste C'est combien l'heure?

Hôtesse Je ne sais pas. Il faut vous renseigner là-bas mais si vous jouez souvent, vous pouvez certainement prendre une carte d'abonnement.

Touriste Je n'ai pas ma raquette de tennis avec moi. On peut louer une raquette au club?

Hôtesse Je pense que oui.

Touriste Vous pouvez me donner l'adresse du club, s'il vous plaît?

Hôtesse Mais oui, la voilà.

Activity 6

How would you ask:

a Where can I (use **on**) play tennis?
b Where do I (use **on**) book the court?
c How much is it for one hour?
d Can one hire a racket?
e Can you give me the address of the club?

Activity 7

You are working at the **office du tourisme** in Vittel. An English family comes in. The members are all very eager to join in the various activities organized by the town (see below). Can you answer their questions?

● **ACTIVITÉS SPORTIVES ET DE LOISIRS avec JEAN-LOUIS et ANNE**

Jogging: dans le parc en petites foulées sur un rythme progressif.
Gymnastique: en salle, assouplissement et tonification musculaire.
Tir à l'arc: initiation et perfectionnement de la maîtrise du tir.
Promenades et randonnées (pédestre, vélo): parcourir la campagne et les bois environnants.
Self défense: initiation, découverte des gestes d'auto-défense.
Volley et sports collectifs, ✎
Gym, danse et stretching.
Promenade VTT: initiation. ✎ ✳

● **ACTIVITÉS TENNIS et GOLF avec BRUNO**

Usage des cours et du practice, du putting green. Initiation golf et tennis en groupe. ✎
Cours particuliers. ✎ ✳

● **L'OFFICE DU TOURISME EST A VOTRE DISPOSITION POUR**
Ses locations ou prêts de vélos, matériels de golf ✳, de tennis de table, jeux de société.
Son coin lecture (journaux, hebdomadaires).

✳ Activité avec participation financière.
✎ Activité avec inscription.

a The woman is very keen on playing tennis:
  i Can she have private classes?
  ii Can she hire a tennis racket?

b The husband would like to go for a bicycle ride:
  i Can he hire a bicycle?
  ii Does he need to enrol if he goes on an organized trip?

c Her youngest son would like to try out mountain biking (**VTT – vélo tous terrains**).
  i Is it free?
  ii Does he need to enrol?

d Her daughter is very keen on doing archery. They have been told that the town runs archery classes:
  i Is it true?
  ii Does she have to pay?

e If it rains what can they do indoors?
  i ....
  ii ....

Mini-test on Units 14, 15 and 16

1 If you saw the following signs in a French station, would you know what they meant?
  a composter
  b sortie
  c correspondance
  d consigne
  e quai
  f guichet

2 Can you ask for:
  a a book of ten tickets
  b a return ticket
  c a timetable
  d a bus stop
  e the information office
  f a single ticket?

Complete the three following sentences by choosing the ending **a**, **b**, or **c**.

3 Si vous voulez faire un pique-nique vous cherchez le panneau (*sign*)

 a sortie.
 b restaurant.
 c aire de pique-nique.

4 Pour faire une excursion vous allez
 a au musée.
 b à la piscine couverte.
 c chez un excursionniste ou à l'office du tourisme.

5 L'entrée dans les parcs et les monuments historiques est souvent plus chère
 a en pleine saison.
 b hors saison.
 c les jours fériés.

6 Fill in the blanks:
 a (au cinéma) Je voudrais une p..... pour la séance de 17.30.
 b Le lundi, c'est t..... réduit pour les étudiants.
 c J'adore danser; je voudrais aller dans une b..... d..... n.....
 d Il y a une très bonne a..... dans ce piano-bar.
 e Demandez le programme des s..... à l'office du tourisme.

Before going on to Unit 17 take the **Self-assessment test 2** (Units 14–16). Once you have done it, check your answers in the **Key to the exercises and tests** and write your score in the box below. If you score between 40 and 50 points, you can go straight on to Unit 17. If your score is between 20 and 40 points, you need to spend more time revising the **Dialogues** and **Key words and phrases**. Below 20 points, go back over Units 14, 15 and 16 and take the test again to see how much you have improved.

Self assessment score (Units 14–16)

Points: _____/50

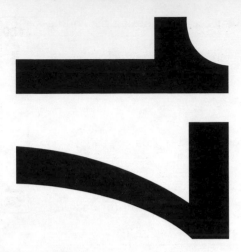

bonne route
safe journey

In this unit you will
- learn useful information for travelling on French roads
- learn some French road signs
- practise asking directions
- buy some petrol and get your tyre pressures checked
- find out what to do in case of breakdown
- learn some essential words for describing what's wrong with your car

Before you start, revise

- asking the way and understanding directions (page 50)
- asking for assistance (page 83)
- understanding what you need to do (page 84)
- numbers (page 233)

Les routes françaises French roads

Pour avoir des informations sur la circulation, les itinéraires conseillés et la météo, consultez les sites suivants:

- Les autoroutes françaises:**www.autoroutes.fr**
- Bison Futé: **www.bison-fute.equipement.gouv.fr**
- Chaîne d'hôtels situés en bord de routes, près des aéroports, aux centre villes avec réservation automatique de chambre 24h/24.

  www.hotelformule1.com
  www.etaphotel.com
  www.accorhotels.com

Le réseau routier français est l'un des plus denses du monde; il est donc facile de visiter le pays en prenant les autoroutes qui sont payantes ou les petites routes 'de campagne'. Comme dans la plupart des pays, la circulation se fait à droite. N'oubliez pas, avant de partir, de vous munir de la carte verte d'assurance internationale.

Par temps sec, la vitesse est limitée à 50 km/h en agglomération, 90 km/h sur route nationale (N) ou départementale (D), 110 km/h sur route à deux voies séparées et à 130 km/h sur autoroute (A). Par temps de pluie, la vitesse maximale est abaissée à 110 km/h sur autoroute et 100 km/h sur route à deux voies séparées.

Tout au long des autoroutes vous pouvez vous restaurer, faire le plein d'essence ou dire achats dans les aires de service. Une quarantaine d'aires disposent de bornes Internet ou d'espaces WiFi pour envoyer les courriels et surfer sur le Web. Les aires de repos, plus nombreuses, sont espacées de 15 kilomètres environ. Elles sont de véritables espaces de détente et sont équipées de tables de pique-nique et d'espaces de jeux pour les enfants.

Les jours fériés en France ne tombent pas nécessairement le lundi. Quand, par exemple, ils tombent un jeudi, beaucoup de Français 'font le pont'. Ils ne travaillent pas le vendredi et prennent un long week-end du mercredi soir au dimanche soir. La circulation à l'entrée et à la sortie des grandes villes, et aux péages des autoroutes devient alors très difficile. Pour éviter les bouchons (longues files de voitures qui avancent très lentement), consultez avant votre départ les sites Internet (voir ci-dessus), et suivez les conseils de Bison Futé (*a 'clever Red Indian' character*).

Activity 1

To see how well you've understood the passage above, try to answer the following questions (see **Key words and phrases** on page 174).

a Do you need to pay a toll on motorways?
b Does the speed limit change according to dry and wet conditions?
c What does N stand for on a French road map?
d What can one do in most *aires de service*?
e Is Internet accessible on motorways?
f What happens when the French *font le pont*?

Activity 2

Study the 'Calendrier du trafic routier' prepared by Bison Futé and answer the questions:

a Quels sont les mois où la circulation est moins dense?
b À quelles fêtes nationales ou religieuses correspondent les périodes de circulation difficile?
c Quels sont les deux week-ends de l'été où la circulation est extrêmement difficile?
d Quel conseil donneriez-vous à un Anglais qui doit circuler en France pendant les mois de juillet et août?

Calendrier du trafic routier 2008

Légende

- ☐ Circulation habituelle
- ▨ Circulation difficile
- ▤ Circulation très difficile
- ■ Circulation extrêmement difficile

DÉPART Sens départ vers les lieux de vacances.

RETOUR Sens retour depuis les lieux de vacances.

Mai	DÉPART	RETOUR	Juin	DÉPART	RETOUR	Juillet	DÉPART	RETOUR	Août	DÉPART	RETOUR
1 J	Ascension		1 D			1 M			1 V	très difficile	
2 V			2 L			2 M			2 S	extrêmement difficile	très difficile
3 S		difficile	3 M			3 J			3 D		difficile
4 D		très difficile	4 M			4 V	très difficile		4 L		
5 L			5 J			5 S	très difficile		5 M		
6 M			6 V			6 D			6 M		
7 M	très difficile		7 S			7 L			7 J		
8 J	Victoire 1945		8 D			8 M			8 V		difficile
9 V			9 L			9 M			9 S	très difficile	très difficile
10 S			10 M			10 J			10 D		difficile
11 D	Pentecôte (très difficile)		11 M			11 V	très difficile		11 L		
12 L		très difficile	12 J			12 S	extrêmement difficile		12 M		
13 M			13 V			13 D		difficile	13 M		
14 M			14 S			14 L	Fête Nationale (très difficile)		14 J	difficile	
15 J			15 D			15 M			15 V	Assomption	
16 V			16 L			16 M			16 S	très difficile	très difficile
17 S			17 M			17 J			17 D		très difficile
18 D			18 M			18 V	très difficile		18 L		
19 L			19 J			19 S	très difficile	difficile	19 M		
20 M			20 V			20 D			20 M		
21 M			21 S			21 L			21 J		
22 J			22 D			22 M			22 V		difficile
23 V			23 L			23 M			23 S	difficile	très difficile
24 S			24 M			24 J		très difficile	24 D		très difficile
25			25			25	très difficile		25		
26 L			26 J			26 S	très difficile	difficile	26 M		
27 M			27 V	difficile		27 D		difficile	27 M		
28 M			28 S	difficile		28 L			28 J		
29 J			29 D			29 M			29 V		difficile
30 V			30 L			30 M			30 S	difficile	
31 S						31 J			31 D		très difficile

Key words and phrases

Quelles sont les directions pour...?	How do you get to ... ? (lit. *what are the directions to...?*)
l'autoroute (f)	*motorway*
la rocade	*ring road, bypass*
la sortie	*exit*
la (route) nationale (N)	similar to an 'A' road in Britain
à péage	*toll payable*
une aire de repos	*service area*
suivez le panneau	*follow the sign*
c'est indiqué	*it is signposted*
le carrefour	*the crossroads*
les feux (m.pl.) rouges	*traffic lights* (often shortened to **les feux**)
une station-service	*petrol station*
où peut-on se garer?	*where can I park?*
le parking	*car park*
défense de stationner	*no parking*
le parcmètre	*parking meter*
je suis en panne	*I've broken down*
le service de dépannage	*breakdown service*
le moteur ne marche pas	*the engine does not work*
vérifier la pression des pneus	*to check the tyre pressure*
le gonflage des pneus est gratuit	*pumping up the tyres is free*
faire le plein	*filling up the car with petrol*
je vous en remets?	*shall I top it up for you?*
l'essence	*petrol*
le sans plomb	*lead-free (petrol)*
le gazole	*diesel*
l'huile (f)	*the oil*
réparer	*to repair*
la carte	*map*
la route à deux voies séparées	*dual carriageway*
une agglomération	*built-up area*
la (route) départementale (D)	equivalent to a 'B' road in the UK
le jour férié	*bank holiday*
le jour de congé	*day's leave*
le bouchon	*bottleneck, traffic jam*
la plupart de	*most of*
le pompiste	*petrol pump attendant*

i When driving in France, remember that at junctions you normally give way to traffic from the right (**priorité à droite**). But you always have right of way on a priority road marked with a yellow-on-white sign.

▶ Dialogue 1: *Les directions pour …?* The way to …?

*You may want to look at the road map of **Bordeaux et son Agglomération** on page 176 before listening to the recording.*

In this telephone conversation a tourist is calling the manager of the Bordeaux Aéroport Hôtel to enquire about accommodation and directions. When is reception open?

Gérant Allô, Hôtel Bordeaux Aéroport, j'écoute.

Touriste Bonjour, Monsieur. Voilà, j'ai l'intention de descendre dans votre hôtel dans deux semaines et je voudrais connaître les directions pour y arriver.

Gérant Vous viendrez d'où?

Touriste De Bayonne, donc j'arriverai **soit** par la A63 **soit** la N10.

Gérant **Il vaudrait mieux** prendre la A63 car la N10 **ne débouche pas sur** la rocade.

Touriste La rocade?

Gérant Oui … c'est **la voie rapide** qui **contourne** Bordeaux. Alors c'est très simple. **Une fois sur** la rocade il faut prendre direction aéroport Mérignac puis la sortie 11.

Touriste Bon, **j'ai compris**. Et après?

Gérant Après? L'hôtel est très bien indiqué. Suivez les panneaux. Il est dans le grand centre hôtelier de l'aéroport entre le Novotel et le Mercure.

Touriste Pour avoir une chambre, que faut-il faire?

Gérant Soit vous réservez directement sur Internet, soit vous nous téléphonez quelques jours à l'avance en nous laissant le numéro de votre carte de crédit, soit vous arrivez le jour même – il y a quelqu'un à la réception à partir de 17 heures … et vous nous laissez alors juste votre nom.

Touriste Et si j'arrive tard?

Gérant Si vous arrivez au-delà des heures de réception, donc après 22 heures, vous devez insérer dans le distributeur votre carte bancaire. La carte sera débitée du **montant** de la chambre et vous obtiendrez le numéro de votre chambre.

Touriste Ah bon … ça a l'air très simple … Et c'est combien?

Gérant	31€ la nuit. Le petit déjeuner est en extra: 3€90.
Touriste	Et pour se garer, il y a un parking?
Gérant	Nous avons un parking fermé.
Touriste	Il faut réserver à l'avance?
Gérant	Oh là, là oui, je vous le conseille surtout en périodes de vacances.
Touriste	Bon, alors je vais **m'en occuper** tout de suite.

soit ... soit	*either ... or*
il vaudrait mieux	*it would be better*
ne débouche pas sur	*does not merge with*
la voie rapide contourne	*the expressway goes round*
une fois sur	*once on*
j'ai compris	*I have understood*
vous nous laissez	*you give us (you leave to us)*
le montant	*the amount*
s'en occuper	*to deal with something*

Activity 3

Have you understood the conversation between the manager and the tourist? Look at the **Formule 1** brochure below, then read the directions and put them in the right sequence.

a Une fois sorti de la rocade, suivez les panneaux
b puis la sortie 11
c Quand vous arrivez sur la rocade,
d il faut prendre la direction aéroport Mérignac
e Il vaudrait mieux prendre la A63

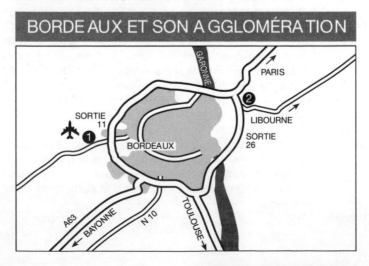

BORDEAUX ET SON AGGLOMÉRATION

Activity 4

Looking at the **Formule 1** brochure, you decide that Est-Artigues is the most conveniently placed hotel in the area around Bordeaux for your journey from Bayonne to Paris. You phone the **gérante**, asking her for the directions. Fill in your part.

a *You*   *Tell her that you would like to stay one night in the hotel. Ask her politely how to get to Est-Artigues.*

Gérante   Vous arrivez d'où?

b *You*   *From Bayonne.*

Gérante   De Bayonne? Alors c'est très simple. La A63 vous mène directement sur la Rocade. Prenez la direction est vers Paris, puis sortie 26 ... Aux ...

c *You*   *Can you repeat, please?*

Gérante   Oui, alors vous allez prendre la rocade direction est, Paris–Libourne, sortie 26. Une fois sorti, prenez à droite aux feux, sortie CourtePaille, et nous sommes à 500 mètres de là.

d *You*   *Repeat her instructions from exit 26.*

Gérante   Voilà, l'hôtel est indiqué. Suivez les panneaux.

e *You*   *Is there a restaurant?*

Gérante   Oui, nous avons un restaurant sur place.

f *You*   *Ask at what time you can arrive.*

Gérante   Il y a quelqu'un à la réception à partir de 17 heures jusqu'à 22 heures.

Stationnement Parking

i Le stationnement dans la plupart des villes est payant, sous forme d'horodateurs. Le tarif horaire varie en moyenne entre un et deux euros.

Activity 5

Here are the kind of instructions which are displayed on **horodateurs** or **distributeurs** in France. Read them, then answer the questions with vrai or faux. Correct the false ones:

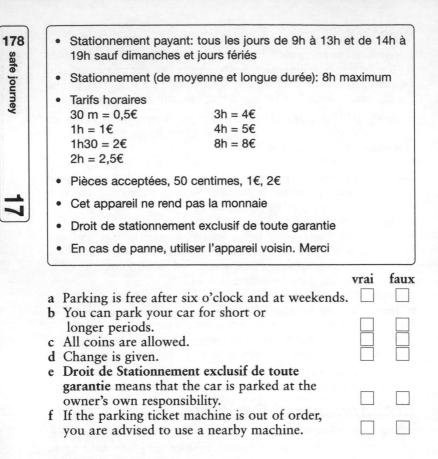

- Stationnement payant: tous les jours de 9h à 13h et de 14h à 19h sauf dimanches et jours fériés

- Stationnement (de moyenne et longue durée): 8h maximum

- Tarifs horaires
30 m = 0,5€	3h = 4€
1h = 1€	4h = 5€
1h30 = 2€	8h = 8€
2h = 2,5€	

- Pièces acceptées, 50 centimes, 1€, 2€

- Cet appareil ne rend pas la monnaie

- Droit de stationnement exclusif de toute garantie

- En cas de panne, utiliser l'appareil voisin. Merci

		vrai	faux
a	Parking is free after six o'clock and at weekends.	☐	☐
b	You can park your car for short or longer periods.	☐	☐
c	All coins are allowed.	☐	☐
d	Change is given.	☐	☐
e	**Droit de Stationnement exclusif de toute garantie** means that the car is parked at the owner's own responsibility.	☐	☐
f	If the parking ticket machine is out of order, you are advised to use a nearby machine.	☐	☐

Le flash trafic Traffic news

▶ Activity 6

Imagine that you are driving in France on the A6 motorway towards Paris. Your car radio is switched on, and the traffic news suddenly comes on. Can you get the gist of what is being said? Look at the map of the area to help you, then answer the questions:

a How would you describe the traffic situation?
b The report recommends caution to the drivers. Why?
c The problem starts at the **barrière de péage** in Fleury-en-Bière. Give the translation for **barrière de péage**.
d A different itinerary is suggested to reach the East of Paris. What is it?

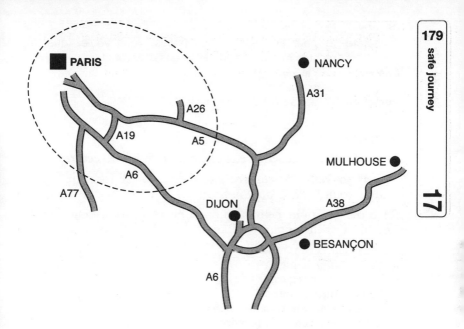

Faire le plein Filling up with petrol

i When travelling through France you'll probably buy **l'essence** or **le carburant** at a self-service station. If you don't and are faced with an attendant, **pompiste**, ask for **le plein**, to have the tank filled up or buy so many Euros' worth, say 50€ or 60€ . There is usually a choice between **l'octane 95 sans plomb** (lead-free petrol with an octane rating of 95), **l'octane 98 sans plomb** (super-plus lead-free petrol) and **le gazole** (diesel).

▶ Dialogue 2

A motorist is filling up her car with petrol. The attendant tells her that something is free. What is it?

Pompiste	Bonjour, Madame, qu'est-ce que vous voulez? Du sans plomb?
Cliente	Je prends du sans plomb 95.
Pompiste	Je vous fais le plein?
Client	Non, seulement pour 46€ ... et vous pouvez aussi vérifier l'huile?
Pompiste	Oui, bien sûr ... votre niveau d'huile est un peu bas, je vous en remets un peu?

Cliente	Oui, un litre alors.
Pompiste	Et pour la pression des pneus, vous voulez que je regarde? Le gonflage des pneus est gratuit.
Cliente	Oui, je veux bien.
	(*after a while*)
Pompiste	Voilà, ça fait 53€50 avec l'huile.

Activity 7

Most of the dialogue above is based on two key structures:

vous pouvez …?	*can you …?*	to ask for help
vous voulez …?	*do you want …?*	to offer something

Read the questions below; can you guess who's asking them? The client or the **pompiste**? Put a tick in the correct column.

	Cliente	Pompiste
a Vous voulez le plein?	....	....
b Vous pouvez regarder le niveau d'eau?	....	....
c Vous voulez du super?	....	....
d Vous pouvez me faire le plein?	....	....
e Vous pouvez vérifier la pression des pneus?	....	....
f Vous voulez 1 litre d'huile?	....	....

Activity 8

Now it's your turn: you need some unleaded petrol and want to have your oil checked.

a **You**	*Say hello. Ask for unleaded petrol.*	
Pompiste	Vous voulez le plein?	
b **You**	*Say no. 58€'s worth.*	
Pompiste	C'est tout?	
c **You**	*Ask if he can check the oil.*	
Pompiste	Oui, effectivement, vous avez besoin d'huile. Vous en voulez combien?	
d **You**	*Say one litre.*	
Pompiste	Un litre, bon très bien. Vous voulez que je vérifie la pression des pneus? Le gonflage est gratuit.	
e **You**	*Say no thank you; it's OK (**ça va**).*	
Pompiste	Ça fait 65€. Vous payez à la caisse.	

En panne Breaking down

i In case of accidents and thefts (**accidents et vols**) phone the police. In case of breakdowns look in the yellow pages (**annuaire professions**) under **dépannage** or call the police.

If you break down on the motorway, go to the nearest emergency telephone (tall orange pillars marked 'SOS'). All you need to do is press the emergency button, release it and wait for the operator to connect you.

▶ Dialogue 3

Une femme est tombée en panne sur l'autoroute. Elle appelle le service de dépannage.

A woman has broken down on the motorway. She rings the breakdown service.

Listen to the recording or read the dialogue and try to answer the following questions: On which motorway has the woman broken down? Where is she going? How long is it going to take the mechanic to get there?

Femme	Allô, le service de dépannage?
Mécanicien	Ici, Dépannage Ultra-rapide, j'écoute.
Femme	Voilà, je suis en panne; je ne comprends pas, le moteur ne marche plus. Vous pouvez m'aider?
Mécanicien	Où êtes-vous, Madame?
Femme	Je suis sur l'autoroute A26, entre Reims et St. Quentin.
Mécanicien	Et dans quelle direction allez-vous?
Femme	Vers Calais.
Mécanicien	Elle est comment votre voiture?
Femme	C'est une Peugeot 307 bleue.
Mécanicien	Bon, j'arrive dans une demi-heure.

Activity 9

Let's hope you won't be so unlucky! But to be prepared for all emergencies practise the following situation: look at the map overleaf; you've broken down with your English Ford and you've just got through to the breakdown service. Fill in your part:

Homme	Allô, service de dépannage.
a *You*	*Ask if they can help you – say you've broken down.*
Homme	Quel est le problème?
b *You*	*Say that you don't know; the engine is not working.*

Homme	Où êtes-vous?
c *You*	*Say you are on the motorway A10 between Orléans and Blois.*
Homme	Où allez-vous?
d *You*	*Say which direction you're going in (towards Tours).*
Homme	Qu'est-ce que vous avez comme voiture?
e *You*	*Say that it's an English car: a white Ford Focus. Ask him when he's arriving.*
Homme	D'ici une heure (*within an hour*).

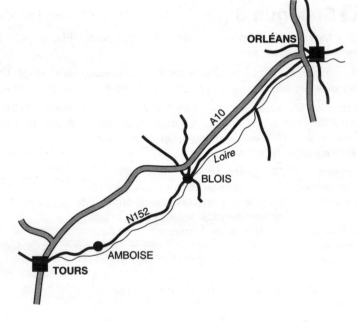

▶ Activity 10

Nothing seems to work in Michel's car. Study the illustrations and explanations opposite describing what's wrong with his car.

Now listen to him explaining his trouble to the mechanic. What he says is not in the same order as below. Fill in the boxes with **1, 2, 3, 4, 5, 6, 7, 8** to show the order in which you hear it. (Check your answers at the back of the book.)

a

☐ Mon pneu est crevé.
I have a puncture.

b

☐ La batterie est à plat.
The battery is flat.

c

☐ Mon phare avant gauche
ne marche pas.
*The front light on the left
side does not work.*

d

☐ Mon pare-brise est cassé.
My windscreen is broken.

e

☐ L'essuie-glace arrière ne
fonctionne pas.
*The back wiper does
not work.*

f

☐ Le moteur chauffe et
fait un drôle de bruit.
*The engine is heating up
and makes a strange
noise.*

g

☐ Ma roue de secours est à
plat.
My spare wheel is flat.

h

☐ Les freins ne marchent
plus.
*The brakes aren't working
any more.*

18

l'argent
money

In this unit you will
- find out how to ask for change
- familiarize yourself with French coins and notes
- practise changing traveller's cheques
- learn to say that there is an error in a bill

Before you start, revise

- saying what you want (page 62)
- asking for help (page 83)
- expressions of time, days of the week **Key words and phrases** (page 36)
- numbers (page 233)

Pièces et billets de banque en euros
Euro coins and banknotes

i En région parisienne, les banques sont principalement ouvertes du lundi au vendredi de 10 à 17h. En province, elles ouvrent du mardi au samedi et ferment entre 13 et 15h.

L'euro est la devise nationale de la France et aujourd'hui de treize autres pays membres de l'Union européenne. Il y a sept billets de couleurs et de tailles différentes: 5, 10, 20, 50, 100, 200 et 500€. Sur les billets on peut voir au recto des fenêtres et portails, et au verso des ponts. Ces éléments illustrent différentes périodes de la culture européenne: le classique, le roman, le gothique, la Renaissance, le baroque, etc.

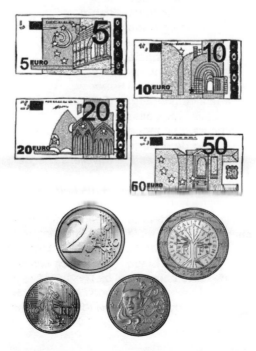

Activity 1

i Il y a huit pièces: 1, 2, 5, 10, 20, 50 centimes, 1€, 2€. Dans un euro il y a 100 centimes. Chaque pièce a deux faces. La première est européenne. Commune avec les autres pays membres de l'Union, elle représente la valeur en euro et douze étoiles, symbole de l'Europe. La deuxième est nationale. Propre à chaque pays, elle représente les symboles caractéristiques de chaque pays. Sur la face française sont représentés trois symboles: la Marianne, symbole de la liberté et de la République, la Semeuse (*sower*), symbole de la fécondité, et l'Arbre, symbole de la vie.

a Do banks shut over lunchtime in France?
b Are euro coins the same throughout the EU?
c In what ways do they differ?

Key words and phrases

If you have not got the recording, check the pronunciation of the words preceded by an * in the **Pronunciation tips** opposite.

* **une pièce**	*coin*
* **un billet**	*banknote*
* **un franc**	*franc* (old currency)
* **un euro**	*a euro*
* **la monnaie**	*small change, currency*
la devise étrangère	*foreign currency*
* **l'argent (m)**	*money*
la livre (sterling)	(English) *pound*
le dollar	*dollar*
* **le cours du change**	*exchange rate*
le taux de change	*to withdraw money*
* **le traveller**	*traveller's cheque*
(or chèque de voyage)	
en bas	*at the bottom*
un stylo	*a pen*
une pièce d'identité	*means of identification*
un changeur de monnaie	*coin changing machine*
une télécarte	*telephone card*
la carte bleue	*the French banker's card*
une carte bancaire	*banker's card*
la note	*hotel bill*
l'addition (f)	*bill* (drinks, snacks)

régler	to settle (bill)
une erreur	a mistake
le chiffre	number
un distributeur automatique	a cashpoint machine

For you to say

vous pouvez changer ... euros?	can you change... euros?
vous avez de la monnaie svp?	do you have any change please?
il me faut des pièces de 1€	I need 1€ coins
changer de l'argent	change some money
la livre est à combien?	what's the rate of exchange for the pound?
vous acceptez les cartes de crédit?	do you accept credit cards?

Worth knowing

faites (faire) l'appoint	put in the exact money
l'appareil ne rend pas l'argent	no change given
retirer de l'argent	to withdraw money

ℹ Pronunciation tips

You do not need to know many words when changing money but they need to be pronounced correctly; here is an opportunity to practise saying them:

pièce	pee–esse
billet	bee–yeah
franc	remember not to pronounce the **c**
euro	ir (as in *sir*) – ro
monnaie	mo–nay
argent	make sure the r is pronounced otherwise it could sound like **agent (de police)**. ʊʊﬂɦ.ɐɾɪɑɾɪ
cours	don't pronounce the s
traveller	as in English but with a French **r**

And now re-read the **Key words and phrases**, checking your pronunciation.

Faire de la monnaie Getting small change

Activity 2

Try to answer the following, using the phrases in the box on the previous page.

a How would you ask: Can you change 10€ please?
b How would you say: I need 1€ coins?
c What does **la machine ne rend pas l'argent** mean?

(Check your answers in the **Key to the exercises and tests**.)

▶ Dialogue 1

Listen to the dialogue or read the conversation that takes place between a passer-by and a motorist, who needs some small change for the pay-and-display machine. Then do the activity.

Femme	Pardon, Madame, vous pouvez changer mon billet de 5€, s'il vous plaît?
Passante	Je ne sais pas, mais je vais regarder. Qu'est-ce qu'il vous faut?
Femme	C'est pour l'horodateur. Il me faut cinq pièces de 1€, ou alors une pièce de 1€ et deux pièces de 2€.
Passante	La machine ne rend pas la monnaie?
Femme	Non, et elle **n'**accepte **que** des pièces de 50 centimes, 1€ et 2€.
Passante	Et vous n'avez pas de carte bancaire?
Femme	Euh, non, je n'en ai pas.
Passante	Eh bien, **vous avez de la chance!** J'ai quatre pièces de 1€ et deux pièces de 50 centimes. **Ça vous va?**
Femme	Merci beaucoup, Madame.

ne ... que	*only*
vous avez de la chance	*you're lucky, you're in luck*
ça vous va?	*is that OK (for you)?*

Activity 3

Find the French for the following phrases:

a Don't you have a bank card?
b I need five coins of 1€
c it only accepts ...
d Can you change ...?

e I haven't got any (card)
f I don't know
g Is that OK?
h you're lucky
i I am going to see

Activity 4

You want to make a phone call but only have a 5€ note on you.
Fill in your part of the dialogue.

a You *Stop a man in the street. Ask him if he has any small change for the telephone.*

Passant Qu'est-ce qu'il vous faut?

b You *Say: I've only got a 5€ note and I need 1€ coins.*

Passant Je suis désolé mais je n'ai pas de monnaie. Pourquoi n'achetez-vous pas une télécarte?

c You *Ask: a 'télécarte'? What is it?*

Passant Une carte pour téléphoner. Toutes les cabines téléphoniques marchent avec des télécartes.

d You *Ask: where can I buy a phone card?*

Passant Dans les tabacs, les postes, les gares de métro ... un peu partout.

Changer de l'argent Changing money

Pour connaître le taux de change: **www.oanda.com/convert/classic**
www.xe.com

i On trouve de nombreux bureaux de change dans les grandes villes (gares, aéroports, grandes agences de banque, points de change). Les grandes postes changent aussi les devises étrangères et les chèques de voyage. Leurs taux sont souvent meilleurs qu'ailleurs. Le nombre de distributeurs automatiques de billets (DAB) augmente régulièrement en France. On y retire de l'argent avec une carte bancaire, la carte Visa/Carte bleue étant la plus acceptée en France suivie de MasterCard (Eurocard).

▶ Dialogue 2

Un étranger change des travellers dans une banque.

A foreigner is in a bank changing traveller's cheques.

Listen to the recording or read below and find out: How many dollars does he want to change? What does he need before he can sign his traveller's cheques?

Étranger	Je voudrais changer des chèques de voyage, s'il vous plaît.
Employée	Oui, très bien. Vous avez une pièce d'identité?
Étranger	Oui, voici mon passeport.
Employée	Bon, qu'est-ce que vous voulez?
Étranger	Je voudrais changer 350 dollars en euros.
Employée	D'accord, alors vous allez signer en bas des chèques de voyage.
Étranger	Euh … vous avez quelque chose pour écrire s'il vous plaît?
Employée	Un instant … voici un stylo.
Étranger	Le dollar est à combien aujourd'hui?
Employée	Aujourd'hui le cours du dollar est à 0,68.
Étranger	Il y a une commission à payer?
Employée	Pas pour les chèques de voyage American Express. Mais pour les autres chèques de voyage il y a une commission de 4%.
Étranger	Ah c'est très bien …

Activity 5

Without looking at the text above, fill in the missing words.

a Je voudrais ……… des chèques de voyage.
b Vous avez une ……… d'identité?
c Vous allez ……… en bas des chèques de voyage.
d Vous avez quelque chose pour ………?
e Le dollar est à ……… aujourd'hui?
f Il y a une commission à ………?

Activity 6

Take part in this conversation in **le bureau de change** at the **Gare du Nord** in Paris.

a *You*	*Say that you would like to change some dollars.*
Employé	Des dollars américains, canadiens, australiens?
b *You*	*Say American dollars.*
Employé	Oui; vous voulez changer des billets ou des travellers?
c *You*	*Say bank notes.*
Employé	Combien voulez-vous changer?
d *You*	*Say 200 dollars. Ask the exchange rate.*
Employé	Le dollar est à 0,70 aujourd'hui.
e *You*	*Ask if they are open on Sundays.*
Employé	Oui, tous les jours de 7h à 21.30. …(*later*) Voici votre argent!

Une erreur dans la note An error in the bill

ℹ️ *Pour régler la note* Paying your hotel bill

- It's a good idea to ask for the bill in advance in order to check it.
- You ask for **la note** to pay for your hotel bill and for **l'addition** to pay for food and drink.
- Remember to check the price of hotel rooms which, by law, should be displayed at the reception and in each room.
- Extras (telephone, mini-bar, etc.) should be charged separately.
- TTC (toutes taxes comprises) means inclusive of tax.
- TVA (taxe à la valeur ajoutée) means 'VAT'.

▶ Activity 7

It is essential for you to be confident in using and understanding numbers, particularly when paying bills! You can revise them at the back of the book, where they are all listed.

Here is some extra practice to help you cope with French prices. Listen to Michel and write down the prices you hear.

a ....   f ....
b ....   g ....
c ....   h ....
d ....   i ....
e ....   j ....

▶ Dialogue 3

A guest is about to leave the hotel. Having asked for the bill, he spots a mistake. Listen to the recording, or read the dialogue below, and say what mistake was made.

Guest Je voudrais régler ma note, s'il vous plaît.
Réceptionniste Bien, vous partez aujourd'hui?
Guest Oui, après le petit-déjeuner.
Réceptionniste Bon, c'est pour quelle chambre?
Guest Chambre quatorze. Vous acceptez les cartes de crédit?
Réceptionniste Oui, bien sûr. Alors un instant … nous allons vérifier. Si vous voulez bien repasser après votre petit-déjeuner votre note sera prête.
(after breakfast)

Guest	Pardon, Madame, il y a une erreur. Qu'est-ce que c'est 'mini-bar 10€'?
Réceptionniste	Ce sont les boissons du mini-bar **que vous avez consommées** dans votre chambre.
Guest	Mais **je n'ai rien pris** du mini-bar.
Réceptionniste	Vraiment? Bon, eh bien c'est sans doute une erreur de notre part...! **Nous avons dû nous tromper** de chambre. Je m'excuse Monsieur. Donc ça fait 94€ moins 10€ pour la boisson... euh 84€.
Guest	C'est avec service et taxes?
Réceptionniste	Oui, taxes de séjour et service sont compris.

que vous avez consommées	*that you've drunk*
je n'ai rien pris	*I haven't taken anything*
nous avons dû nous tromper	*we must have made a mistake*

Activity 8

Have you understood the dialogue well enough to answer the following questions?

a When does the client intend to leave the hotel?
b What was the number of his room?
c Was the bill correct?
d What does the amount of 10€ correspond to?
e Is the bill inclusive of tax and service?

Mini-test on Units 17 and 18

How would you ask/say:

1 Is there a car park near here?
2 I need four 1€ coins for the parking meter.
3 Can you help me please? I've broken down.
4 I need 1 litre of oil.
5 Have you any small change?
6 Do you accept credit cards?
7 I would like to settle my bill.
8 Can you check the tyre pressure?
9 Can you fill up my car with petrol?
10 I would like to change £150 into euros.

19

savoir faire face
troubleshooting

In this unit you will

- find out how to ask for medicine at the chemist's
- familiarise yourself with the French health system
- practise making an appointment with the doctor/dentist
- find out about the telephone in France
- learn some key expressions to describe your problems

Before you start, revise

- saying what you want (page 62)
- how to describe things (page 63)
- how to spell in French (page 123)
- how to say my, your, his, etc. (page 32)
- expressions of time, days of the week **Key words and phrases** (page 36)
- numbers (page 233)

Sign for a French chemist's

La pharmacie en France The chemist's in France

ℹ️ The French chemist's is easily recognizable, with its green neon cross sign outside. For minor ailments you'll find that the trained pharmacist, **pharmacien(-ne)** is usually happy to give you advice. You will not be able to buy medicines (even aspirin!) anywhere except at the **pharmacie**.

Chemist's shops/pharmacies are generally open from 8.00 to 20.00. Some stay open later. Their opening times on Sundays and bank holidays are fixed by a rotating schedule. When they are shut, the address of the nearest duty/night chemist's shop is displayed on the door. In Paris the following chemist's shops stay open all night long:

- Pharmacie Dhéry (24h) inside the shopping arcade at 84, avenue des Champs-Elysées (8e), tél: 01 45 62 02 41
- Pharmacie Européenne de la Place de Clichy (24h), 6 place de Clichy (17e), tél: 01 48 74 65 18 and 01 42 89 01 04
- British and American Pharmacy, 1 rue Auber (9e), tél: 01 47 42 49 40
- Pharmacie Anglaise, 62 Avenue Champs Elysées, (8e), tél: 01 43 59 22 52

Le service médical Medical treatment

ℹ️ Before leaving for France

Check whether your country has signed a bilateral agreement with the French Social Security (**Centre des Liaisons Européennes et Internationales de Sécurité Sociale: www.cleiss.fr**). In all cases, it is more prudent to take out a travel insurance policy.

If you are a EU resident, remember to take your European Health Insurance Card (EHIC) with you. It can be obtained online (**www.dh.gov.uk/travellers**), by phone (0845 606 2030) or by post (pick up the EHIC form and pre-addressed envelope from the Post Office).With the EHIC you can obtain a refund of generally 70 per cent on the cost of prescriptions and standard doctors' and dentists' fees.

Before making an appointment with a doctor or dentist, make sure that they are **conventionné** and belong to the category **Secteur 1. Conventionné** practitioners fall into one of two categories: in **Secteur 1** they charge the official social security rate, in **Secteur 2** an extra charge is added to the official rate.

Show the doctor (general practitioners and specialists) your EHIC before paying him/her directly. He/She will fill out a **feuille de soins** (*treatment form*) and **une ordonnance** (*prescription*) if necessary.

You can obtain your medication from any chemist's shop/pharmacy on presenting the **feuille de soins** and **ordonnance**. The price of the medicine is printed on a second **feuille de soins** that the chemist will give back to you with the prescription. The **vignettes** (*stickers*) on the medicine packaging must be removed and stuck on the **feuille de soins** in the space provided. The amount left to the patient to pay (approximately 30 per cent) is what the French call the **ticket modérateur**.

Once you have dated and signed the **feuille de soins,** attached the vignettes and filled in your permanent address and bank details (name of bank, address, SWIFT code, account number and IBAN or BIC), you should send the form to the nearest Sickness Insurance Office (**Caisse Primaire d'Assurance-Maladie** or **CPAM**) while you are still in France, together with the prescription and a copy of your European Health Insurance Card. The refund will be sent to your home address later. This refund process normally takes around two months.

Emergencies

In an emergency, phone:

- **SAMU**/24 hour ambulance: 15

- **SOS Médecins**/Doctors – 24h house calls: 01 47 07 77 77

- **Urgence Médicales de Paris** (Paris Medical Emergencies): 01 53 94 94 94

- **SOS Helpline** (in English, 3–11 p.m.): 01 47 23 80 80

- **SOS Dentaire/** Dental emergency: 01 43 37 51 00

- **Hôpital Américain de Paris**, 63, boulevard Victor-Hugo, 92 202 Neuilly, tél: 01 46 41 25 25. The hospital provides consultations in English (24/7) for all dental and medical emergencies.

Key words and phrases

For you to say

la pharmacie	*chemist's*
le pharmacien, la pharmacienne	*chemist*
chez le médecin	*at the doctor's*
chez le dentiste	*at the dentist's*
le cabinet médical/dentaire	*doctor's/dentist's surgery*
prendre rendez-vous	*to make an appointment*
souffrir	*to suffer, be in pain, feel ill*
depuis quand	*since when*
je voudrais quelque chose pour...	*I would like something for ...*
* la piqûre d'insectes	*insect bite*
le mal de gorge	*sore throat*
le mal de dents	*toothache*
le mal de tête	*headache*
j'ai mal à la gorge	*I've got a sore throat*
j'ai mal aux dents	*I've got toothache*
j'ai mal à la tête	*I've got a headache*
j'ai mal au ventre	*I've got stomachache*
il a de la fièvre	*he's got a temperature*
le dentifrice	*toothpaste*
le shampooing	*shampoo*
contre	*against*
j'ai perdu (il a perdu)...	*I've lost (he's lost)*

j'ai laissé (il a laissé)...	I've left (he's left)
... est cassé(e)	... is broken
... sont cassés(ées)	... are broken
on a volé	... was stolen
le sac à main	handbag
le portefeuille	wallet
le porte-monnaie	purse
les lunettes	glasses

For you to understand

un médicament	medicine
une crème	cream
une huile	oil
une aspirine effervescente	soluble aspirin
en comprimés	in tablet form
je vous conseille	I advise you, I recommend to you

* **piqûre** is pronounced 'pic-oore' (with French **u**)

▶ Dialogue 1: *À la pharmacie* At the chemist's

Listen to the recording or read below: What's wrong with the customer's husband? Has he got a temperature? Name at least three items the customer buys.

Pharmacien	Bonjour, Madame. Vous désirez?
Cliente	Vous avez quelque chose pour le mal de gorge?
Pharmacien	C'est pour vous, Madame?
Cliente	Non, c'est pour mon mari.
Pharmacien	Il a de la fièvre?
Cliente	Non, mais il a aussi mal à la tête.
Pharmacien	Bon, pour le mal de gorge je vous donne des pastilles. Il en prend une quand il a mal. Pour le mal de tête, je vous donne de l'aspirine effervescente. Deux comprimés toutes les quatre heures. Il n'est pas allergique à l'aspirine?
Cliente	Non, non … merci. Je voudrais aussi du dentifrice et quelque chose contre le soleil.
Pharmacien	Vous préférez une crème ou une huile?
Cliente	Une crème.
Pharmacien	Alors voici du dentifrice et une crème pour le soleil; c'est tout?
Cliente	Oui, merci.
Pharmacien	Bon, eh bien ça fait 38€15.

Activity 1

Read the dialogue again and choose the right answers for the patient's medical record card below. (Check your answers in the

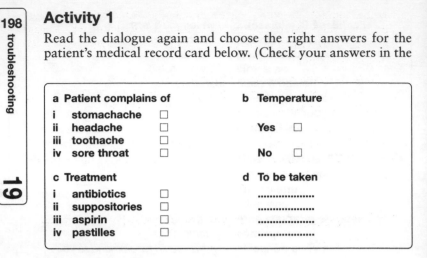

a Patient complains of
i   stomachache   ☐
ii headache   ☐
iii toothache   ☐
iv sore throat   ☐

b Temperature
Yes   ☐
No   ☐

c Treatment
i   antibiotics   ☐
ii suppositories   ☐
iii aspirin   ☐
iv pastilles   ☐

d To be taken
....
....
....
....

Key to the exercises and tests.)

Activity 2

Now it's your turn to go to the chemist's to get some medicine for your daughter, who has toothache.

Pharmacienne Bonjour, Monsieur/Madame. Vous désirez?
a You *Say: my daughter has toothache.*
Pharmacienne Elle a de la fièvre?
b You *Say: yes, a little.*
Pharmacienne Depuis quand souffre-t-elle?
c You *Say: since yesterday.*
Pharmacienne Bon, je vais vous donner de l'aspirine vitaminée et si ça continue dans un jour ou deux il faudra aller chez le dentiste.
d You *Thank her. Ask for something for insect bites.*
Pharmacienne Pour les piqûres d'insectes? Certainement. Je vous conseille cette crème anti-démangeaisons ... elle est très bonne ...
e You *You didn't get everything she said but you understood that she was recommending the cream. Say: I'll take it and ask to pay.*

i EU residents are covered for emergency medical treatment throughout the European Union. US visitors with private health insurance are also covered for a limited period. Canadians with a valid **Assurance-maladie du Québec** card can receive reimbursement in some cases. Australian Medicare provides absolutely no coverage in France. However any foreigner who is sick can receive treatment in the casualty ward of any public hospital. In emergencies phone:

> **SAMU**/*24 hour ambulance*: 15 or 01 45 67 50 50
> **SOS Médecins**/*Doctors – 24h house calls*: 01 47 07 77 77
> **SOS Dentaire**/*Dental emergency*: 01 43 37 51 00

If you come from the UK, remember that form E111 has been replaced by the European Health Insurance Card (EHIC), which will enable you to obtain a refund after receiving medical and/or dental treatment. (See page 195.)

▶ Dialogue 2: *Chez le docteur* At the doctor's

Mrs Jones phones Dr Leroux's surgery to make an appointment. Why does Mrs Jones phone? Who is the patient? Has the patient got a temperature? What other symptom?

Réceptionniste	Allô, le cabinet du docteur Leroux, j'écoute.
Mrs Jones	Je voudrais prendre rendez-vous, s'il vous plaît.
Réceptionniste	Bon, c'est pour une consultation ou une visite?
Mrs Jones	Je ne comprends pas, vous pouvez expliquer?
Réceptionniste	Pour une consultation vous venez ici, pour une visite le médecin va chez vous. Vous êtes la patiente?
Mrs Jones	Non, c'est ma fille. Elle a beaucoup de fièvre …
Réceptionniste	Alors, vous voulez une visite … Écoutez, le docteur **est pris** toute la journée mais il pourrait **passer voir** votre fille dans la soirée vers … peut-être 19.30. Qu'est-ce qu'elle a, votre fille?
Mrs Jones	Je ne sais pas, peut-être **la grippe**. Elle a très mal à la tête.
Réceptionniste	Vous pouvez me donner votre nom et adresse?
Mrs Jones	Jones J-O-N-E-S et j'habite appartement 8, 10 rue Legrand, à côté de la piscine.
Réceptionniste	Bon, eh bien Mme Jones, le docteur Leroux passera voir votre fille vers 19.30.
Mrs Jones	Merci beaucoup. Au revoir, Madame.

est pris	*is busy* (lit. is taken)	**la grippe**	*flu*

i Using the phone in France may seem like a daunting experience but it doesn't need to be. Here are two useful tips when speaking on the phone.

- Speak clearly and open your mouth wide, particularly when pronouncing the vowels **i**, **o**, **u**, **é**.

- If you don't understand what is being said, don't be afraid to ask the person at the other end to repeat using one of the following expressions:

>   **Vous pouvez répéter, s'il vous plaît?**
>   **Vous pouvez parler plus lentement?**
>   **Je ne comprends pas.**
>   **Vous pouvez expliquer?**

Activity 3

Here are a few French words which appear on the **feuille de soins** and which you may need to recognize in order to fill it in correctly. Match the words in the left column with their equivalent in the right column, then check your answers at the back of the book.

a la facturation du pharmacien	**i**	*the social security office*
b le remboursement	**ii**	*signed statement of treatment given*
c les honoraires perçus		
d le médecin traitant	**iii**	*the GP*
e la feuille de soins	**iv**	*keep the original prescription*
f conserver l'original de l'ordonnance	**v**	*refund*
g coller les vignettes	**vi**	*the chemist's bill*
h l'organisme d'assurance maladie	**vii**	*the received fee (by the GP)*
	viii	*stick on the (detachable) labels*

Activity 4

It's your turn to make an appointment at the dentist's. Say your part.

Réceptionniste Allô, allô.
a *You*   *Say: I would like to make an appointment.*
Réceptionniste Oui, très bien; c'est pour vous?
b *You*   *Say: no, it's for my son. We are English, on holiday here and he has had toothache since Tuesday.*
Réceptionniste Il a quel âge votre fils?

c **You**	Say: he's 12.
Réceptionniste	Oui, je vois. Et quand peut-il venir?
d **You**	Say: today, this morning or this afternoon.
Réceptionniste	Bon; eh bien cet après-midi, à 3.45. Ça vous va?
e **You**	Ask her to repeat the time.
Réceptionniste	À 3.45. Votre nom, s'il vous plaît?
f **You**	Say your name and spell it.
Réceptionniste	Merci, nous attendons donc votre fils à 3.45. Au revoir Monsieur/Madame.

La poste, le téléphone et l'Internet en France Using the post office, the phone and the Internet in France

Pour tous renseignements pratiques sur Paris:
http://en.parisinfo.com/guide-paris

i La poste

Les bureaux de poste sont ouverts de 8 heures à 19 heures du lundi au vendredi, et le samedi matin de 8 heures à midi. À la poste, on peut acheter des timbres, poster son courrier, changer de l'argent, téléphoner et consulter l'Internet.

Le téléphone

La plupart des cabines téléphoniques s'utilisent avec des télécartes de 50 ou 120 unités, vendues dans les bureaux de poste, les principales stations de métro et de RER, les tabacs et les caisses des supermarchés.

Pour téléphoner depuis la France, faites les dix chiffres indiqués dans la cabine. Le premier commence toujours par un 0 et le second indique la zone de votre correspondant. La France est divisée en cinq zones. Pour Paris et l'Île-de-France, faites le 01.

Pour téléphoner à l'étranger, composez le préfixe international 00, le code du pays et le numéro de la zone (sans le 0). Pour ne pas payer la communication, vous pouvez vous faire rappeler dans la cabine téléphonique en donnant le code de la France (33), le numéro de la zone sans le 0, puis les huit chiffres de la cabine téléphonique.

L'Internet

On peut accéder à l'Internet:

- en libre-service en payant la connexion avec une télécarte aux bornes Internet (**www.netanoo.com**). Ces bornes sont situées dans de nombreux sites publics et privés, galeries marchandes (*shopping centres/malls),* hôtels, points d'accueil des offices de tourisme, etc.

- avec WiFi, accessible dans certains hôtels, gares et différents offices de tourisme.

- dans les cybercafés. Ceux-ci abondent à Paris et vous en trouverez toujours un situé près de votre lieu de résidence.

Activity 5

Answer the following statements with **vrai** or **faux**. Correct the false ones:

	vrai	faux
a The post office is open on Saturday afternoon.	☐	☐
b Phone cards are only used with public phones.	☐	☐
c Phone cards are often sold in supermarkets.	☐	☐
d French numbers have ten digits, the first being 0 and the second indicating one of the five telephone zones in France.	☐	☐
e WiFi is only accessible in some hotels.	☐	☐
f Internet cafés are not so frequent in Paris.	☐	☐

Activity 6

Look at the call charges below and fill in the blanks, using the correct word from the box.

Pour la France, l'Australie, le Royaume-Uni et les USA, les heures pleines sont de a _____ à b _____ tous les jours de la c _____. Le week-end et jours d _____ les heures sont creuses à partir de 12.00. Le tarif est le même que l'on téléphone au Royaume-Uni ou aux e _____. Pour f _____, le tarif est de 0,49 €/min. pendant les heures g _____ et de 0,34 €/min. pendant les heures h _____.

---

fériés   semaine   l'Australie   8.00   creuses   USA   19.30   pleines

JOURS	Heures pleines	Heures creuses
lundi	8–19.30	19.30–8
mardi	8–19.30	19.30–8
mercredi	8–19.30	19.30–8
jeudi	8–19.30	19.30–8
vendredi	8–19.30	19.30–8
samedi	8–12	12–8
dimanche	8–12	12–8
jours fériés	8–12	12–8

PAYS	Tarif par min. Heures pleines	Tarif par min. Heures creuses
France	0,19	0,07
UK	0,23	0,12
USA	0,23	0,12
Australie	0,49	0,34

Activity 7

Here are some instructions you might see in a **cabine téléphonique** when using a **télécarte**. Can you find for each French instruction its English equivalent?

a décrochez
b introduisez la carte ou
  faites numéro libre
c patientez SVP
d crédit
e numéro appelé
f retirez votre carte
g appel arrivé

i *incoming call*
ii *credit*
iii *number being connected*
iv *remove card*
v *insert card or dial*
  free number
vi *wait*
vii *lift receiver*

Au commissariat de police At the police station

i Pour tout papier d'identité perdu ou volé, vous devez faire **une déclaration** (*statement*) au **commissariat de police** (*police station*) le plus proche. Vous pouvez aussi informer votre consulat. Pour un objet personnel perdu à Paris, présentez-vous en personne au 36, rue des Morillons, 15ème. Pour une carte de crédit, faites une déclaration au commissariat de police après avoir téléphoné au service d'urgence de votre carte.

▶ Activity 8

To familiarize yourself with some of the vocabulary you need to describe the kind of problems you may experience in France, listen to Michel's various mishaps and fill in the blanks using the correct items from the box. Even without the recording, you may be able to work out what goes where.

> identité   faire   voiture   cartes   téléphone
> portefeuille   lunettes   clés   stylo

a Hier matin, j'ai perdu mes …….. d'appartement dans le métro.

b Après ça, j'ai laissé mon …….. en or et mes …….. à la banque.

c Juste avant midi, on m'a volé au restaurant mon …….. avec tout mon argent et mes …….. de crédit.

d Hier soir, j'ai oublié au commissariat de police ma carte d'…….. et mon parapluie tout neuf.

e Ce matin, j'ai téléphoné au commissariat, mais personne ne m'a répondu. Je crois que mon …….. est cassé.

f Alors j'ai pris ma …….., mais je ne comprends pas, elle ne démarre plus. Mais qu'est-ce que je vais …….. ?

▶ Dialogue 3

A man is at the police station reporting the theft of his car. Can you give the make, colour and number plate of his car?

Agent Monsieur?
Homme Je suis anglais, en vacances avec ma famille … On m'a volé ma voiture.

Agent	Quand ça?
Homme	La nuit dernière.
Agent	Où **était** votre véhicule?
Homme	Ma voiture? Dans la rue Gambetta devant l'hôtel du Lion d'Or.
Agent	C'est quoi votre voiture?
Homme	C'est une Volvo S70 rouge.
Agent	Quel est le numéro d'immatriculation?
Homme	Euh … AB08 PLM
Agent	Bon, nous allons essayer de la retrouver. **En attendant**, il faut faire une déclaration par écrit. Vous pouvez remplir cet imprimé?
Homme	Euh … maintenant?
Agent	Oui, tout de suite car vous en avez besoin pour vos assurances en Angleterre; mais c'est facile … c'est traduit en anglais.

était *was*   **en attendant** *in the meantime*

Activity 9

Read the dialogue again and try to spot the French version of the following phrases then write them out:

a my car was stolen ....
b what make of car is it? ....
c what's the registration number? ....
d write a statement ....
e fill in this printed form ....
f you need it for your insurance ....

Activity 10

In this last exercise, following the examples given, practise saying who lost what, where, and what it looked like. Revise how to say my, your, his, etc. (see Unit 4).

J'ai perdu ma montre en or dans le train.
I have lost my gold watch on the train.

Mon amie a perdu son sac à main en cuir marron dans le bus.
My friend has lost her brown, leather handbag on the bus.

Who	What	Description	Where
a you	your pen	gold	office
b my brother	his suitcase	brown	airport
c your sister	her purse	leather white	park
d his father	his passport	British	street
e my friend	her scarf	in silk	bus

Mini-test on Unit 19

How would you say:

1 I would like something for headaches.
2 I would like to make an appointment.
3 I've got a sore throat.
4 My handbag was stolen in the cinema.
5 My glasses are broken.

Take the final section of **Self-assessment test 2** (Units 17–19). Once you have done it, check your answers in the **Key to the exercises and tests** and write your score in the box below. If you score between 40 and 50 points, congratulate yourself. You are now a truly competent speaker of basic French. If your score is between 20 and 40 points, you need to spend more time revising the **Dialogues** and **Key words and phrases**. Below 20 points, go back over Units 17, 18 and 19, and take the test again to see how much you have improved.

Self-assessment score (Units 17–19)

Points: _____ /50

taking it further

In the **Introduction** and **Unit 4** we emphasize how important it is for language learners to create every opportunity to speak the language with other learners or French speakers, listen to some French regularly and read French material. If the idea at first seems a little daunting we give some tips in **Unit 7** to help you get the gist of what you read or listen to, or make the most of your conversations in French. Ideally you should find a 'study buddy' with whom you could work through the course and try your French out. Learning French would then become more meaningful and fun as speaking a language is about communicating with others. Going to France or one of the francophone countries would also be a most valuable experience to try the language out whilst getting direct feedback from the people you talk to. Anyhow, if this is not possible you can still get a real flavour of French in your own home by using the following:

- Newspapers (*Libération*; *Le Parisien* – found in Paris and easy to read; *Le Figaro* – the weekend issue is particularly interesting).

- Magazines (*Paris-Match*, *Marie-Claire*, *Elle*, *Cosmopolitan*).

- Satellite and/or cable TV channels (e.g. TV5 Europe, *Canal +*, *La 5ème*. For news: *CNN* and *Euronews*).

- Radio stations on long wave (*France Inter*, *RTL*, *Europe 1*), or via satellite.

- Websites:
  a to find out information relating to France:
  www.yahoo.fr or **www.wanadoo.fr** or **www.google.fr**

b to familiarize yourself with French society and institutions:

www.diplomatie.fr (a site prepared by *Le Ministère des Affaires Étrangères*)

c to read the French press on-line:

www.lemonde.fr, www.lefigaro.fr, www.liberation.fr, www.leparisien.fr

d to listen to French news in easy French with their transcription:

www.rfi.fr/lffr/statiques/accueil_apprendre.asp

- In London you can also get information and activities at *l'Institut Français*, 17 Queensberry Place, London SW7 2DT (telephone 020 7073 1350 or visit **www.institut-francais.org.uk**).

To help you monitor your overall progress with *Teach Yourself Beginner's French* we have prepared two **Self-assessment tests** covering Units 1–10 and 11–19. Each **Self-assessment test** includes a series of short self-assessment tasks after every third or fourth unit with points allocated to the answers. You will find the answers to the test questions in the **Key to the exercises and tests**. When the questions require individual responses, we usually give you model answers to guide you.

We indicate the number of points allocated to each answer, so that you can keep your own score (out of a total of 50 points per test). Here are a few guidelines to help you grade your performance:

40–50 points	Congratulations! You are ready to start the next units.
30–40 points	Very good. You have mastered most of the points covered in the last units. Try to identify the areas which still need some work and go over them again.
20–30 points	Well done, but it might be advisable to revise the areas where you are not quite so confident before moving on to the next units
Below 20 points	Not bad, but we would strongly advise you to go back over the last units. When you have done so, take the test again and see how much you have improved.

Always remember that learning a new language may take more time than you think. If you feel that it seems a bit difficult, don't be discouraged. Look back at the tips in the section **Be successful at learning languages** on page ix as well as those marked with the 🔢 symbol, and try to put them into practice. They do work!

Bon courage!

Self-assessment test 1

Units 1–3   Points: _____/50

This test covers the main vocabulary and phrases, skills and language points in Units 1–3. You can check your answers in the **Key to the exercises and tests. Bonne chance!** *Good luck!*

1   Can you do the following? Say the answers out loud and write them down. Two points for each correct answer. Check your pronunciation with the **Pronunciation guide**.

a   Introduce yourself and ask someone to introduce themselves.
b   Ask someone for their name using the formal way.
c   Ask a friend how he/she is.
d   Answer the previous question and return the question (informally).
e   Tell someone what you do in life.
f   Ask someone what their job is.
g   Say where you live (town and country).
h   Say what nationality you are and what language(s) you speak.
i   Say whether you are married or single and whether you have children.
j   Say that you don't understand.
k   Ask someone if they speak English.
l   Ask someone to speak more slowly.
m   Say your age.

Points _____ /26

2   Fill in the blanks with the right endings of the verbs *to have* or *to be*. One point for each correct answer:.

Je **a** .... anglais mais ma mère **b** ...... française. Mon père et ma mère **c** ...... mariés depuis 50 ans. J' **d** ..... trois frères qui ne **e** .... pas mariés et une soeur qui **f** ..... deux enfants. Ils **g** .... quinze et dix ans. Ma soeur et moi **h** .....un mari anglais et nous **i** .... professeures de français en Angleterre. Je n' **j** .... pas d'enfants.

Points _____ /10

▶ 3 Rôle-play

You are travelling on the train to Paris. The person sitting next to you strikes up a conversation. You are happy to practise your French. Take part in the conversation.

One point for each correct sentence. Two points when your answer consists of two correct sentences.

Points: _____ /14

Units 4–7   Points: _____/50

This test covers the main vocabulary and phrases, skills and language points in Units 4–7. For how to read your score, refer back to page 209. You can check your answers in the **Key to the exercises and tests. Bonne chance!**

4   Can you ask and say the following? Say the answers out loud and write them down. One point for each correct answer.

   a   Is it far?
   b   No, it is not far.
   c   Is there a bank nearby?
   d   No, there is not a bank nearby.
   e   Have you a stamp?
   f   No, I haven't any.
   g   What is the film like?
   h   Where is the bus stop?
   i   It is ten minutes away on foot.
   j   When does the shop open?

Points: _____ /10

5   Complete the questions by selecting the appropriate endings. One point for each correct answer.

   a   Il y a   i   c'est?
   b   Quel âge   ii vous appelez-vous?
   c   Qu'est-ce que   iii commencez vous le matin?
   d   À quelle heure   iv une île?
   e   Comment   v   une cabine téléphonique
                                   près d'ici?

Points: _____ /5

6   Using the example as a model, say these dates out loud in French, then write them out in full for practice. One point for each correct answer.

Tuesday, the 9th of November: **le mardi neuf novembre**

a   Sunday, the 31st of March
b   Wednesday, the 2nd of June
c   Friday, the 18th of January
d   Tuesday the 24th of October
e   Saturday, the 11th of May
f   Monday, the 23rd of August
g   Thursday, the 19th of September

Points: ____/7

7   Can you say the following in French? Say the answers out loud and write them down. Two points for each correct answer.

a   I have breakfast at 8.00 in the morning.
b   My mother does the cooking every day.
c   My husband and I often take the train on Mondays.
d   What do you do this weekend?
e   She always works until lunchtime.
f   At what time do you finish work?
g   Today he goes home around 20.00.
h   You have been watching TV since 10 in the morning.
i   I do not work on Sundays.

Points: ____/18

▶ 8 Rôle-play

This is the continuation of your conversation on the train (Question 3). Give yourself one point for each correct answer and two when your answer consists of two correct sentences.

Points: ____/10

Units 8–10   Points: ____/50

This test covers the main vocabulary and phrases, skills and language points in Units 8–10. You can check your answers in the **Key to the exercises and tests. Bonne chance!**

9   Look at the box overleaf and say out loud the likes and dislikes of Sophie and Mohamed. Then write down your own hobbies. One point for each correct answer.

		Sophie	Mohamed	Yourself
a	playing football	1	3	
b	cooking	3	1	
c	watching TV	3	2	
d	listening to music	4	3	
e	swimming	2	4	
f	skiing	4	1	
g	going to restaurants	2	3	
h	playing tennis	1	4	

Adore	Aime beaucoup	N'aime pas	Déteste
4	3	2	1

Points: _____/24

10 Fill in the part of the reflexive verbs which is missing. Half a point for each correct ending.

a je ..... lève
b tu ..... habilles
c il ..... lave
d nous ..... baignons
e vous ..... reposez
f elles ..... couchent

Points: _____/3

11 Talk about the weather in France, incorporating each icon on the map overleaf into a full sentence:

e.g. **chaud** → **il fait chaud.**

a À Lille, ...
b En Bretagne, ...
c Dans le Sud-Ouest ....
d Sur la Côte d'Azur ....
e Dans les Alpes...................................
f À Strasbourg ....
g À Paris ....

Points: _____/7

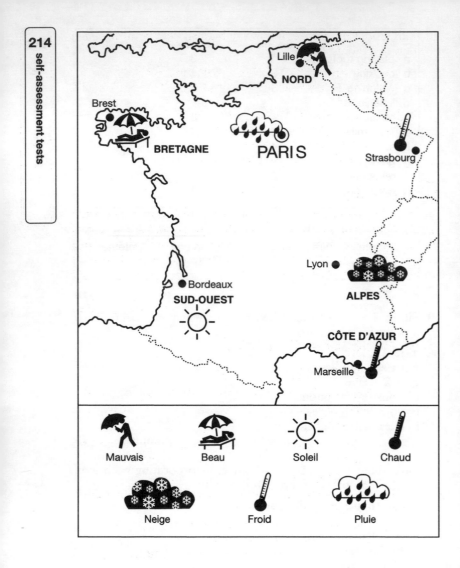

12 Talk about the future. Fill in the blanks. One point for each correct ending.

    a Qu'est-ce que vous ...... faire pour vos vacances?

    b Nous ...... passer deux semaines de vacances au bord de la mer.

    c Jane ...... visiter le sud de la France

    d Tu ...... aller voir le film ce soir?

    e Je ...... me reposer chez moi.

    f Les Durand ...... se baigner tous les jours

                                      Points: ____/6

▶ **13 Rôle-play**

On your last trip to France you stayed with a very nice French family. When you left, you invited them to go and see you. Eva phones you to arrange their visit. Agree on suitable dates. Give yourself one point for each correct answer and two when your answer consists of two correct sentences.

                                      Points: ____/10

Self-assessment test 2

Units 11–13   Points: ____/50

This test covers the main vocabulary and phrases, skills and language points in Units 11–13. You can check your answers in the **Key to the exercises and tests. Bonne chance!**

1 Can you do the following? Say the answers out loud and write them down. Three points for each correct answer.

    a Say that you are looking for a cotton dress.

    b Give the English translation for **Vous faites quelle taille?**

    c Ask whether you can try it on.

    d Say that it is a bit too expensive/big/small.

    e Ask: Do you have anything else?

                                   Points: ____/15

2 Say the following out loud and write them down. Three points for each correct answer.

    a Say good evening and ask if they have a double room with bathroom.

    b Say that it is for two nights.

    c Ask for the price.

    d Ask if breakfast is included.

e Ask whether there is a restaurant in the hotel.
f Say that the television does not work.

Points: _____/18

▶ 3 Rôle-play

You are on holiday in France. It is lunchtime and you are hungry. You see a restaurant which looks attractive. You enter and order some food. Give yourself one point for each correct answer and two when your answer consists of two correct sentences.

Points: _____/17

Units 14–16   Points: _____/50

This test covers the main vocabulary and phrases, skills and language points in Units 14–16. You can check your answers in the **Key to the exercises and tests. Bonne chance!**

4   You are in the **Office de Tourisme** in Paris. Can you do the following? Say the answers out loud and write them down. Three points for each correct answer.

   a Find out whether they can book a room for you.
   b Ask for a town map.
   c Find out how to go to the Eiffel tower.
   d Ask what they've got in the way of excursions.
   e Ask what there is to do for the children.
   f Ask for a list of restaurants.
   g Ask the attendant to show you the **grands magasins** on the map.

Points : _____/21

▶ 5 Rôle-play

You are at the ticket office in the Gare du Nord in Paris. You want to go and spend a weekend in Brussels with your partner. Give yourself one point for each correct answer and two when your answer consists of two correct sentences.

Points:_____ /15

6   The text overleaf describes the range of excursions available to tourists visiting Paris and the Île-de-France. Read the text and say whether the assertions are **vrai** or **faux**. One point when your assertions are correct. Two points when you give a full answer.

Excursions et balades

Dans un grand autocar de prestige avec climatisation, dans un minibus tout aussi confortable, installés à ciel ouvert sur la plate-forme panoramique du pont supérieur de l'autobus à impériale ou à bord d'un train touristique de quartier, pour deux heures ou pour une journée, découvrez Paris avec des guides polyglottes, des commentaires culturels et des circuits à thème. Les audio-guides fournis disposent de commentaires en plusieurs langues (jusqu'à 14 différentes). Dans les minibus, les chauffeurs sont multilingues. Les programmes sont organisés en journée et en soirée, été comme hiver. Nos fiches vous donnent le détail de leurs offres et vous pourrez réserver auprès des excursionnistes ou par l'intermédiaire de l'Office de Tourisme la formule que vous préférez: une matinée, un après-midi ou une journée, avec ou sans repas.

	vrai	faux
a The publicity refers to coach and minibus excursions.	☐	☐
b Tourists can sit on open top buses.	☐	☐
c Tourists have access to films and polyglot guides to discover Paris.	☐	☐
d Tourists are advised to buy audio-guides.	☐	☐
e Audio-guides are necessary because drivers do not speak foreign languages.	☐	☐
f Excursions are organized during daytime in summer and in winter.	☐	☐
g The Tourist Office books the tours.	☐	☐

Points: ___/14

Units 17–19   Points: _____/50

This test covers the main vocabulary and phrases, skills and language points in Units 17–19. You can check your answers in the **Key to the exercises and tests. Bonne chance!**

7 You are staying in 'Les Edelweiss', 7, Boulevard Latapie-Flurin in the centre of Cauterets. Some French friends from Paris phone you and want to go hiking with you. Can you do the following? Look at the information below and say the answers out loud. Three points for each correct answer.

a Ask whether they are coming by car or train (translate: *take the car or train*).

b Give directions if they choose to come by train.

c Give directions if they choose to come by car and tell them that they can park the car opposite the hotel.

d Give them your address and say that the hotel is in the centre of Cauterets.

e Fix a date and time: Friday 22nd April around seven o'clock in the evening.

Points : _____/15

CAUTERETS

Hautes-Pyrénées (65) - Midi-Pyrénées – Altitude 932 m. – 1336 habitants - Paris 899 km – Capacité d'accueil: 22 000 lits

Accès par avion: Aéroport de Tarbes: 35 km de Cauterets
Accès par train: Gare SNCF à Lourdes puis bus jusqu'à Cauterets (30 km)
Accès par voiture: Autoroute jusqu'à Tarbes, puis la N21 et la D921

---

8 Match up the words in the left-hand column with the correct English translation in the right-hand column. One point for each correct answer.

a	la monnaie	i	*banknote*
b	un changeur de monnaie	ii	*banker's card*
c	un distributeur automatique	iii	*bill (drinks, snacks)*
d	une carte bancaire	iv	*exchange rate*
e	la pièce	v	*coin changing machine*
f	la télécarte	vi	*a cashpoint machine*
g	un billet	vii	*means of identification*
h	le cours du change	viii	*bill (hotel)*
i	l'addition	ix	*telephone card*
j	la note	x	*coin*
k	la pièce d'identité	xi	*small change*

Points: _____/11

▶ **9 Rôle-play**

You want to change some money in a French bank. Follow the prompts. One point for each correct sentence. Two points when your answer consists of two correct sentences.

Points: ___/10

10 You have damaged your knee after two days of skiing in Cauterets. As you need to see the doctor you speak to the hotel receptionist. Say the answers out loud and write them down. Two points for each correct answer.

a Tell the receptionist that you need to see a doctor.
b Ask for his/her address.
c Ring the doctor and say that you want an appointment.
d Explain that your knee (**le genou**) is sore.
e Say that you have been suffering for three days.
f Say that you cannot walk.
g Tell the receptionist that you can come tomorrow morning at ten o'clock.
h Say your name and spell it.

Points: _____/14

key to the exercises and tests

Unit 1

Activities: 1 **a** Bonjour Madame/Mademoiselle **b** Bonjour
Monsieur **c** Bonsoir Madame/Mademoiselle **d** Bonjour
Messieurs-dames **e** Bonne nuit, Monsieur **f** Bonsoir Messieurs-
dames 2 Bonsoir Monsieur 3 **c** 4 Bonne nuit 5 Comment ça
va? Très bien merci. 6 **a** s'il vous plaît **b** ça va **c** au revoir
d madame **e** bonsoir **f** non merci 7 **a** iii, **b** ii, **c** iii, **d** iii
Mini-test: 1 Bonjour, comment ça va? 2 Parlez plus
lentement, s'il vous plaît 3 Pardon 4 D'accord

Unit 2

Have a go!: Bonjour Madame. Je voudrais une baguette, s'il
vous plaît.
Dialogue: Beer, wine and two bottles of mineral water; no,
she doesn't get any beer
Activities: 1 **a** un café **b** une bière **c** un journal **d** des
bouteilles **e** un euro **f** un timbre 2 une chambre, un café, un
journal 3 **a** Je voudrais quatre cartes, s'il vous plaît **b** Vous
avez quatre timbres? **c** Et de l'aspirine, s'il vous plaît? **d** C'est
combien? 4 trois 5 **a** ii, **b** iv, **c** iii, **d** i 6 **a** Messieurs-dames
b café **c** bière **d** voudrais **e** addition 7 **a** cinq **b** neuf **c** dix
d neuf **e** deux **f** quatre **g** neuf **h** huit
Mini-test: 1 I haven't got any 2 Je voudrais l'addition 3 Vous
avez de l'aspirine, s'il vous plaît? Merci, au revoir 4 Je
voudrais une bouteille d'eau minérale

Unit 3

Have a go!: Je voudrais deux bouteilles de bière et un kilo
d'oranges.
Dialogue: Yes, part-time in a travel agency; 3 children – a girl
and 2 boys; Jane is not married, she has a boyfriend.

Practise!: travaille, travailles, travaille, travaillons, travaillez, travaillent
Activities: 1 a 13 **b** 18 **c** 4 **d** 12 **e** 7 **f** 19 **g** 5 **h** 15 **i** 11 **j** 9 **2 a** treize **b** quinze **c** vingt **d** treize **e** dix-neuf **f** onze **g** cinq **h** six **i** quatre **j** douze **3 a** est **b** ont **c** Elles **d** enfants, un **e** n'a pas **f** n'est pas **g** dix **h** a, ans **4 a** n'ai pas de timbres **b** n'a pas de café **c** n'est pas marié **d** n'est pas secrétaire **e** n'ai pas de chambre **f** n'ont pas d'enfants **g** n'est pas dans le nord de l'Angleterre **h** ne parle pas français **i** n'a pas 18 ans
5 a Je m'appelle Anne **b** Non, je suis mariée **c** Oui, j'ai deux enfants **d** Une fille et un garçon **e** Ils ont douze et dix ans **f** J'habite Chaville **g** Oui, je suis secrétaire **6 a** Vous êtes marié?
b Vous avez des enfants? **c** Vous travaillez? **d** Vous habitez Paris? **e** Vous avez des frères et soeurs? **f** Ils ont quel âge?
g Vous êtes français? **h** Vous parlez anglais?
Mini-test: 1 Parlez plus lentement, s'il vous plaît **2 b 3** I don't understand **4** Je voudrais une bouteille de vin, s'il vous plaît
5 C'est combien? **6 a** Je m'appelle **b** Je ne suis pas marié(e)
c J'habite (à) Brighton **d** Je travaille à Londres

Unit 4

Have a go!: Vous êtes français(e)? Vous êtes marié(e)? Je m'appelle … et vous? Vous travaillez?
Dialogue: Yes; Yes; Yes; 3 children
Activities: 1 a v **b** i **c** vii **d** viii **e** iii **f** ii **g** vi **h** iv **2** (*Note that there are alternative ways of asking these questions*) **a** Il y a un restaurant dans l'hôtel? **b** Il y a une pharmacie près d'ici?
c Il y a des magasins près d'ici? **d** La banque est ouverte? **e** Il y a un train direct pour Paris? **f** C'est loin la gare? **g** Où sont les toilettes? **3 a** Il y a une pharmacie mais il n'y a pas d'aspirine
b Il y a une pâtisserie mais il n'y a pas de croissants **c** Il y a une gare mais il n'y a pas de trains **d** Il y a un arrêt d'autobus mais il n'y a pas de bus **e** Il y a un bar mais il n'y a pas de bière **f** Il y a une cabine téléphonique mais il n'y a pas de téléphone **4 a** Vous êtes en vacances? **b** Vous êtes mariée?
c Vous avez des enfants? **d** Vous habitez Londres? **e** Vous travaillez? **5 a** combien **b** où **c** quand **d** où **e** où **f** comment
6 a 49€50 **b** 3€75 **c** 8€60 **d** 56€15 **e** 68€
Mini-test: 1 Vous vous appelez comment? **2** Vous travaillez?
3 Vous habitez où? J'habite dans la banlieue de Londres **4** J'ai … ans **5** Il y a une banque près d'ici au bout de la rue

Unit 5

Have a go!: Vous avez un plan, s'il vous plaît? Il y a une banque et une cabine téléphonique près d'ici? *You can find more questions to ask in* **Key words and phrases** *of Unit 4.*
Practise!: on rentre quand? on peut prendre le petit-déjeuner quand? le concert finit quand? **Dialogue:** 8.30 a.m. and 5.30 p.m.; school canteen
Activities: 2 a prends **b** commencent **c** arrive **d** apprend **e** déjeune **f** prenez **g** fais **h** est **i** finit **j** faites **k** attendons **l** comprennent **3 a** iii, **b** vii, **c** v, **d** i, **e** ii, **f** iv, **g** vi **4 f**, e, a, c, g, d, h, b **5 a** prends **b** prennent **c** commence **d** travaille **e** déjeune **f** finit **g** fait **h** regardent **6** le 1er mai, le 10 juin, le 3 février, le 13 octobre, le 21 mars, le 30 septembre, le 15 juillet, le 6 août **7 a** mercredi **b** vendredi **c** dimanche **d** lundi **e** jeudi **f** samedi **g** mardi **8 a** il est neuf heures dix (du matin) **b** midi moins vingt **c** une heure et demie (de l'après-midi) **d** six heures vingt-cinq (du soir) **h** minuit moins dix
Mini-test: 1 dimanche, samedi, vendredi, jeudi, mercredi, mardi, lundi **2** Quand est-ce que la banque ferme?/la banque ferme quand? **3** Il y a un train pour Lille? **4** Est-ce que je peux prendre le petit-déjeuner à l'hôtel? **5** (Nous sommes le …) Aujourd'hui c'est le … Il est …

Unit 6

Have a go!: 1 Vous pouvez parler plus lentement? Vous pouvez répéter, s'il vous plaît? **2** *Use the dialogue and* **Key words and phrases** *of Unit 5*
Dialogue: As you leave the house turn left, go to the end of rue Vaugirard, turn right into rue Vincennes and the park is 200 metres on your left. It takes approximately 25 minutes.
Activities: 1 a Pour aller à la piscine? **b** Pour aller à la gare? **c** Pour aller à l'église St. Paul? **d** Pour aller au musée? **e** Pour aller à l'office du tourisme? **2 a** C **b** E **c** A **d** D **e** B **4** à Brighton, en France, l'Allemagne, à Berlin, à Bonn, au Danemark, aux États-Unis, au Japon, à Londres **5 a** en face du **b** à côté de la **c** au coin de **d** entre **e** au bout de **f** grands magasins **g** bar **h** pâtisserie **i** dans la rue **j** sur la place

Unit 7

Have a go!: 1 dans **2** sur **3** entre **4** à côté du **5** sous **6** devant **7** derrière
Dialogue: the big scarves are too expensive, Vous pouvez me faire un paquet-cadeau, s'il vous plaît?

Activities: 1 cet, ces, ce, ces, ce, cet, cette, cette **2** Mme Durand a 35 ans. Elle a les cheveux blonds et longs. Elle a les yeux verts. Elle fait 1,70 mètre et pèse 65 kg. Elle porte des lunettes rondes. Elle porte un ensemble vert uni, des chaussures légères et une chemise blanche. Jane a 23 ans. Elle a les cheveux bruns et courts. Ses yeux sont bleus (Elle a les yeux bleus). Elle fait 1,62 mètre et pèse 55 kg. Elle porte un jean bleu pâle et un pull-over blanc. Elle a (porte) des bottes noires. **3 a** une boîte de petits pois français **b** une tarte aux pommes **c** un baba au rhum **d** une glace à la vanille **e** un sorbet au citron **f** un grand verre de vin rouge **g** un café au lait sans sucre **h** un poulet à 6€80 **i** un petit café noir **j** un sandwich au fromage **k** une bouteille de lait **4 a** Chère **b** famille **c** tout **d** sympathique **e** bonnes **f** confortable **g** grande **h** longues **i** jours **j** meilleure **k** anglaise **l** mieux **m** prochaine **5 a** un grand café noir **b** deux pressions **c** et un petit crème **d** non, deux pressions, un petit crème et un grand café noir **e** Vous avez des croissants? **f** J'en voudrais quatre
Mini-test: 1 a au bout de la rue **b** Prenez la route pour Lille **2 b 3 a 4** Vous avez autre chose? C'est de quelle couleur? Je vais prendre le plus petit

Unit 8

Have a go!: Je cherche quelque chose pour ouvrir les bouteilles de vin.
Dialogue: Cooking French dishes; squash, swimming, wind-surfing.
Activities: 1 a Comment vous appelez-vous? Je m'appelle Roger Burru. **b** Quel âge avez-vous? J'ai 35 ans. **c** Vous êtes marié? Oui, je suis marié? **d** Vous avez des enfants? Non, je n'ai pas d'enfants. **e** Qu'est-ce que vous faites dans la vie? Je suis professeur. **f** Depuis quand? Depuis 10 ans. **g** Où habitez-vous? J'habite Lille. **h** Qu'est-ce que vous faites comme sport? Je fais de la natation. **i** Vous faites quoi pendant vos loisirs? J'aime beaucoup faire la cuisine. **2** e, c, a, adore, d, g aime beaucoup, f, b n'aime pas, h déteste **3 a** la regarde **b** le connaissez **d** les **a e** l'ai **f** l'aiment **g** la fais **h** l'attendons **i** la regarde **j** les écoutons **4 a** viii, **b** vii, **c** iv, **d** ii, **e** ix, **f** x, **g** iii, **h** vi, **i** v, **j** i, **5 a** F **b** F **c** V **d** V **e** V **f** F **g** V **h** V **i** F **j** F **k** V **l** F
Mini-test: 1 Je joue au squash mieux que Fabrice **2** La France est plus grande que l'Angleterre **3** Elle a des lunettes et des cheveux longs **4** Je cherche quelque chose pour réparer ma voiture **5** J'aime le squash mais je préfère jouer au tennis **6** J'aime beaucoup la cuisine française.

Unit 9

Have a go!: 1 a Vous pouvez répéter, s'il vous plaît? b Vous pouvez parler plus lentement s'il vous plaît?

Activities: 1 a v, b vii, c ix, d vi, e iii, f viii, g ii, h iv, i i 2 a iv, b v, c i, d vi, e ii, f iii 3 a C b F c B d D e A f E; i 7 ii add pepper and salt iii 30 g of butter iv when the butter is hot v a fork 4 a v, b iv, c vii, d vi, e i, f ii, g iii

Practise!: It is strictly forbidden to take photographs using a tripod or flash; to damage the sculptures or the vases; to pick flowers or fruit; to climb on the sculptures; to walk on the lawn or to climb on the seats; to lunch outside the area reserved for the cafeteria; to bring animals into the museum's grounds; to ride a bicycle; to play ball games; to drop rubbish except in the litter baskets.

Mini-test: 1 Aujourd'hui il fait froid mais il ne pleut pas. 2 Qu'est-ce qu'il faut faire? 3 Il me faut une télécarte pour téléphoner. 4 a la direction de la gare? b où est la station de métro la plus proche? c l'adresse du docteur?

Unit 10

Have a go!: 1 Out of order 2 Qu'est-ce qu'il faut faire pour utiliser l'Internet?

Dialogue: 4 weeks; to the seaside and to the mountains; swimming, play tennis, go for long walks and see regional historic monuments. No, she prefers to stay at home or go out to a night club with friends.

Practise!: Je m'habille, tu t'habilles, il/elle/on s'habille, nous nous habillons, vous vous habillez, ils s'habillent

Activities: *Activities 1, 2, 3, 4, 5, could have alternative answers to the ones given below:* 1 a D'abord je me lève à 7 heures b puis je me lave c ensuite je prends le petit-déjeuner avec les enfants d À 8h30 j'emmène les enfants à l'école e ensuite je fais des courses f À midi je prépare le déjeuner g L'après-midi, je joue au tennis h ou je vais chez mes amis i ou je vais au cinéma j Le soir, je regarde la télévision k ou j'écoute la radio l enfin je me couche à 23 heures. 2 a …il/elle se lève … b …il/elle se lave … c …il/elle prend … d il/elle emmène … e …il/elle va … f …il/elle rentre, prépare … g il/elle joue … h …il/elle va chez ses amis … i il/elle va … j il/elle regarde … k il/elle écoute … l il/elle se couche … 3 *Robert:* a en août b 3 semaines c à Oxford en Angleterre d Je vais apprendre l'anglais, visiter des monuments historiques, voir des amis, sortir le soir, jouer au tennis. *Jeanine:* a le 21 juin b 10 jours c à Anglet près de Biarritz dans le sud de la France d Je vais me baigner, lire beaucoup, regarder un peu la télévision, faire de longues promenades, me coucher tôt. **4 a** Vous allez partir quand en vacances? **b** Où allez-vous aller? **c** Comment allez-vous passer vos vacances? **5 a** beaucoup **b** mari **c** Grande-Bretagne **d** finit **e** samedi **f** après-midi **g** rester **h** jours **i** visiter **j** habitent **k** besoin **l** prendre **6 a** téléphoner à Marc **b** aller chez le dentiste **c** aller à la banque **d** faire des courses et acheter 2 steaks, une bouteille de vin et une glace à la fraise **e** écrire une lettre à sa mère **f** poster la lettre **g** jouer au tennis **h** faire la cuisine **i** inviter Anne à dîner

Mini-test: 1 a Vous pouvez m'aider s'il vous plaît? **b** Je ne comprends pas. Vous pouvez répéter s'il vous plaît? **2 a** il a besoin d'un jus de fruit/d'un verre d'eau/de boire **b** avons besoin d'une banque/d'un distributeur automatique **c** ont besoin de manger/de sandwiches **d** ai besoin d'un docteur/d'aller chez le docteur **3 a** vont **b** va **c** vont **d** vas **e** vais **f** allons

Unit 11

Activities: 1 a 7/8 p.m. **b** shut **c** Monday **d** pâtisseries, charcuteries **e** No **3 a**, **c** boucherie, **d**, **e**, **g** épicerie, **b** boulangerie, **f** charcuterie **4 c**, **f**, **h**, **a**, **e**, **d**, **g**, **i**, **b 5 b**, **d**, **g**, **l 7 a** Confection **b** Pressing **c** Généraliste **d** Librairie **e** Informatique **f** Bijouterie **g** Chaussures **h** Lingerie – Vêtements **i** Traiteur **j** Cave – Marchand de Vin **8 a** bargain lovers **b** come down **c** reduction **d** special offers **e** F – also for fashion and thousands of other items **f** F – the previous season's **g** F – they cannot exceed six weeks **h** V **9 a** Je cherche une jupe noire **b** Vous faites quelle taille? **c** quelque chose de moins cher **d** Je vais essayer **e** la jupe à 63€ **f** Elle vous va bien? **10 a** Je voudrais un journal, s'il vous plaît. Vous avez/vendez quels journaux anglais? **b** Je vais prendre le *Times* et ces trois cartes postales. C'est combien un timbre pour l'Angleterre? **c** Je vais prendre huit timbres **d** Je vais aussi acheter le magazine 'Elle' pour ma femme **11 a** pullover **b** white/pale yellow **c** it's too big **d** he doesn't like the colour **e** 68€50 **f** at the cash desk

Mini-test: 1 J'ai besoin de kleenex **2** Je voudrais quelque chose de plus grand, s'il vous plaît **3** Vous avez autre chose? **4** C'est tout **5** Vous acceptez les cartes de crédit?

Unit 12

Activities: 1 a villa meublée et équipée **b** hôtel **c** résidence de tourisme **d** chambre d'hôte **2 a** ii **b** xiv **c** xii **d** vi **e** xv **f** iv **g** viii **h** xvii **i** xi **j** i **k** x **l** ix **m** iii **n** v **o** vii **p** xiii **q** xvi **3 a** Je viens d'arriver **b** Vous pouvez me réserver une chambre? **c** C'est où le seizième arrondissement? **d** Nous voulons aussi une douche ou une salle de bains **e** J'espère que l'hôtel n'est pas complet **f** Il y a des chambres de libre **4 a** F – on the second **b** F – it is on top **c** F – from 7.30 **d** V **e** F – at the end of the corridor on the right **f** V **g** V **5** Bonsoir, vous avez une chambre, s'il vous plaît? Non, une chambre double à deux lits et avec salle de bains. C'est pour quatre nuits. C'est combien? C'est quoi, une promotion? Est-ce que le petit-déjeuner est compris? À quelle heure servez-vous le petit-déjeuner? On peut prendre un repas dans l'hôtel? Haussman c'est qui? **6 a** Le radiateur ne marche pas **b** Il n'y a pas de savon **c** Il n'y a pas d'eau chaude **d** La lampe ne marche pas **e** Il n'y a pas de serviettes **f** La douche ne marche pas **g** La télévision ne marche pas **h** Il n'y a pas de couvertures **7 a** electricity, water facilities, water sewage **b** restaurant, food shop, launderette, ironing, television, children's playground, organized entertainment **c** cycling, swimming in the pool, fishing, mini-golf **d** bowling **9 i** l'entretien **ii** remboursement **iii** caution **iv** retard **v** draps et linge **vi** aviser **10** Suggestions **a** Combien de personnes peuvent dormir dans le mobil-home? **b** Faut-il/Est-ce qu'il faut amener les draps et les serviettes? **c** Acceptez-vous/Est-ce que vous acceptez le chiens sans supplément? **d** Quand faut-il/est-ce qu'il faut payer la caution/Il faut payer la caution quand?
Mini-test: 1 Je cherche un hôtel à deux étoiles **2** Vous pouvez me réserver une chambre, s'il vous plaît? **3** Le petit-déjeuner est compris? **4** Il n'y a pas de téléphone dans la chambre **5** Il y a un camping près d'ici? **5** C'est combien l'emplacement pour une voiture, deux personnes et une caravane pour huit jours?

Unit 13

Activities: 1 a a variety of cuisines **b** can easily be found **c** usually cheap **d** meat, vegetables or noodles **e** a limited range of dishes **f** today's special **g** a crêperie **h** le menu touristique **2 c** e b f d a **3 a** Je voudrais un croque-monsieur **b** Vous avez des omelettes? **c** Qu'est-ce que c'est 'Parmentier'? **d** Je vais prendre l'omelette Parmentier **e** Qu'est-ce que vous avez comme jus de fruit? **f** Je voudrais un jus d'ananas et l'addition, s'il vous plaît **5 a** C'est quoi 'L'oeuf cocotte au foie gras'? **b** C'est deux oeufs cuits au four **c** Je crois que je préfère … **d** Vous le servez avec quoi le steak? **e** Vous pouvez me conseiller pour le vin? **f** Vous pouvez expliquer le nom de la tarte? **g** Amenez l'addition après le dessert **6 a** Pour commencer je vais prendre un filet de hareng **b** Alors je vais prendre un avocat à la vinaigrette **c** Qu'est-ce que c'est le cassoulet? **d** Je n'aime pas les haricots. Je préfère prendre la grillade du jour avec frites **e** A point. Je voudrais aussi une bouteille de Sauvignon **f** Qu'est-ce que vous avez comme desserts? **g** Je vais prendre une glace à la vanille **h** Qu'est-ce que vous avez comme autres parfums? **i** Je vais prendre une glace à la fraise **7** L'Auberge Au boin coin. It provides special menus for children and offers a family type atmosphere in the country.

Mini-test: 1 a Où est le restaurant le plus proche? **b** Je cherche quelque chose de moins cher **c** Vous avez autre chose? **2 a 3 a** Il n'y a plus de sandwiches au fromage **b** Comme dessert, je vais prendre une glace à la vanille **c** Qu'est ce que vous avez comme boissons?

Unit 14

Activities: 1 a V **b** F **c** F **d** F **e** V **f** V **g** F **2 a** direction **b** prenez **c** changer **d** mener **e** manquerez **3** He needs to take the underground link to Antony, then the RER B direction Charles de Gaulle or Mitry-Claye and get off at the station Gare du Nord which is after Châtelet-Les Halles **4 a** go up **b** crossroads **c** carry straight on **5 a** C'est quelle ligne pour aller à la Gare d'Austerlitz? **b** C'est direct? **c** C'est loin à pied? **d** Le prochain bus part à quelle heure? **e** Où est-ce que je peux acheter un ticket? **f** Je voudrais acheter un (ticket) aller-retour pour les Invalides **g** Je vais prendre un carnet **h** Il faut combien de temps pour arriver à la gare? **6 a** Je voudrais un (billet) aller-retour pour Paris **b** le 8 octobre dans l'après midi **c** Il (le train) met combien de temps? **d** Je ne veux pas arriver à Paris après 19 heures **e** Le train de 15.29 me convient. C'est combien le billet en deuxième classe? **f** C'est un peu cher. Il y a moins cher? **g** Je peux changer le billet? **h** Le train arrive à Paris à quelle heure? ('est trop long/ Il met trop de temps. Je vais prendre le train de 15.20. **7 a** F – in any station 'Vélib' **b** V **c** V – from the terminals you can access information, hire a bicycle and take a short term subscription using your bank card **d** F **e** V

Mini-test: 1 Je voudrais un sandwich au fromage **2** Qu'est-ce que vous avez à boire? **3** Je voudrais un carnet (de tickets) **4** A quelle heure part le prochain train pour Paris?

Unit 15

Activities: 1 a iv **b** x **c** v **d** vi **e** vii **f** viii **g** xi **h** iii **i** i **j** ix **k** ii
2 a Je voudrais un plan de la ville **b** Qu'est-ce qu'il y a à voir?
c Qu'est-ce qu'il y a à faire pour les enfants? **d** Il y a une
piscine couverte? **e** Pour aller au Parc floral, il y a un bus?
3 a Yes. There are animals, a children's play area, a miniature
golf and a little train for a ride around the park. **b** Yes. There
is a picnic area. **c** Exotic butterflies in a glasshouse and an
exhibition on insects. **4 a** C'est combien l'entrée? **b** C'est quoi
la serre? **c** douze ans; il faut payer pour le 'petit train' et le golf
miniature? **d** On peut pique-niquer? **e** Merci Madame. À
quelle heure ferme le parc? **5 a** B **b** A, C and D: on the 1st
Sunday of each month **c** A: every evening except Tuesdays
until 9 p.m. + late-night openings with some exhibitions; C:
late-night opening on Wednesdays and Fridays; D: late-night
opening on Thursdays; **d** B because of its dynamic approach in
teaching sciences and techniques: interactive games, spectacles,
etc. **6 a** 7.15 a.m. **b** one hour **c** have lunch, visit the Hospices,
the wine museum and the wine cellar **d** 184€ **7 a** Nous
voulons faire l'excursion de la route des vins de Bourgogne
b Nous voulons deux places pour le 22 juillet **c** Le car part
d'ici? **d** Vous pouvez répéter, s'il vous plaît? **e** Merci. À quelle
heure part le car? **f** On peut acheter du vin dans la cave?
8 a dimanche **b** 9.15 **c** 7 heures environ **d** le matin, visite des
appartements du château et des jardins, déjeuner dans le
restaurant du Château, l'après-midi visite du Grand Trianon et
du petit village construit pour la Reine Marie-Antoinette **e** Le
prix de l'entrée est compris dans le prix de l'excursion
f Michel offre l'excursion à Agnès parce que c'est son anniversaire
Mini-test: 1 Je voudrais un plan de la ville et des
renseignements sur la cathédrale, s'il vous plaît **2** Est-ce que le
musée ferme entre midi et deux heures? **3** Il y a une visite
guidée?

Unit 16

Activities: 1 a F in the evenings **b** F they like to dance and eat
well **c** F it is a restaurant with music, open all night **d** V **e** V **f** V
2 a E **b** D **c** C **d** B **e** A **3 a** Monday **b** his wedding anniversary
c dinner by candlelight **d** Spanish **e** 2 am **f** a dozen red roses **4**
a Je voudrais des places pour dimanche prochain. **b** Ça finit à
quelle heure le concert? **c** C'est combien la place? **d** C'est tarif
réduit. **e** Ma soeur doit payer? **5** 29, boulevard des Italiens,
those who are students, seniors, from large families,

servicemen, under 18. From 18.00 Monday to Friday except on public holidays and the days before. **6 a** Où est-ce qu'on peut jouer au tennis? **b** Où est-ce qu'on réserve le court? **c** C'est combien l'heure? **d** On peut louer une raquette? **e** Vous pouvez me donner l'adresse du club, s'il vous plaît? **7 a** i yes ii no; **b** i yes ii no; **c** i no ii yes **d** i yes ii no **e** i play table tennis ii board games
Mini-test: 1 a date-stamp **b** exit **c** connection **d** left luggage **e** platform **f** ticket office **2 a** un carnet (de tickets), s'il vous plaît **b** un aller-retour svp **c** un horaire svp **d** l'arrêt d'autobus svp? **e** le bureau de renseignements svp? **f** un aller (simple) svp? **3** c **4** c **5** a **6** place, tarif, boîte de nuit, ambiance, spectacles

Unit 17

Activities
1 a Yes **b** Yes, in wet conditions the speed limit is lowered to 110 km/h on motorways and 100 km/h on dual carriageways **c** route nationale **d** get some food, fill up the vehicle with petrol, do some shopping **e** Internet and WiFi facilities are provided in 40 service areas **f** they extend the weekend (between a public holiday and the weekend)
2 a mai, juin, **b** Ascension, Victoire 1945, Pentecôte, Fête Nationale, Assomption **c** 11–13 juillet, 1–3 août **d** avoid travelling at the weekend **3** e, c, d, b, a **4 a** Je voudrais passer une nuit dans votre hôtel. Quelles sont les directions pour Est-Artigues? **b** De Bayonne **c** Vous pouvez répétez s'il vous plaît? **d** Une fois sorti, il faut prendre aux feux à droite, sortie CourtePaille, et c'est à 500 mètres **e** Il y a un restaurant? **f** Je peux (on peut) arriver à quelle heure? **5 a** F it is free from 1 to 2 p.m., after 7 o'clock, on Sundays and bank holidays **b** V **c** F only 50 centimes, 1€, 2€ **d** F **e** V **f** V **6 a** quite difficult **b** because of a 4 kilometre long tailback on the A6 on the outskirts of Paris **c** toll gate **d** leave the A6 at Courtenay, divert onto the A19, then join the A5 to reach the Eastern part of Paris **7** pompiste a, c, f; client: b, d, e **8 a** Bonjour, je voudrais de l'essence sans plomb, s'il vous plaît **b** Non, pour 58€ **c** Vous pouvez vérifier l'huile? **d** Un litre **e** Non, merci, ça va **9 a** Vous pouvez m'aider, je suis en panne **b** Je ne sais pas, le moteur ne marche pas **c** Je suis entre Orléans et Blois sur l'autoroute A10 **d** direction/vers Tours **e** C'est une voiture anglaise: une Ford Focus blanche. Vous arrivez quand? **10 a** 2 **b** 1 **c** 4 **d** 3 **e** 5 **f** 8 **g** 6 **h** 7

Unit 18

Activities: 1 a not in the Paris region but outside Paris they do **b** the side with the € is common, the other is not **c** each country shows its national symbols **2 a** Vous pouvez changer 10€, svp? **b** Il me faut des pièces de 1€ **c** No change given **3 a** vous n'avez pas de carte bancaire? **b** il me faut cinq pièces de 1€ **c** elle n'accepte que … **d** vous pouvez changer … **e** je n'en ai pas **f** je ne sais pas **g** ça vous va? **h** Vous avez de la chance. **i** Je vais regarder. **4 a** Pardon Monsieur, vous avez de la monnaie pour le téléphone, s'il vous plaît? **b** Je n'ai qu'un billet de 5€ et il me faut des pièces de 1€ **c** Une télécarte, qu'est-ce que c'est? **d** Où est-ce que je peux acheter une télécarte? **5 a** changer **b** pièce **c** signer **d** écrire **e** combien **f** payer **6 a** Je voudrais changer des dollars **b** des dollars américains **c** des billets **d** 200 dollars; il est à combien le dollar? **e** Vous êtes ouverts le dimanche? **7 a** 5€40 **b** 7€22 **c** 19€75 **d** 22€ **e** 89€56 **f** 172€ **g** 315€40 **h** 632€15 **i** 918€30 **j** 72 centimes **8 a** after breakfast **b** 14 **c** no **d** drinks from the mini-bar **e** yes

Mini-test: 1 Il y a un parking près d'ici? **2** Il me faut quatre pièces de 1€ pour le parcmètre **3** Vous pouvez m'aider, s'il vous plaît? Je suis en panne **4** Il me faut un litre d'huile **5** Vous avez de la monnaie? **6** Vous acceptez les cartes de crédit? **7** Je voudrais régler ma note **8** Vous pouvez vérifier la pression des pneus, s'il vous plaît? **9** Vous pouvez faire le plein, s'il vous plaît? **10** Je voudrais changer cent cinquante livres en euros.

Unit 19

Activities: 1 a ii, iv **b** No **c** iii, iv **d** iii two every four hours and iv one when needed **2 a** Ma fille a mal aux dents. **b** Oui, un peu. **c** Depuis hier. **d** Merci; vous avez quelque chose pour les piqûres d'insectes? **e** Je vais la prendre; c'est combien? **3 a** vi, **b** v, **c** vii, **d** iii, **e** ii, **f** iv, **g** viii, **h** i **4 a** Je voudrais prendre rendez-vous **b** Non, c'est pour mon fils. Nous sommes anglais, en vacances ici et il a mal aux dents depuis mardi. **c** Il a 12 ans **d** aujourd'hui, ce matin ou cet après-midi **e** À quelle heure, s'il vous plaît? **f** Monsieur/ Madame … **5 a** F – it shuts at 12 **b** F – also with the Netanoo Internet terminals **c** V **d** V **e** F – WiFi is also accessible in some stations and tourist offices **f** F – they are plentiful **6 a** 8h **b** 19.30h **c** semaine **d** fériés **e** USA **f** l'Australie **g** pleines **h** creuses **7 a** vii, **b** v, **c** vi, **d** ii, **e** iii, **f** iv **g** i **8 a** clés **b** stylo, lunettes **c** portefeuille, cartes **d** identité **e** téléphone **f** voiture, faire **9 a** on m'a volé ma voiture **b** C'est quoi votre voiture? **c** quel est le numéro d'immatriculation **d** faire une déclaration par écrit **e** remplir cet imprimé **f** vous en avez besoin pour vos assurances **10 a** J'ai perdu mon stylo en or au bureau **b** mon frère a perdu sa valise marron à l'aéroport **c** ma soeur a perdu son porte-monnaie en cuir blanc au parc **d** son père a perdu son passeport britannique dans la rue **e** mon amie a perdu son foulard en soie dans l'autobus

Mini-test: 1 Je voudrais quelque chose pour le mal de tête **2** Je voudrais prendre rendez-vous **3** J'ai mal à la gorge **4** On m'a volé mon sac au cinéma **5** Mes lunettes sont cassées

Self-assessment test 1 (Units 1–10)

1a Je m'appelle …. et vous? **b** Vous vous appelez comment? / Comment vous appelez-vous? / Quel est votre nom? **c** Comment vas-tu? **d** Je vais très bien et toi? **e** Je suis dentiste. / Je travaille pour Air France/dans une banque. **f** Vous travaillez? / Qu'est-ce que vous faites dans la vie? **g** J'habite Brighton en Angleterre (dans le Sud de l'Angleterre). **h** Je suis anglais(e) et je parle anglais et allemand. **i** Je suis marié(e) et j'ai trois enfants. / Je ne suis pas marié(e) et je n'ai pas d'enfants. **j** Je ne comprends pas. **k** Vous parlez anglais? (*raise the voice on the last syllable*) **l** Parlez plus lentement. **m** J'ai … ans. **2 a** suis **b** est **c** sont **d** ai **e** sont **f** a **g** ont **h** avons **i** sommes **j** ai **4 a** C'est loin? **b** Non, ce n'est pas loin. **c** Il y a une banque près d'ici? **d** Non, il n'y a pas de banque près d'ici. **e** Avez-vous/Vous avez un timbre? **f** Non, je n'en ai pas. **g** C'est comment le film? / Le film est comment? **h** C'est où l'arrêt d'autobus? **i** C'est à dix minutes d'ici à pied. **j** Le magasin ouvre quand? / Quand est-ce que le magasin ouvre? **5 a** v **b** iv **c** i **d** iii **e** ii **6 a** le dimanche trente-et-un mars **b** le mercredi deux juin **c** le vendredi dix-huit janvier, **d** le mardi vingt-quatre octobre **e** le samedi onze mai **f** le lundi vingt-trois août **g** le jeudi dix-neuf septembre. **7 a** Je prends le petit déjeuner à huit heures du matin **b** Ma mère fait la cuisine/cuisine tous les jours **c** Mon mari et moi prenons souvent le train le lundi **d** Qu'est-ce que vous faites ce week-end? **e** Elle travaille toujours jusqu'à midi **f** À quelle heure finissez-vous le travail? **g** Aujourd'hui il rentre à la maison vers 20 heures **h** Tu regardes la TV depuis 10 heures du matin **i** Je ne travaillle pas le dimanche **9 a** Sophie déteste, Mohamed aime beaucoup, je n'aime pas jouer au football. **b** Sophie aime beaucoup, Mohamed déteste, j'adore faire la cuisine. **c** Sophie aime beaucoup, Mohamed n'aime pas, j'adore regarder la télévision. **d** Sophie adore, Mohamed aime beaucoup, j'adore écouter de la musique. **e** Sophie n'aime pas, Mohamed adore, j'aime beaucoup faire de la natation. **f** Sophie adore, Mohamed déteste, je n'aime pas faire du ski. **g** Sophie n'aime pas, Mohamed aime beaucoup, j'adore aller au restaurant. **h** Sophie déteste, Mohamed adore, et je n'aime pas jouer au tennis **10 a** me **b** t' **c** se **d** nous **e** vous **f** se **11 a** il fait mauvais **b** il fait beau **c** le soleil brille **d** il fait chaud **e** il neige **f** il fait froid **g** il pleut **12 a** allez **b** allons **c** va **d** vas **e** vais **f** vont

Self-assessment test 2 (Units 11–19)

1 a Je cherche une robe en coton **b** What size are you? **c** Je peux essayer? **d** C'est un peu trop cher/grand/petit. **e** Vous avez autre chose? **2 a** Bonsoir. Vous avez une chambre double avec salle de bains? **b** C'est pour deux nuits. **c** C'est combien? **d** Le petit-déjeuner est compris? **e** Il y a un restaurant dans l'hôtel / On peut manger dans l'hôtel? **f** La télévision ne marche pas. **4** These are only possible answers: **a** Vous pouvez (me/nous) réserver une chambre, s'il vous plaît? **b** Vous avez un plan de Paris? **c** Pour aller/Je voudrais aller à la Tour Eiffel. **d** Qu'est-ce que vous avez comme excursions? **e** Qu'est-ce qu'il y a à faire pour les enfants? **f** Vous avez une liste de restaurants? **g** Vous pouvez me montrer les grands magasins sur le plan? **6a** F – also to tourist trains **b** V – and also on air-conditioned coaches, comfortable minibuses and tourist trains **c** F – guides, cultural commentaries and theme tours **d** F – they are provided **e** F – drivers are multilingual **f** F – also during the evenings **g** F – also tour companies **7 a** Vous prenez la voiture ou le train? **b** En train vous descendez à la gare de Lourdes, puis vous prenez l'autobus jusqu'à Cauterets. Cauterets est à 30 km de Lourdes. **e** En voiture, vous prenez l'autoroute jusqu'à Tarbes, puis la N 21 et la D 921. Vous pouvez garer la voiture en face de l'hôtel. **d** 'L'Edelweiss' est situé au 7, Boulevard Latapie Flurin, au centre de Cauterets. **e** le vendredi 22 avril vers sept heures du soir. **8 a** xi **b** v **c** vi **d** ii **e** x **f** ix **g** i **h** iv **i** iii **j** viii **k** vii **10 a** J'ai besoin d'un docteur / Il me faut (voir) un docteur. **b** Quelle est son adresse? / Vous pouvez me donner son adresse? **c** Allô, je voudrais prendre rendez-vous. **d** J'ai mal au genou. **e** J'ai mal/Je souffre depuis trois jours. **f** Je ne peux pas marcher. **g** Je peux venir demain matin à dix heures. **h** Check with the **French alphabet** on page 122.

0	zéro	21 vingt et un	70 soixante-dix
1	un	22 vingt-deux	71 soixante et onze
2	deux	23 vingt-trois	72 soixante-douze,
3	trois	24 vingt-quatre	etc.
4	quatre	25 vingt-cinq	80 quatre-vingts
5	cinq	26 vingt-six	81 quatre-vingt-un
6	six	27 vingt-sept	82 quatre-vingt-deux,
7	sept	28 vingt-huit	etc.
8	huit	29 vingt-neuf	90 quatre-vingt-dix
9	neuf	30 trente	91 quatre-vingt-onze
10	dix	31 trente et un	92 quatre-vingt-douze,
11	onze	32 trente-deux, etc.	etc.
12	douze	40 quarante	100 cent
13	treize	41 quarante et un	101 cent un
14	quatorze	42 quarante-deux, etc.	102 cent deux, etc.
15	quinze	50 cinquante	200 deux cents
16	seize	51 cinquante et un	210 deux cent dix
17	dix-sept	52 cinquante-deux, etc.	300 trois cents
18	dix-huit	60 soixante	331 trois cent trente
19	dix-neuf	61 soixante et un	et un
20	vingt	62 soixante-deux, etc.	

1,000 mille   1,000,000 un million
2,000 deux mille   2,000,000 deux millions

rôle-play scripts

Unit 4

Activity 7

Tourist	Pardon, euh ... vous parlez français?
You	Seulement un petit peu.
Tourist	Je cherche une pharmacie. C'est loin d'ici?
You	Parlez plus lentement, s'il vous plaît.
Tourist	Il y a une pharmacie près d'ici?
You	Oui, Boots est à dix minutes à pied.
Tourist	Elle est ouverte maintenant?
You	Oui. Vous êtes en vacances?
Tourist	Oui, je suis en vacances avec mon fils depuis une semaine. Il y a une piscine ici?
You	Oui, il y en a une, mais elle est fermée.
Tourist	Quel dommage! Et il y a peut-être un cinéma?
You	Oui, il y en a un. Il est loin, mais l'arrêt d'autobus est au bout de la rue.
Tourist	C'est quel numéro pour l'autobus?
You	C'est le 27.

Unit 5

Activity 9

Journalist	Bonjour, je voudrais vous poser des questions sur vos occupations pendant la semaine. Vous travaillez?
You	Je travaille à Londres pour une compagnie d'assurances.
Journalist	Vous prenez le train pour aller à Londres?

You	Je prends le train à 7.20.
Journalist	Et vous commencez le travail à quelle heure?
You	Je commence à 9 heures du matin.
Journalist	Et où déjeunez-vous? À la cantine? En ville?
You	À midi, je déjeune toujours dans un restaurant avec mes collègues.
Journalist	Et le soir, vous finissez le travail à quelle heure?
You	Je finis souvent à 17.30 et quelquefois à 18.30.
Journalist	Et vous travaillez le soir chez vous?
You	Non, je regarde la télé avec ma femme.
Journalist	Ah bon. Et le week-end qu'est-ce que vous faites?
You	Le samedi après-midi, je vais à la piscine avec mes deux enfants.

Unit 6

Activity 7

Passer-by	Je ne suis pas d'ici. Vous pouvez m'aider, s'il vous plaît? Où est la banque?
You	La banque est à côté de la pharmacie.
Passer-by	Merci beaucoup. Je voudrais acheter quelques souvenirs pour ma famille. Où sont les grands magasins?
You	Ils sont en face du supermarché.
Passer-by	Il faut combien de temps pour aller au supermarché?
You	Il faut environ 15 minutes à pied.
Passer-by	Merci. Et ... où est la poste?
You	Elle est en face du café.
Passer-by	Elle est ouverte maintenant?
You	Elle est fermée mais elle ouvre à 2 heures.
Passer-by	Et où est la piscine à Chatou?
You	Il faut aller tout droit jusqu'au pont, tourner à gauche, prendre la première à droite. La piscine est en face du parc.
Passer-by	Ah merci beaucoup.

Unit 7

Activity 6

| Paul | Allô Rosine, c'est Paul ici. Tu arrives quand à Paris? |
| You | J'arrive le 13 février. |

Paul	Le mardi 13 février?
You	Non, le 13 février c'est un mercredi.
Paul	Ah pardon. Et tu arrives comment?
You	Je prends l'Eurostar de Londres à Paris.
Paul	Ah très bien. Tu arrives mercredi matin?
You	Non, l'après-midi. Le train arrive à 17.19 à la Gare du Nord.
Paul	Bon je viendrai te chercher à la gare. Je suis grand et mince et j'ai les yeux bleus. Et toi, tu es comment?
You	Je suis petite et mince et je porte des lunettes.
Paul	Tu as les cheveux comment?
You	Ils sont longs et blonds.
Paul	Écoute, je porterai un jean et un T-shirt rouge, et toi?
You	Des bottes noires, une chemise verte et un pantalon blanc.
Paul	D'accord, et j'aurai aussi le journal *Le Monde* à la main. Eh bien, à mercredi Rosine, et bon voyage.

Unit 8

Activity 6

Presenter	Alors vous faites beaucoup de sport?
You	Je déteste le sport, mais mon petit ami fait du sport trois fois par semaine.
Presenter	Et la cuisine vous aimez la faire?
You	Je n'aime pas faire la cuisine. Je cuisine pendant la semaine et mon petit ami toujours le week-end.
Presenter	Bien. Et vous faites quoi pendant vos loisirs?
You	J'adore écouter de la musique classique.
Presenter	Et votre ami, qu'est-ce qu'il aime?
You	Il écoute du jazz et regarde la télé.
Presenter	Et vous la télé, vous la regardez?
You	Je ne la regarde plus, parce qu'il n'y a rien à regarder.
Presenter	Et vous sortez ensemble? Vous allez au cinéma?
You	J'aime le cinéma français, mais mon petit ami ne regarde que les films américains.
Presenter	Et le restaurant vous y allez souvent?
You	Nous adorons aller au restaurant et nous y allons deux ou trois fois par mois.
Presenter	Quelles cuisines aimez-vous?
You	J'aime la cuisine française, mais il aime la cuisine italienne.

Presenter Eh bien, il me semble qu'il faut vous trouver un autre petit ami!

Unit 9

Activity 5

You Pardon, Monsieur, je voudrais utiliser l'Internet. Vous pouvez m'aider?

Man Mais bien sûr. Alors il faut d'abord mettre l'ordinateur en marche. Puis après ça, il faut aller dans « menu » et ...

You Je ne comprends pas. Vous pouvez parlez plus lentement s'il vous plaît?

Man Il faut appuyer sur le bouton « marche/arrêt » sur le clavier et puis il faut aller dans « menu » et ...

You Où est l'Internet?

Man L'Internet? Il faut aller dans « menu », sélectionner Internet et cliquer dessus.

You C'est quoi « cliquer »?

Man « Cliquer »? ça veut dire que vous appuyez dessus avec la souris.

You Mais ça ne marche pas.

Man Vous avez dû mal cliquer. Il faut cliquer deux fois avec le doigt ...

You Vous pouvez me montrer?

Man Euh ... je suis occupé pour le moment. Donnez-moi cinq minutes et je viens vous aider.

You D'accord, je vais attendre.

Unit 10

Activity 7

Michel Qu'est-ce que vous allez faire pour vos vacances cet été?

You Je vais aller au Portugal.

Michel Vous y allez seul où avec votre famille?

You Avec ma femme et mes deux enfants qui ont treize et onze ans.

Michel Quand partez-vous au Portugal?

You Nous y allons pendant le mois d'août.

Michel Et vous y resterez combien de temps?

You Nous allons passer deux semaines au bord de la mer.

Michel Vous allez descendre à l'hôtel? Vous allez faire du camping?

You	Nous avons de très bons amis anglais au Portugal.
Michel	Ah c'est bien. Et comment allez-vous passer vos vacances?
You	Les enfants vont jouer au tennis le matin et se baigner l'après-midi.
Michel	Et vous et votre femme, qu'allez-vous faire pendant la journée?
You	Nous allons nous reposer et nous promener.
Michel	Et le soir?
You	Nous allons lire ou parler avec nos amis.
Michel	Et les enfants? Ils vont sortir le soir?
You	Oui, ils peuvent sortir en boîte avec leurs amis.

Self-assessment test 1

Activity 3

Man	Vous êtes anglaise?
You	Non, je suis américaine. (1)
Man	Vous habitez en Angleterre?
You	J'habite à Cambridge, /mais je suis de Chicago. (2)
Man	Et qu'est-ce que vous faites à Cambridge? Vous étudiez? Vous ...
You	Parlez plus lentement, s'il vous plaît. (1)
Man	Vous travaillez à Cambridge?
You	Oui, je travaille pour les touristes américains. (1)
Man	Vous êtes mariée avec un Anglais?
You	Je ne suis pas mariée/mais j'ai un petit ami anglais. (2)
Man	Il travaille aussi à Cambridge?
You	Il travaille à Londres./Il est comptable. (2)
Man	Et vous avez des enfants?
You	J'ai deux enfants. (1)
Man	Des filles ou des garçons?
You	Une fille et un garçon. (1)
Man	Ils ont quel âge?
You	Ils ont dix ans et cinq ans. (1)
Man	Et vos parents, ils habitent avec vous?
You	Non, ils habitent aux USA. (1)
Man	Vous parlez bien le français?
You	Non, seulement un peu. (1)

Activity 8

Man	Vous connaissez déjà Paris?
You	Non, c'est la première fois/que je vais à Paris. (2)

Man	Et vous restez combien de temps à Paris?
You	Une semaine. (1)
Man	Vous allez dans un hôtel?
You	Non, j'ai des amis américains/qui habitent Paris. (2)
Man	Qu'est-ce qu'ils font dans la vie?
You	Il est journaliste/et elle ne travaille pas. (2)
Man	Ah, c'est bien ... et ils habitent où à Paris?
You	Ils habitent dans le seizième arrondissement près du Bois de Boulogne. (1)
Man	Quelle coïncidence! J'habite aussi dans le seizième. Vous prenez un taxi pour aller chez vos amis?
You	Non, les taxis sont trop chers. (1)
Man	Eh bien, ma femme m'attend à la gare avec la voiture. Venez avec nous!
You	Merci beaucoup, Monsieur.

Activity 13

Eva	Allô, c'est Eva ici. Lionel et moi aimerions vous rendre visite pour nos vacances. Vous pouvez nous recevoir cet été?
You	Je ne parle pas très bien français./Vous pouvez parler plus lentement? (2)
Eva	Est-ce que nous pouvons rester chez vous pendant le mois d'août?
You	Vous voulez venir quand au mois d'août? (1)
Eva	Nous souhaitons venir du 1er au 15 août.
You	Je suis vraiment désolée/mais je ne peux pas en août. (2)
Eva	Ah quel dommage!
You	Mon mari et moi sommes au Canada du 20 juillet au 20 août. (1)
You	Je voudrais beaucoup vous voir./Vous pouvez changer les dates de vos vacances? (2)
Eva	Si vous préférez, on peut venir au début du mois de septembre?
You	Ces dates sont plus pratiques pour nous. (1)
Eva	Alors c'est parfait. Je peux prendre le billet pour septembre?
You	Oui. Vous pouvez acheter le billet. (1)

Self-assessment test 2

Activity 3

You	J'ai très faim/et je voudrais manger. (2)
Waiter	Alors ... c'est pour une personne? Suivez-moi. Cette table vous convient?
You	Oui, c'est parfait./Qu'est-ce que vous avez comme menus? (2)
Waiter	Nous avons le menu touristique à 15€ et le menu gastronomique à 21€.
You	Je vais prendre le menu à 15€. (1)
Waiter	Très bien. Alors comme entrée il y a l'assiette de crudités et comme plat principal du magret de canard.
You	C'est quoi le magret de canard? (1)
Waiter	C'est du filet cuit selon notre recette maison. Vous la voulez comment la cuisson?
You	Bien cuite./Je déteste la viande saignante. (2) Qu'est-ce que vous servez comme légumes? (1)
Waiter	Alors le canard est servi avec du riz et de la ratatouille. Vous voulez boire quelque chose?
You	Une bouteille d'eau minérale. (1)
Waiter	Très bien. Je vous apporte cela tout de suite.
You	Vous pouvez/me donner le menu? (2)
Waiter	D'accord je vous amène ça ...
You	Je voudrais une glace à la vanille et au chocolat. (1)
Waiter	Ah, je regrette, mais nous n'avons plus de chocolat.
You	Qu'est-ce que vous avez/comme autres parfums? (2)
Waiter	Fraise, citron et café.
You	Je vais prendre citron./Vous pouvez m'apporter l'addition avec le café? (2)
Waiter	Mais, bien sûr.

Activity 5

You	Bonjour. Je voudrais un billet aller-retour/pour Bruxelles pour deux personnes. (2)
Ticket clerk	C'est pour quel jour?
You	Je voudrais partir le 17 janvier/et revenir le 21 janvier. (2)
Ticket clerk	Très bien. Alors sans réductions, le billet aller-retour pour deux personnes coûte 372€.
You	C'est un peu trop cher./Vous avez quelque chose de moins cher? (2)
Ticket clerk	Oui, justement nous avons en ce moment une promotion: un aller-retour Paris-Bruxelles pour deux personnes pour 148€.

You	Le prix est meilleur./Quelles sont les conditions? (2)
Ticket clerk	Il faut voyager du vendredi au dimanche, et le billet n'est ni échangeable, ni remboursable.
You	À quelle heure le train part de Paris? (1)
Ticket clerk	Vous désirez voyager le matin ou l'après-midi?
You	Le matin entre 9.30 et 10.30. (1)
Ticket clerk	Vous avez plusieurs trains. Il y en a un à 9.25, un autre à 10.25 ...
You	Je vais prendre le train de 10.25. (1)
Ticket clerk	Très bien. Pour le retour, il y a un train à 14.43. Un autre à 16.13 ...
You	Je voudrais prendre le train de 16.13. (1)
You	Il faut combien de temps/pour aller de Paris à Bruxelles? (2)
Ticket clerk	Le train met 1 heure 22 minutes. Alors le billet vous va?
You	D'accord. Je peux payer avec ma carte de crédit? (1)
Ticket clerk	Oui, tout à fait.

Activity 9

You	Je voudrais changer de l'argent, s'il vous plaît. (1)
Bank clerk	Oui, bien sûr. Vous avez une carte de crédit?
You	J'ai une carte Visa. (1)
Bank clerk	Eh bien, c'est facile. Utilisez le distributeur automatique de billets?
You	Il ne marche pas/et l'hôtel n'accepte pas les cartes bancaires. (2)
Bank clerk	Vous avez des chèques de voyage?
You	Non, je n'en ai pas. (1)
Bank clerk	Bon, eh bien ... je vais vous faire une avance sur votre carte visa. Vous voulez changer combien?
You	Il me faut 300 euros pour payer l'hôtel. (1)
Bank clerk	Pas de problème. Vous avez une pièce d'identité avec vous? Votre passeport?
You	J'ai laissé mon passeport dans ma chambre à l'hôtel. (1)
Bank clerk	Ah ... malheureusement Il me le faut pour cette transaction.
You	La banque ferme à quelle heure? (1)
Bank clerk	Elle ferme dans 45 minutes. Il est loin votre hôtel?
You	Il est à quinze minutes à pied. (1)
Bank clerk	C'est bon. Vous avez juste le temps d'y aller et de revenir.
You	D'accord. Merci beaucoup, Madame. (1)

French–English vocabulary

à *to, in*
abord *see* d'abord
accord *see* d'accord
abricot (m) *apricot*
achat (m) *shopping*; faire des achats *to do some shopping*
acheter *to buy*
addition (f) *bill, sum*
adorer *to adore, to love*
adresse (f) *address*
affaires (f pl) *business*; homme d'affaires *businessman*
âge (m) *age*
agence de voyages (f) *travel agency*
aider *to help*
aimer *to like, to love*
aire (f) de pique-nique *picnic area*
alcool (m) *spirit*
alimentation (f) *grocer's shop*
aller *to go*
aller (m) simple *single ticket*
aller-retour (m) *return ticket*
allô *hello (on phone)*
alors *well, then*
ambiance (f) *atmosphere*
ami (m), amie (f) *friend*
amende (f) *fine*
an (m) *year*
ancien(ne) *ancient, former*
anglais(e) *English (often used for British)*
Angleterre (f) *England*
année (f) *year*
après *after*
après-midi (m) *afternoon*
apprécier *to appreciate*
août *August*
apparaître *to appear*

s'appeler *lit. to be called* je m'appelle *my name is*
apprendre *to learn*
argent (m) *money*
arrêt (m) *stop*
arrivée (f) *arrival*
arriver *to arrive*
arrondissement (m) *district in large towns*
ascenseur (m) *lift*
aspirine (f) effervescente *soluble aspirin*
assez *enough, fairly*
assiette (f) *plate*
attendre *to wait for*
aujourd'hui *today*
au revoir *goodbye*
aussi *also, too, as well*
autobus (m) *bus*; en autobus *by bus*
autocar (m) *coach*; en autocar *by coach*
automne (m) *autumn*; en automne *in autumn*
autoroute (f) *motorway*
autre *other*; autre chose *something else*
avec *with*
avion (m) *aeroplane*
avoir *to have*; avoir l'air *to seem*
avril *April*

se baigner *to go for a swim*
baguette (f) *'French stick' (bread)*
balle (f) *ball*
banlieue (f) *suburb*
banque (f) *bank*
bar (m) *bar*
bas(se) *low*

bas (m) *bottom, lower part*
bâtiment (m) *building*
battre *to beat*
beau (belle) *handsome, beautiful*
beaucoup (de) *much, a lot*
belle *see* beau
besoin (m) *need*; avoir besoin *to need*
beurre (m) *butter*
bien *well*; bien sûr *certainly*
bientôt *soon*; à bientôt *see you soon*
bière (f) *beer*
billet (m) *ticket, (bank) note*
blanc (blanche) *white*
bleu(e) *blue*; bleu marine *navy blue*; bleu pâle *pale blue*
blond(e) *blond*
boeuf (m) *beef, ox*
boire *to drink*
boîte (f) *box, can, tin*
boîte aux lettres *letter box*
boîte (f) (de nuit) *disco, nightclub*
boisson (f) *drink*
bol (m) *bowl*
bon(ne) *good*; bon marché *cheap*
bonjour *good day, hello*
bonsoir *good evening*
botte (f) *boot*
boucherie (f) *butcher's*
bouchon (m) *cork, bottleneck*
boulangerie (f) *baker's*
boulevard (m) *boulevard*
bout (m) *end*; au bout de *at the end of*
bouteille (f) *bottle*
brasserie (f) *pub-restaurant*
briller *to shine*
britannique *British*
brouillard (m) *fog*
bruit (m) *noise*
brun (brune) *brown (hair, complexion)*
bureau (m) de location *box office*
bureau (m) de renseignements *information office*
bureau (m) des réservations *booking office*
bus (m) *see* autobus

cabine téléphonique (f) *telephone box*
cabinet de toilette (m) *small room containing wash basin and bidet*
cadeau (m) *present*
café (m) *coffee, café*; café au lait (m) *white coffee*; café crème *coffee served with cream*

caisse (f) *cash desk, cashier's ticket office*
ça *that, it*; ça va? *how are things?*; ça va *things are OK*
cabine (f) d'essayage *fitting room*
campagne (f) *country*; à la campagne *in (to) the country*
camping (m) *camping, campsite*
car (m) *see* autocar
carnet (m) *book (of tickets), ten metro tickets*
carrefour (m) *crossroads*
carte (f) *map, card, menu*; carte bancaire *banker's card*; carte d'abonnement *season ticket*; carte de crédit *credit card*; carte d'identité *identity card*; carte postale (f) *postcard*
cassé(e) *broken*
ce, cet, cette *this, that (adjective)*
ceci *see* ce
célèbre *famous*
célibataire (m and f) *single, bachelor*
cent *a hundred*
centime (m) *centime*
centre (m) *centre*; au centre de *in the centre of*; centre ville *town centre*
centre commercial (m) *shopping centre*
certain(e) *certain*
certainement *certainly*
ces *these, those*
c'est *it is, this is*
c'est ça *that's it*
cet, cette *see* ce
chambre (f) *(bed)room*
champignon (m) *mushroom*
chance (f) *luck*
changer *to change*
changeur (m) de monnaie *coin changing machine*
chaque *each, every*
charcuterie (f) *selling cooked meats*
chaud(e) *hot*; avoir chaud *to be hot*
chauffer *to heat up*
chaussure (f) *shoe*
chemise (f) *shirt*
chèque de voyage (m) *see* traveller
cher (chère) *expensive, dear*
chercher *to look for*; aller chercher *to go and fetch*
cheveux (m pl) *hair*
chez *at the home of*; chez moi *at my house, at home*

choisir *to choose*
choix (m) *choice*
chose (f) *thing*
chocolat (m) *eating or drinking chocolate*
cinq *five*
cinquante *50*
circulation (f) *traffic*
citron (m) *lemon*
classe (f) *class*
classique *classical*
clé (f) *key*
coin (m) *corner*
combien (de)? *how much? how many?*
commander *to order*
comme *as, like, in the way of*
commencer *to start, to begin*
comment *how, how to, what*
complet(ète) *full*
composer *to dial (a telephone number)*
composter *to date-stamp (a ticket)*
comprendre *to understand*
comprimé (m) *tablet*
compris *understood, included*
connaître *to know (a person or a place)*
connu(e) *known*
conseiller *to advise*
consigne (f) *left luggage*; consigne automatique *luggage lockers*
content(e) *pleased*
continuer *to continue*
copain/copine *(boy, girl) friend*
correspondance (f) *connection*
côté (m) *side*; à coté de *next to*; de l'autre côté *on the other side*
costume (m) *suit for men*
couchette (f) *couchette*
se coucher *to go to bed*
couleur (f) *colour*
coup (m) de fil *telephone call*
cours (m) particulier *private lesson*
cours (m) de change *exchange rate*
courses (f pl) *shopping*
court(e) *short*
court (m) de tennis *tennis court*
coûter *to cost*
couverture (f) *blanket, cover*
cravate (f) *tie*
crème (f) *cream*
crêperie (f) *pancake house*
croire *to believe*

croissant (m) *croissant*
croque-monsieur (m) *toasted cheese sandwich with ham*
en cuir *in leather*
cuisine (f) *kitchen, cooking*
cuit (e) *cooked*

d'abord *firstly*
d'accord *OK, agreed*
dans *in, into*
danser *to dance*
date (f) *date*
de *of, from*
décembre *December*
décider *to decide*
décrocher l'appareil *to lift the receiver*
déjeuner *to lunch, lunch*; petit-déjeuner (m) *breakfast*
demain *tomorrow*
demi(e) *half*; demi-kilo (m) *half a kilogram*; demi-heure (f) *half an hour*
dent (f) *tooth*
dentifrice (m) *toothpaste*
dépannage: le service de dépannage *breakdown service*
dépendre de *to depend on*
depuis *since*; je suis marié depuis dix ans *I've been married for ten years*
déranger *to disturb, to inconvenience*; en dérangement *out of order*
dernier(ière) *last*
descendre *to go down*
désirer *to wish for*
desservir *to serve*
détester *to hate*
deux *two*
deuxième *second*
devoir *must, should, ought*
différent(e) *different*
dimanche *Sunday*
diminuer *to decrease*
dîner (m) *dinner, to have dinner*
dire *to say*
direct(e) *direct*
directement *directly*
direction (f) *direction*
disque (m) *record*
dix *ten*
dix-huit *18*
dix-neuf *19*
dix-sept *17*
doit, ça doit *see* devoir
donner *to give*

dormir *to sleep*
douche (f) *shower*
douze *12*
droit(e) *straight*; tout droit *straight on*
à droite *right (hand)*; avoir droit *to be entitled*

eau (f) *water*
  eau minérale (f) *mineral water*
école (f) *school*
écouter *to listen*
église (f) *church*
élève (m and f) *pupil*
écrire *to write*
  par écrit *in writing*
émetteur(rice) *issuing*
emmener *to take (someone somewhere)*
emplacement (m) *pitch*
en *in, on, of it, of them*
enfant (m and f) *child*
ensemble *together*
ensemble (m) *outfit, suit (woman)*
ensuite *then*
entre *between*
entrée (f) *way in, admission charge*
environ *about*
environs (m pl) *surroundings*
envoyer *to send*
équitation (f) *riding*
erreur (f) *mistake*
espérer *to hope*
essayer *to try*
essence (f) *petrol*
essuie-glace (m) *windscreen wiper*
est (m) *east*
et *and*
étage (m) *floor*
été (m) *summer*; en été *in summer*
étoile (f) *star*
être *to be*
eux *them (people)*
exuier *to excuse*

excursion (f) *excursion, trip*; faire une excursion *to go on an excursion*
excuser *to excuse*
expliquer *explain*
en face (de) *facing*

facile *easy*
faim (f) *hunger*; avoir faim *to be hungry*
faire *to do, to make*

famille (f) *family*
il faut *it is necessary, one has to*
il faudra *it will be necessary*
faux (fausse) *false*
favori (favorite) *favourite*
femme (f) *wife, woman*
fenêtre (f) *window*
fermé(e) *closed*
fermer *to close*
fête (f) *feast-day, celebration*
feux (m pl) (rouges) *traffic lights*
février *February*
fièvre (f) *fever, temperature*
figurer *to appear*
fille (f) *daughter, girl*
fils (m) *son*
finalement *finally*
finir *to finish*
fleur (f) *flower*
fois (f) *time*; une fois *once*
fond (m) *back, far end*; au fond du couloir *at the far end of the corridor*
fondre *to melt*
forme (f) *shape*
formidable *great*
foulard (m) *scarf*
fourchette (f) *fork*
fraise (f) *strawberry*
franc (m) *franc*
français(e) *French*
France (f) *France*
frère (m) *brother*
frein (m) *brake*
frite (f) *chip*; *(adjective) fried*
froid(e) *cold*; avoir froid *to be cold*
fromage (m) *cheese*
fruit (m) *fruit*

garçon (m) *boy, waiter*
garder *to keep*
gare (f) *station*; gare routière (f) *bus, coach station*; gare SNCF (f) *railway station*
garer *to park*
garni(e) *served with vegetables, salads, etc.*
à gauche *left*
généralement *generally*
glace (f) *ice cream*
gonflage (m) des pneus *pumping up the tyres*
gorge (f) *throat*
gourmet (m) *gourmet*

grand (e) *big, tall*
Grande-Bretagne (f) *Great Britain*
gratuit (e) *free*
grillade (f) *grilled meat*
grippe (f) *flu*
gros (grosse) *fat, large*
guichet (m) *ticket office*

(s')habiller *to dress*
habiter *to live*
haricot (m) *bean*; haricot vert *green bean*
heure (f) *hour*; quelle heure est-il? *what time is it?*
hiver (m) *winter*; en hiver *in winter*
homme (m) *man*; homme d'affaires *businessman*
hôpital (m) *hospital*
horaire (m) *timetable*
hôtel (m) *hotel*; hôtel de ville (m) *town hall*
hors *outside*; hors-d'oeuvre *starter*; hors de service *out of service*
huile (f) *oil*
huit *eight*

ici *here*
île (f) *island*; Ile de France *Paris area*
indicatif (m) *dialling code*
indiquer *indicate*
ingénieur (m) *engineer*
intéressant(e) *interesting*
introduire *to insert*
inviter *to invite*
inscription (f) *enrolment*

jamais *never*
jambon (m) *ham*
janvier *January*
jardin (m) *garden*
jardinage (m) *gardening*
jaune *yellow*
jean (m) or jeans (m pl) *jeans*
jeu (m) *game*; jeu de société *parlour game*
jeudi *Thursday*
jeune *young*
joli(e) *pretty*
jouer *to play*
jour (m) *day*; jour férié *bank holiday*
journal (m) *newspaper*
journée (f) *day, day-time*
joyeux(se) *joyful, merry*
juillet *July*

juin *June*
jupe (f) *skirt*
jus (m) de fruit *fruit juice*
jusqu'à *until, as far as*

kilo(gramme) (m) *kilogram*

la *the, her, it*
là(-bas) *(over) there*
lait (m) *milk*
laisser *to leave*; laissé *left*
large *wide, big*
(se) laver *to wash*
le *the, him, it*
léger (légère) *light*
légume (m) *vegetable*
lentement *slowly*
lequel, laquelle *who, which*; sur laquelle *on which*
lettre (f) *letter*
leur(s) *their, to them*
se lever *to get up*
libre *free (but for free of charge use gratuit)*; libre service (m) *small supermarket*
ligne (f) *number* (bus), *line* (métro)
lire *to read*
lit (m) *bed*; à deux lits *twin-bedded*; le grand lit *double bed*
litre (m) *litre*
livre (m) *book*; (f) *pound*
location (f) *hire*
loin *far*
loisir (m) *hobby*
long (longue) *long*
louer *to let, to hire, to book*
lourd(e) *heavy*
lui *to him, to her, he, as for him*
lundi *Monday*
lunettes (f pl) *glasses*

Madame *Madam, Mrs*
Mademoiselle *Miss*
magasin (m) *shop*; grand magasin *department store*
mai *May*
maillot de bain (m) *swimming costume, swimsuit*
maintenant *now*
mais *but*
maison (f) *house*; à la maison *at home*
mal *badly*; avoir mal *to have a pain*; mal (m) de dos *backache*

malheureusement *unfortunately*
manger *to eat*
manquer *to be lacking, missing*
marché (m) *market*; bon marché *cheap*
marcher *to walk, to work (for a machine)*
mardi *Tuesday*
mari (m) *husband*
marié(e) *married*
marron *brown*
mars *March*
matin (m) *morning*
mauvais(e) *bad*
médecin (m) *doctor, physician*
médicament (m) *medicine*
meilleur(e) *better*
mélange (m) *mixture*, mélanger *to mix*
même *same, even*
menu (m) *set meal*
mer (f) *sea*; au bord de la mer *at the seaside, by the sea*
mère (f) *mother*
merci *thank you*
mercredi *Wednesday*
mesurer *to measure*
Messieurs-dames *ladies and gentlemen*
métro (m) *underground*
mettre *to put*
midi *midday, lunch time*
mieux *better*
milieu (m) *middle, milieu*
mille *a thousand*
mince *thin*
minuit *midnight*
moi *me, I*
moins *less*
mois (m) *month*
moitié (f) *half*
mon, ma, mes *my*
monument (m) *monument*
monde (m) *world*; tout le monde *everybody*
monnaie (f) *small change*
Monsieur *Sir, Mr*
montagne (f) *mountain*; à la montagne *in, to the mountains*
monter *to go up*
montre (f) *watch*
montrer *to show*
morceau (m) *piece*
moteur (m) *engine*

motif (m) *pattern, design*
moyen(ne) *medium, average*
musée (m) *museum*

natation (f) *swimming*
neiger *to snow*
neuf *nine*
neuf (neuve) *new*
niveau (m) *level*
nocturne *late-night opening*
Noël (m) *Christmas*
noir(e) *black*
nom (m) *name*
non *no*
nord (m) *north*
note (f) *bill (hotel, telephone)*
notre, nos *our*
nouveau (elle) *new*; à nouveau *again*
novembre *November*
nuit (f) *night*
numéro (m) *number*, numéro d'immatriculation *number plate*

occupé(e) *busy*
s'occuper *to deal with, to attend to*
octobre *October*
office du/de tourisme (m) *tourist office*
oeil (m) *eye*
oeuf *egg*
oeuvre (f) *work of art*
omelette (f) *omelette*
on *one (used also for 'we' and 'I')*
onze *11*
(en) or *(made of) gold*
ou *or*; ou … ou *either … or*
où *where*
ouest (m) *west*
oui *yes*
ouvert(e) *open*
ouvrir *to open*

pain (m) *bread*
panne (f) *breakdown*
panneau (m) *sign*
pantalon (m) *trousers*
paquet (m) *packet*
paquet-cadeau (m) *gift-package*
parcmètre (m) *parking meter*
pardon *pardon, sorry, excuse me*
parfum (m) *perfume, flavour (ice cream)*
parking (m) *car park*
parler *to speak*
en particulier *particularly*

partir *to go, to leave*
à partir de *from, as*
pas *not*; pas du tout *not at all*
passant(e) *passer-by*
passer *to pass*
pâté (m) *pâté*; pâté de campagne
  country pâté
pâtisserie (f) *a cake shop, pastry, cake*
payer *to pay*
pays (m) *country; area*
à péage *toll payable*
pendant *during*
penser *to think*
perdre *to lose*; perdu *lost*
père (m) *father*
personne (f) *person*; personne (+ ne)
  nobody
peser *to weigh*
pétanque (f) *petanque (kind of bowls)*
petit(e) *small*; petit-déjeuner
  breakfast
(un) peu *(a) little, few*
pharmacie (f) *chemist's*
pharmacien(ne) *chemist*
pied (m) *foot*; à pied *on foot*
pièce (f) *room, coin*; pièce d'identité
  identification
pique-nique (m) *picnic*
piscine (f) (couverte) *(indoor)
  swimming pool*
plan (m) (de la ville) *(town) map*
place (f) *square, space, seat*
plaisir (m) *pleasure*; faire plaisir *to
  please*; avec plaisir *with pleasure*
planche à voile (f) *windsurfing board*
plat (m) *dish, course*
plein(e) *full*; le plein, s'il vous plaît
  (at the garage) fill it up, please
il pleut *it is raining*
sans plomb (m) *lead-free petrol*
(la) plupart *most*
plus *more, plus*; plus … que *more
  than*;
  en plus *in addition, extra*; ne …
  pas *no longer, no more*
pneu (m) *tyre*
poêle (f) *frying pan*
poids (m) *weight*
à point *medium done (meat)*
pois, petits pois (m pl) *peas*
poisson (m) *fish*
pointure (f) *size shoes*
poivre (m) *pepper*; poivrer *to pepper*
pomme (f) *apple*; pomme de terre (f)

potato; pommes frites (f pl) *chips*
pompiste (m) *pump attendant*
pont (m) *bridge*
portefeuille (m) *wallet*
porte-monnaie (m) *purse*
porter *to carry, to wear*
poste (f) *post, post office*
pourboire (m) *tip*
poulet (m) *chicken*
pour *for, in order to*
pouvoir *can, be able to*; vous pouvez
  you can
pratique *practical, convenient*
pratiquer *to practise, to do*
préférer *to prefer*
premier(ière) *first*
prendre *to take*; pris *taken*
près (de) *near*; près d'ici *near by*
pression (f) *pressure (tyre)*; *draught
  (beer)*
presque *nearly*
printemps (m) *spring*; au printemps
  in spring
prix (m) *price*
prochain(e) *next*
proche *near*
professeur(e) *teacher*
profession (f) *profession*
promenade (f) (à pied) *walk*
se promener (à pied) *to go for a walk*
puis *then*
pull-over (m) *pullover*

quai (m) *platform*
quand? *when?*
quarante *40*
quatorze *14*
quatre *four*
quatre-vingts *80*
quatre-vingt-dix *90*
quel(le)? *which?, what?*
quelque(s) *some (a few)*; quelque
  chose *something*
quelqu'un *someone*
quelquefois *sometimes*
que *that, than*
(ne) … que *only*
qu'est-ce que *what*
qui *who, which*
quinze *15*
quinzaine (f) *15 or so*
quitter *to leave*
quoi? *what?*

raide *straight (hair)*
randonnée (f) *hike*
rapide *rapid*
raquette (f) *racket*
régler *to settle (bill)*
regretter *to be sorry*
regarder *to watch*
remplir *to fill in*
rendez-vous (m) *appointment*
rendre *to give back*
rendre visite *to pay a visit*
renseignement (m) *(piece of) information*
se renseigner *to inquire*
rentrer *to go back, to go home*
réparer *to repair*
repas (m) *meal*
répéter *to repeat*
se reposer *to rest*
RER *fast extension of the underground in the suburbs*
restaurant (m) *restaurant*
réserver *to reserve, to book*
rester *to stay*
retourner *to go back, to return*
rien *nothing*; de rien *don't mention it*
robe (f) *dress*
rocade (f) *ring road, bypass*
rouge *red*
route (f) *road*
rue (f) *street*

sac à main (m) *handbag*
saignant(e) *bleeding, rare (meat)*
saison (f) *season*; hors saison *out of season*; en pleine saison *in high season*
saler *to salt*
salle (f) *hall, auditorium, room*; salle de bains *bathroom*; salle à manger *dining room*
sandwich (m) *sandwich*
sans *without*
saucisson (m) *kind of salami*
savoir *to know (a fact or how to do something e.g.* je sais faire la cuisine *I know how to cook)*
savon (m) *soap*
scène (f) *scene*
séance (f) *session*
secrétaire (m and f) *secretary*
seize *16*
sel (m) *salt*
selon *according to*

semaine (f) *week*
sept *seven*
septembre *September*
servir *to serve*
serviette (f) *towel, napkin*; serviette de toilette *hand towel*
shampooing (m) *shampoo*
s'il vous plaît *please*
situé(e) *situated*
six *six*
ski (m) *ski*; ski de fond *cross-country ski-ing*, de piste *downhill*
SNCF *French railways*
soeur (f) *sister*
soie (f) *silk*; en soie *made of silk*
soif (f) *thirst*; avoir soif *to be thirsty*
soir (m) *evening*
soirée (f) *evening, evening entertainment*
soixante 60
soixante-dix 70
en solde *in the sale*
soleil (m) *sun*
son, sa, ses *his, her, its*
sortie (f) *exit*
sortir *to go out*
souffrir *to suffer*
source (f) *spring*
souvenir (m) *souvenir, memory*
souvent *often*
spectacle (m) *show*
sport (m) *sport*
station (f) de métro *underground station*
station thermale (f) *spa*
station-service (f) *petrol station*
stationnement (m) (interdit) *(no) parking*
stationner *to park*
stylo (m) *pen*
sucre (m) *sugar*, sucreries (f pl) *sweet things*
sud (m) *south*
suivre *to follow*
supermarché (m) *supermarket*
surtout *mainly, especially*
svp (s'il vous plaît) *please*
sympathique *friendly, pleasant*
syndicat d'initiative (m) *tourist office*

tabac (m) *tobacconist's-cum-newsagent's*

taille (f) *size, waist*

tarif (m) *price list, rate;* tarif réduit *reduced rate*

tarte (f) *pie*

taxi (m) *taxi*

télécarte (f) *phone card*

téléphone (m) *telephone*

téléphoner (à) *to phone*

temps (m) *time, weather*

tête (f) *head*

T.G.V. *high speed train*

thé (m) *tea*

ticket (m) *ticket*

timbre (m) *stamp*

tir-à-l'arc (m) *archery*

tire-bouchon (m) *corkscrew*

toi *you (familiar)*

toilette (f), faire sa toilette *to wash and dress;* les toilettes *lavatory*

ton, ta, tes *your*

tonalité (f) *dialling tone*

toujours *always*

touriste (m and f) *tourist*

tourner *to turn*

tout(e) tous *all;* tout de suite *immediately;* tout droit *straight ahead;* tout le monde *everybody;* tous les deux *both of them;* tous les jours *every day*

train (m) *train;* en train *by train*

trajet (m) *journey*

tranche (f) *slice*

travail (m) *work, job*

travailler *to work*

traveller (m) *travellers' cheque*

traverser *to cross*

treize *13*

trente *30*

très *very*

trois *three*

troisième *third*

se tromper *to make a mistake*

trop *too, too much, too many*

trouver *to find;* se trouver *to be (situated)*

TTC *all taxes included*

un(e) *a, an, one*

uni(e) *plain*

va, vas *see* aller

vacances (f pl) *holiday(s)*

valise (f) *suitcase*

vanille (f) *vanilla*

vase (m) *vase*

il vaut *it costs, it is worth*

veau (m) *veal*

vélo (m) *bicycle*

vendeur (m), vendeuse (f) *sales assistant*

vendredi *Friday*

vent (m) *wind*

ventre (m) *stomach*

vérifier *to check*

verre (m) *glass*

vers *towards*

verser *to pour*

vert(e) *green*

vêtement (m) *garment*

viande (f) *meat*

vie (f) *life, cost of living*

vieux (vieil, vieille) *old*

ville (f) *town*

vin (m) *wine*

vingt *20*

vite *quickly*

vitesse (f) *speed*

visite (f) guidée *guided tour*

visiter *to visit (a place)*

voie (f) *track*

voilà *there is, here is, there you are*

voir *to see*

voiture (f) *car;* voiture-restaurant *restaurant-car;* en voiture *by car*

voler *to steal;* volé *stolen*

votre, vos *your*

je voudrais *I'd like*

vouloir *to want;* vous voulez *you want*

voyager *to travel*

vrai(e) *true*

V.T.T. *mountain biking*

WC (m) (pronounced vé-cé) *toilet*

week-end (m) *weekend*

y *there, to it*

yaourt (m) *yoghurt*

yeux *see* oeil

zéro *zero*

a un, une
about environ
address l'adresse (f)
admission charge l'entrée (f)
after après
afternoon après-midi (m)
again encore, de nouveau
age l'âge (m)
agency l'agence (f); *travel agency* l'agence (f) de voyages
all tout, toute, tous, toutes
also aussi
always toujours
and et
appear apparaître
apple la pomme
appointment le rendez-vous
April avril
arrival l'arrivée (f)
arrive arriver
as comme
aspirin l'aspirine (f)
at à, chez; *at the corner* au coin; *at home* à la maison
August août
autumn l'automne; *in autumn* en automne

bad mauvais(e); *badly* mal
baker's la boulangerie
bank la banque; *bank holiday* le jour férié
bath le bain; *to have a bath* prendre un bain; *bathroom* salle de bains
be être
be able to pouvoir
bean l'haricot (m)
beautiful beau, belle

bed le lit; *double bed* le grand lit; *twin-bedded* à deux lits
beer la bière; *draught (beer)* la pression
before avant
behind derrière
believe croire
better meilleur(e), mieux
between entre
bicycle le vélo
big grand(e)
bill (food, drinks) l'addition (f)
bill (hotel) la note
black noir(e)
blue bleu(e)
book le livre
book louer, réserver
bottle la bouteille
box la boîte; *box office* le bureau de location
boy le garçon
bread le pain
break casser; *broken* cassé(e)
breakdown la panne; *breakdown service* le service de dépannage
breakfast le petit-déjeuner
bridge le pont

brother le frère
brown marron
bus l'autobus (m), le bus; *bus stop* l'arrêt (m) d'autobus
busy occupé(e)
but mais
butcher's la boucherie
butter le beurre
buy acheter

cake, cake shop une pâtisserie
camping, campsite le camping
can peux, peut, pouvez
car park le parking
car la voiture; *by car* en voiture
carry porter
cash desk, cashier's la caisse
catch prendre
certainly bien sûr
change changer
change (small) la monnaie
cheap bon marché; *cheaper* meilleur marché
check vérifier
cheese le fromage
chemist le pharmacien, la pharmacienne
chemist's la pharmacie
chicken le poulet
child l'enfant (m and f)
chips les frites
choose choisir
church l'église (f)
close fermer; *closed* fermé(e)
clothes les vêtements, la tenue
coach l'autocar (m), le car
coffee (black) le café
coin la pièce
cold froid(e); *to be cold* avoir froid
colour la couleur
come venir; *come home* rentrer
cook faire la cuisine
cooking la cuisine
corkscrew le tire-bouchon
cost coûter
country le pays
course le plat
credit card la carte de crédit
cross traverser

dance danser
daughter la fille
day le jour; *the whole day* toute la journée
dear cher, chère
December décembre
dinner le dîner
dish le plat
do faire
doctor le médecin
dress la robe; s'habiller
drink boire; la boisson
during pendant

easy facile
eat manger
egg l'oeuf (m)
end le bout; *at the end* au bout
engine le moteur
England l'Angleterre (f)
English anglais(e)
Englishman l'Anglais; *Englishwoman* l'Anglaise
enough assez
evening le soir, la soirée
every tout, toute
everyday tous les jours; *everybody* tout le monde
everything tout
excuse me pardon
exit la sortie
expensive cher, chère
eye l'oeil (m)

false faux, fausse
family la famille
far loin
fat gros(se)
father le père
February février
fill in remplir; *fill it up (with petrol)* faire le plein
find trouver
finish finir
first premier, première
firstly d'abord
fish le poisson
floor l'étage (m)
follow suivre
foot le pied; *on foot* à pied
for pour
France la France
free (costing nothing) gratuit(e)
French français(e)
Frenchman le Français, *Frenchwoman* la Française
French railways S.N.C.F.
Friday vendredi
friend l'ami (m), l'amie (f)
friendly sympathique
from de, à partir de
fruit juice le jus de fruit
full complet, complète, plein(e)

gardening le jardinage
get up se lever
girl la fille
give donner

glasses les lunettes (f pl)
go aller, partir, *to go up* monter; *to go down* descendre
go and get aller chercher
go out sortir; *go home* rentrer à la maison
good bon, bonne
good evening bonsoir
goodbye au revoir
good night bonne nuit
Great Britain la Grande-Bretagne
green vert(e)
grocer's shop l'alimentation (f)

hair les cheveux (m pl)
half demi(e); *half an hour* demi-heure
ham le jambon
handbag le sac à main
hate détester
have avoir
head la tête
headache le mal de tête
hear entendre
heavy lourd(e)
hello bonjour, allô *(on the phone)*
help aider
here ici
here is voilà
hike la randonnée
hire, hiring louer, la location
hobby le loisir
holiday(s) les vacances (f pl)
home, at home à la maison; *at my home* chez moi
hope espérer
hospital l'hôpital (m)
hot chaud(e); *to be hot* avoir chaud
hotel l'hôtel (m)
hour l'heure (f)
house la maison
how comment
how much/how many combien
hundred (a) cent
hungry, to be hungry avoir faim
husband le mari

I je, moi
ice cream la glace
identification la pièce d'identité
ill malade
immediately tout de suite
in, into à, en, dans
in front of devant

information (piece of) le renseignement
information office le bureau de renseignements
inquire se renseigner
insert introduire
interesting intéressant(e)
invite inviter
it's c'est, il est, elle est

January janvier
jeans le jean, les jeans
journey le trajet
July juillet
June juin

key la clé
know savoir, connaître

ladies and gentlemen Messieurs-dames
large gros(se), grand(e)
last dernier, dernière
late-night opening le nocturne
learn apprendre
leave quitter
left, on the left à gauche
left luggage la consigne
lemon le citron
less moins
letter box la boîte aux lettres
letter la lettre
lift l'ascenseur (m)
like aimer
like comme
line (underground) la ligne
listen écouter
litre le litre
little petit(e); *(a) little* (un) peu
live habiter
long long, longue
look for chercher
lose perdre; *lost* perdu(e)
lot, a lot (of) beaucoup (de)
love aimer
lunch le déjeuner

Madame, Mrs Madame, Mme
make faire
man l'homme (m)
many beaucoup
map la carte; *map (town)* le plan (de la ville)
March mars

market le marché
married marié(e)
May mai
me moi
meal le repas
measure mesurer
meat la viande; *well done* bien cuit(e); *medium* à point
medicine le médicament
menu à la carte
midday midi
middle milieu; *in the middle* au milieu
midnight minuit
milk le lait
Miss Mademoiselle
Monday lundi
money l'argent (m)
month le mois
more plus; *no ... more* ne ... plus
morning le matin, la matinée
mother la mère
motorway l'autoroute (f)
mountain la montagne; *in/to the mountains* à la montagne
much beaucoup
museum le musée
must; one must il faut + infinitive

name le nom
near près (de)
nearby près de; *near here* près d'ici
nearly presque
need avoir besoin
never jamais
new neuf, neuve, nouveau, nouvelle
newspaper le journal
next prochain(e)
next to à côté de
night la nuit
nightclub la boîte (de nuit)
no non
nothing rien
November novembre
now maintenant
number le numéro; *(bus) number* la ligne

October octobre
of, off de
often souvent
oil l'huile (f)
OK d'accord
old vieux, vieil, vielle

omelet l'omelette (f)
on sur, à, en; *on foot* à pied
once une fois
one un, une, on
only seulement
open ouvrir; *opened* ouvert(e)
opposite en face de
or ou
order commander
other autre
out of hors de

packet le paquet
pain la douleur; *to have a pain* avoir mal
park garer
parking meter le parcmètre
particularly particulièrement
passer-by passant(e)
pay payer
peas les petits pois
pepper le poivre
person la personne
petrol l'essence (f); *petrol station* la station-service
petrol: lead-free le sans plomb
phone card télécarte (f)
picnic le pique-nique; *to have a picnic* faire un pique-nique
pie la tarte
piece le morceau
platform le quai
play jouer
please s'il vous plaît
pleased content(e)
postcard la carte postale
post; post office la poste
potato la pomme de terre
pound (sterling) la livre (sterling)
prefer préférer
pressure (tyre) la pression
pretty joli(e)
price le prix
price list le tarif
pullover le pull-over
pump attendant le pompiste
purse le porte-monnaie
put mettre

quick rapide; *quickly* vite

rain la pluie; *it's raining* il pleut
rare (meat) saignant(e)
read lire

record le disque
red rouge
repair réparer
repeat répéter
reserve réserver
rest se reposer
right, on the right à droite
road la route
room la pièce, la salle; *bathroom* salle de bains; *dining room* la salle à manger

sale (on) en solde
sales assistant le vendeur, la vendeuse
salt le sel
same même
sandwich le sandwich
Saturday samedi
say dire
school l'école (f)
sea la mer; *by the sea* au bord de la mer
season la saison; *out of ...* hors ...; *in high ...* en pleine ...
seat la place
secretary le/la secrétaire
see voir
send envoyer
September septembre
serve servir
serve (transport) desservir
shampoo le shampooing
shine briller; *the sun shines* le soleil brille
shirt la chemise
shoe la chaussure; *shoe size* la pointure
shop le magasin
shopping les courses; *to do some shopping* faire les courses
shopping centre le centre commercial
show montrer
show le spectacle
shower la douche; *to have a shower* prendre une douche
sign le panneau
since depuis
single/bachelor célibataire
Sir, Mr Monsieur, M.
sister la soeur
situated situé(e)
size la taille
skirt la jupe
sleep dormir

slice la tranche
slow lent; *slowly* lentement
small petit(e)
snow neiger
soap le savon
some quelque(s)
someone quelqu'un
something quelque chose
something else quelque chose d'autre
sometimes quelquefois
son le fils
soon bientôt
sorry pardon; désolé(e)
speak parler
spend (time) passer
sport le sport; *to do a sport* pratiquer un sport
spring le printemps; *in spring* au printemps
square la place
stamp le timbre
star l'étoile (f)
start commencer
station (rail) la gare (SNCF); *bus/coach station* la gare routière; *underground station* la station
straight raide, droit(e)
straight on tout droit
street la rue
surburbs la banlieue
sugar le sucre
suitcase la valise
summer l'été (m)
sun le soleil
Sunday dimanche
supermarket le supermarché
surroundings les environs (m pl)
swim nager
swimming la natation; *swimming pool* la piscine; *swimming costume, swimsuit* le maillot de bain

take, taken prendre, pris
tall grand(e)
taxi le taxi
tea le thé
teacher le professeur, la professeure
tell dire
telephone téléphoner, le téléphone
telephone box la cabine téléphonique
than que
thank you merci
that's all c'est tout
the le, la, les

then ensuite, puis, alors
there y
these, those ces
thin mince
thing la chose
think penser
thirst la soif; *to be thirsty* avoir soif
this is c'est
this, that ce, cet, cette
thousand mille
throat la gorge
Thursday jeudi
ticket le billet, le ticket
ticket office le guichet
time l'heure (f); *what time is it?*
  quelle heure est-il?
time le temps; *spend time* passer le
  temps
timetable l'horaire (m)
tip le pourboire
to à, en, pour, jusqu'à
tobacconist's/newsagent's le tabac
today aujourd'hui
together ensemble
toilet les toilettes (f pl)
toll payable à péage
tomorrow demain
too; too much; too many trop
tooth la dent; *toothpaste* le dentifrice
tour la visite; *guided tour* la visite
  guidée
tourist le/la touriste
tourist office l'office (m) du/de
  tourisme, le syndicat d'initiative
towards vers
towel la serviette
town la ville
traffic la circulation
train le train; *by train* en train; *on
  the train* dans le train
travel voyager, le voyage
traveller's cheque le traveller
trip l'excursion (f)
trousers le pantalon
true vrai
try essayer
Tuesday mardi
turn tourner
tyre le pneu

underground le métro
understand comprendre
until jusqu'à

very très
visit visiter

wait attendre
walk marcher; *a walk* une
  promenade; *to go for a walk* se
  promener
wallet le portefeuille
wash (oneself) (se) laver
watch regarder; la montre
water (mineral) eau minérale
wear porter
weather le temps
Wednesday mercredi
week la semaine
weigh peser
well bien
what que(le); qu'est-ce que; quoi
when quand
where où
which quel(le)
white blanc, blanche
white coffee le café crème
who qui
wife la femme
windsurf board la planche à voile
wine le vin
winter l'hiver (m); *in winter* en hiver
wish désirer
with avec
without sans
woman la femme
work travailler, marcher (machine)
work le travail
write écrire

year l'an (m), l'année (f)
yellow jaune
yes oui
yoghurt yaourt
you tu, toi
young jeune

index

accents **xi**
adjectives **22, 63**
à
  preceding the name of
    a place **51**
  to describe special
    features **63**
age **23**
aller
  + **à 50**
  + infinitive **93**
au, à la, à l', aux 52
avoir 21
  constructions with
    avoir 21, 93

beaucoup de 62
besoin de 93

capital letters **23, 94**
ce, cet, cette, ces 62
ce que 74
colours **60**
combien 14
comment 31
connaître 75
consonants **xii**
countries, article with **51**

dates **41**

days **36–7**
de 13
depuis 30
du, de la, de l', des 13

en
  meaning one, some, of
    it, of them **31**
  preceding the name of
    a country **51**
-er verbs **20**
est-ce que 39
être 21

faire 42
faut (il) 51, 84
feminine **12**; pronoun **75**

il y a 31
il y en a/il n'y en a pas 31
infinitive **21**
instructions **84**

jouer à 74
jouer de 74

le, la, l', les 12
leur 32
liaison **xiii**

masculine **12**; pronoun **75**
me 84, 92
meilleur 65
mieux 65
moins 64
mon, ma, mes 32
months **37**

ne ... pas 22
ne ... jamais 75
ne ... plus 75
ne ... que 75
ne ... rien 75
notre, nos 32
nouns **12**
numbers **233**

on 21
one **13, 21**
où 31

partir 50
plural **13**
plus 64
pour 93
pouvoir 39, 83
premier, deuxième etc. 52
prendre 42
pronouns **75**

quand 31
quel, quelle 23
qu'est-ce que 40

questions **30**
  by intonation **30, 39**
  by inversion **39**
  using **est-ce que 39**

-re verbs **40**
reflexive verbs **92**

s'appeler 92
savoir 75
son, sa, ses 32
sortir 94

time **41**
ton, ta, tes 32

un, une 12
venir 94
verbs
  + infinitive **39, 42,
    74, 76, 83**
votre, vos 32
voudrais 39
vouloir 83
vowels **xi–xii**

weather **72, 76**
with **63**
without **63**

y 94